THE BEST OF
CORWIN

DIFFERENTIATED
INSTRUCTION

D1412621

The Best of Corwin Series

Classroom Management
Jane Bluestein, Editor

Differentiated Instruction
Gayle H. Gregory, Editor

Differentiated Instruction in Literacy, Math, and Science
Leslie Laud, Editor

Educational Neuroscience
David A. Sousa, Editor

Educational Technology for School Leaders
Lynne M. Schrum, Editor

Equity
Randall B. Lindsey, Editor

Inclusive Practices
Toby J. Karten, Editor

Response to Intervention
Cara F. Shores, Editor

THE BEST OF CORWIN

DIFFERENTIATED INSTRUCTION

GAYLE H. GREGORY
Editor

With contributions by

Gayle H. Gregory • Carolyn Chapman • Marilee Sprenger

Donna Walker Tileston • Lin Kuzmich

Kathy Tuchman Glass • Patti Drapeau • Glenda Beamon Crawford

Carol Ann Tomlinson • Mary Ruth Coleman • Susan Allan

Anne Udall • Mary Slade

CORWIN
A SAGE Company

FOR INFORMATION:

Corwin

A SAGE Company

2455 Teller Road

Thousand Oaks, California 91320

(800) 233-9936

Fax: (800) 417-2466

www.corwin.com

SAGE Ltd.

1 Oliver's Yard

55 City Road

London EC1Y 1SP

United Kingdom

SAGE India Pvt. Ltd.

B 1/I 1 Mohan Cooperative

Industrial Area

Mathura Road, New Delhi 110 044

India

SAGE Asia-Pacific Pte. Ltd.

33 Pekin Street #02-01

Far East Square

Singapore 048763

Acquisitions Editor: Hudson Perigo

Associate Editor: Allison Scott

Editorial Assistant: Lisa Whitney

Production Editor: Melanie Birdsall

Typesetter: C&M Digitals (P) Ltd.

Cover Designer: Rose Storey

Graphic Designer: Nicole Franck

Permissions Editor: Adele Hutchinson

Printed in the United States of America

Library of Congress Cataloging-in-Publication Data

A catalog record of this book is available from the Library of Congress.

978-1-4522-1740-6

This book is printed on acid-free paper.

11 12 13 14 15 10 9 8 7 6 5 4 3 2 1

Contents

Preface

Gayle H. Gregory

Differentiation has been around since the beginning of school days—even in the one-room schoolhouse where all grades were in the same room, with the same teacher, and where a family-type atmosphere developed over time. Students worked together, helping one another and sharing ideas, expertise, and limited materials. Schools evolved as education became more universal, and students were sorted by age and grade into more chronological groupings. Subject disciplines were also isolated. Teachers influenced by Dewey still recognized the differences in students' abilities and interests and often responded accordingly through different learning activities and assessments. As the Carnegie model emerged in the age of industrialization, "sit-and-get" instruction became more common, and teachers (especially those working in high schools) became more specialized in their content areas. Later, in the twentieth century, the standards movement required mandatory testing at various grade levels for all students, even though the diversity in the classroom had grown as a result of immigration from around the world. The rigidity of program, instruction, and assessment did not get the results expected from this standardized approach; teachers recognized that they weren't reaching and teaching all students if they were only preparing them for "the test." Thus, differentiation emerged strongly in the late 1990s as a mindset and model for helping all students succeed (the No Child Left Behind Act).

Emerging research and information on how we learn, based on neuroscience advancement, helped teachers understand how the brain operates, attends, makes meaning, and creates long-term memory, as well as how the brain becomes unique due to plasticity based on genetics (nature) and prior experiences, circumstances, and environments (nurture). All the authors in this book help teachers connect educational neuroscience to classroom environment and strategies.

Each of the chapters in this book was selected to create a tapestry of critical information for teachers implementing differentiation. Several authors foster the need for a climate conducive to learning, based on what we know about the brain's need for safety and innate need to belong. Several suggest that knowing the learner and helping the learner be aware of his or strengths, preferred modes of learning, and interests is essential. Others offer a variety of instructional methods to provide diverse ways for students to process content and develop skills. Templates for both unit planning and lesson planning based on standards are included in two chapters. An in-depth look at adolescent learners and the need for differentiation to satisfy their developmental needs is an appropriate addition for middle and high school.

Introduction

Gayle H. Gregory

This volume is an overview of the concept of differentiated instruction, featuring excerpts from eight works by recognized experts. The following is a synopsis of what you will find in each chapter.

Chapter 1. Creating a Climate for Learning

Gayle H. Gregory and Carolyn Chapman

Carolyn Chapman and I begin with the issues of teacher and student mindsets and beliefs about learning potential and how attitudes and feelings affect student learning. We stress the importance of a climate conducive for learning for all students. When we began the journey of differentiation, we realized that key to student diversity was linked to the brain's need to feel safe. Emotions, positive or negative, can facilitate or block learning in the classroom. Brain research and findings that support this notion are discussed. Theorists and psychologists such as Maslow and Goleman are cited regarding basic needs and emotional intelligences. Chapter 1 offers practical suggestions for creating a positive classroom where learners feel safe, included, and part of the learning community.

Chapter 2. Getting to Know Your Students: Learning Strengths

Marilee Sprenger

Marilee Sprenger, like Carolyn Chapman and me, worked in classrooms for many years and recognized the need to accommodate not only identified students, but all students. Each student is unique in what he or she brings to the schoolhouse; it is important to know the *what* and *how* of the curriculum, but it is also important to identify *who* you are teaching. Chapter 2 focuses on building learning profiles of the students and helping them know themselves as learners so that students may advocate for themselves and optimize their learning experiences through self-knowledge as lifelong learners. Thus, teachers can use the knowledge of students' strengths to provide a variety of ways to garner attention, process information, and create products. Sprenger reminds us that it is critical for teachers to capture students' attention and curiosity through sensory pathways and to help students see the relevancy of the new knowledge, concepts, and skills; the teacher is key to energizing, intriguing, and engaging students through personal connections, pathways, patterns, and metacogniton. This chapter provides an overview of learning styles and techniques to help teachers use that knowledge to teach and re-teach, and tools are provided to help teachers and students identify learner strengths.

Chapter 3. Differentiating for Different Learning Styles

Donna Walker Tileston

In Chapter 3, Donna Walker Tileston looks to educational cognitive research to clarify classroom practices and student needs. She describes the concept of *neuroplasticity* and the ability of the brain's neurons to grow and connect throughout life, citing Marion Diamond's work with dendritic growth in rats in enriched environments. Tileston also describes the auditory, visual, and kinesthetic modalities and behaviors that students exhibit and suggests ways of capitalizing on those strengths through a variety of pathways that tap into each one.

Chapter 4. Curriculum Approaches for Data-Driven Instruction

Gayle H. Gregory and Lin Kuzmich

When Lin Kuzmich and I began the journey of differentiation, we realized that there were lots of fun activities being used in classrooms, but that some lacked substance and were not rooted in targeted standards. Variety of instruction and students' readiness, interests, and preferences are important, but outcomes are crucial as the foundation for planning. Thus, we elaborated on the "backward-design" model from Grant Wiggins and Jay McTighe to marry the planning process and assessment and then differentiated the instructional process based on readiness, interest, learning profiles, and varying content, process, and product. We have offered a practical progression for planning that begins with identifying the standards to be integrated, including the concepts, benchmarks, and skills. Chapter 4 includes tips for designing the final assessment, pre-assessments, formative assessments, and rubrics and provides several detailed examples as well as samples from various grade levels and disciplines.

Chapter 5. Differentiated Instruction and Strategies

Kathy Tuchman Glass

Kathy Tuchman Glass redefines the term *differentiation* and the key components of content, process, and product, as well as the student characteristics related to differentiating—readiness, interests, and learning profiles. Glass then relates Learning styles to readiness-based differentiation. Chapter 5 features a comprehensive chart listing strategies and how to use them, as well as links from strategy to readiness, interests, and learning profiles of all students.

Chapter 6. Graphic Organizers: Tools to Promote Differentiation

Patti Drapeau

In Chapter 6, rationale is given to support the use of graphic organizers and other visual representations in the differentiation process. A chart is provided to show how graphic organizers support differentiation which provides principles and applications. Patti Drapeau offers six ways to differentiate using graphic organizers: (1) open-ended prompts, (2) directed prompts, (3) differentiating, (4) resources for organizers, (5) variety plus, and (6) create your own. Drapeau describes each of the six with steps for each, including the advantages and disadvantages of each, points to remember, and factors to consider. Examples for each type are provided as well as tips on developing critical rubrics.

Chapter 7. Differentiation and Adolescent Development

Glenda Beamon Crawford

Glenda Beamon Crawford begins Chapter 7 by offering six Es—evaluation, expectation, engagement, exploration, extension, and environment—as adolescent-centered design principles. A clear description of adolescent development with implications for the classroom is provided in chart form, and adolescent learner needs are explained. Crawford then aligns differentiation principles with brain-based developmental learning needs. Each of the developmental learning needs is elaborated with a thorough description, supporting brain research, and implications for the classroom. The adolescent brain is a work in progress, and Crawford shares important brain findings that are critical for adolescent educators to know. A useful summary of brain compatible instruction concludes the chapter.

Chapter 8. Interface Between Gifted Education and General Education: Toward Communication, Cooperation, and Collaboration

Carol Ann Tomlinson, Mary Ruth Coleman, Susan Allan, Anne Udall, and Mary Slade

Carol Ann Tomlinson, who has been a forerunner in the field of differentiation, with her colleagues, discusses the relationship between gifted education and general education in Chapter 8. The premise of differentiation is the notion that we must reach all learners on the continuum, but it was never suggested that we leave out the gifted population. All students need the opportunity for creativity and variety. In this chapter, the interface of gifted and general education are explored, as well as the 3Cs—communication, cooperation, and collaboration—as well as the associated cautions, obstacles, benefits, and recommendations.

Chapter 9. Putting It All Together in Your Differentiated Classroom

Gayle H. Gregory and Carolyn Chapman

The key concepts of climate creation, knowing the learner, assessment, adjusting assignments, instruction, and curriculum models can be massive changes for some teachers, but if these concepts are presented piecemeal, teachers will be missing the big picture of how these ideas are integrated in the classroom. In Chapter 9, we provide a lesson-planning template that will help teachers think about the myriad of decisions related to the differentiated classroom. We have provided several completed lesson plans at various grade levels with various subject standards, showing a variety of approaches; sometimes differentiation is provided by adjusted assignments at three levels, and sometimes it requires respecting the interests and preferences of all learners by providing choice. We have also included a reflection checklist linking the process of differentiation to the BRAIN—building safe environments, recognizing and honoring diversity, assessment, instructional strategies, and numerous curriculum approaches.

About the Editor

Gayle H. Gregory is an internationally known consultant who has specialized in brain-compatible learning and differentiated instruction and assessment.

She presents practical teacher- and student-friendly strategies grounded in sound research that educators find easy to use. Her interactive style and modeling of strategies help teachers and administrators transfer new ideas to their classroom and school with ease.

She has had extensive experience in elementary, middle, and secondary schools, and in community colleges and universities. Gayle has also had district leadership roles, including the role of curriculum coordinator and staff development director. She has worked with instructional leadership teams in many schools and districts throughout the country, focusing on data analysis; using assessment, both formative and summative; and differentiating instruction based on readiness, learning profiles, and interests.

Her areas of expertise include brain-compatible learning, block scheduling, emotional intelligence, instructional and assessment practices, differentiated instructional strategies, the use of data to differentiate, literacy, presentation skills, renewal of secondary schools, enhancement of teacher quality, the use of coaching and mentoring, change management, and creation of professional learning communities.

Gayle believes in lifelong learning for herself and others.

Gayle may be contacted at (905) 336-6565 or (716) 898-8716, or by e-mail at gregorygayle@netscape.net. Her website is www.gaylehgregory.com.

About the Contributors

Susan Allan recently retired from the position of assistant superintendent for curriculum, assessment, instruction, and technology for the Grosse Pointe Public School System in Michigan. An educator for more than 30 years, Dr. Allan has served as a high school social studies teacher, a K–12 resource teacher, a gifted education coordinator, a middle school administrator, and a fine-arts director. She has also been an adjunct instructor at the University of Virginia and George Mason University and a guest instructor at various Michigan universities.

Dr. Allan is the author of *Leadership for Differentiating Schools and Classrooms* with Carol Tomlinson and *Local Realities, Local Adaptations: Problems, Process, and Person in a School's Governance* with Frederick Lighthall, as well as many articles on differentiated instruction, grouping practices, and gifted education. Her recent article "Helping Teachers Make Sense of It All: Implementing Differentiated Instruction and Response to Intervention Together," with Yvonne Goddard, appeared in the October 2010 online edition of *Educational Leadership*.

Dr. Allan has presented at many conferences, served on the boards of national and state organizations, and consulted around the country and internationally. She may be contacted at www.differentiatedinstruction.net.

Carolyn Chapman continues her life's goal as an international educational consultant, author, and teacher. She supports educators in their process of change for today's students. She has taught in a variety of settings from kindergarten to college classrooms. Her interactive, hands-on professional development opportunities focus on challenging the mind to ensure success for learners of all ages. All students *do* learn. Why not take control of that learning by putting excitement and quality in effective learning? Carolyn walks her walk and talks her talk to make a difference in the journey of learning in today's classrooms.

Carolyn authored *If the Shoe Fits . . . How to Develop Multiple Intelligences in the Classroom*. She has coauthored *Multiple Assessments for Multiple Intelligences, Multiple Intelligences Through Centers and Projects, Differentiated Instructional Strategies for Writing in the Content Areas, Differentiated Instructional Strategies: One Size Doesn't Fit All*, and *Test Success in the Brain Compatible Classroom*. Video Journal of Education, Inc., features Carolyn

Chapman in *Differentiated Instruction*. Carolyn's company, *Creative Learning Connection, Inc.*, has also produced a CD, *Carolyn Chapman's Making the Shoe Fit*, and training manuals to accompany each of her books. Each of these publications and her trainings demonstrate Carolyn's desire and determination to make an effective impact for educators and students. She may be contacted through the Creative Learning Connection website at www.carolynchapman.com.

Mary Ruth Coleman, PhD, is a senior scientist at the FPG Child Development Institute at the University of North Carolina at Chapel Hill. She directs Project U-STAR~PLUS (Using Science, Talents, and Abilities to Recognize Students—Promoting Learning in Underrepresented Students). Her projects have included ACCESS (Achievement in Content and Curriculum for Every Student's Success), a National Significance Project funded by OSEP, and applications of RTI for young children through the Recognition and Response Project sponsored by the Emily Hall Tremaine Foundation. Dr. Coleman has numerous publications, including the thirteenth edition of the seminal textbook, *Educating Exceptional Children* (2010) with co-authors Samuel A. Kirk, James J. Gallagher, and Nicholas J. Anastasiow. She has served three terms on the Board of Directors for the Association for Gifted (TAG), one of which she was President; three terms on the Board of the National Association for Gifted Children (NAGC); and two terms on the Board of Directors for the Council for Exceptional Children (CEC). She was president of the CEC in 2007.

Glenda Beamon Crawford's experiences with young adolescent learners span nearly thirty years. She has taught Grades 4 through 12 and currently coordinates the Middle Grades Education Program at Elon University where she is a professor. She has written three books, one in its second edition, and published several articles on structuring classrooms for adolescent thinking and learning. Dr. Crawford consults and presents regularly at state, national, and international conferences. She has conducted professional development in Tajikistan and has taught in London and at Southeast University in the Peoples Republic of China. Her research and teaching honors include the 2002 North Carolina Award for Outstanding Contribution to Gifted Education and the 2004 Award for Outstanding Scholarship in the School of Education at Elon University.

Patti Drapeau is teacher, trainer, author, an internationally known presenter, and educational consultant. She has more than twenty-five years of classroom experience teaching students and coordinating programs in Freeport, Maine. Patti currently serves as adjunct faculty at the University of Southern Maine where she teaches graduate courses in Differentiation, Critical and Creative Thinking, Curriculum Integration, Education of the Gifted and Talented, and Curriculum and Methods for Teaching Gifted and Talented Students. Patti is also a certified trainer for the IIM (Independent Investigation Method) Research Model.

Patti developed a curriculum model for the regular classroom called "Affective Perspectives: Combining Critical Thinking, Creative Thinking, and Affect." She has authored a variety of articles for the *Maine Exchange* and is the author of two books published by Scholastic, *Great Teaching With Graphic Organizers* and *Differentiated Instruction: Making It Work.*

Patti is an international presenter in the United States and Canada, where she has appeared at many national, state, and regional conferences. As an educational consultant, she conducts district and school workshops focusing on different ways to meet the needs of all students. She may be contacted through her website, www.pattidrapeau.com.

As a former master teacher who holds current teaching certification, **Kathy Tuchman Glass** consults with schools and districts, presents at conferences, and teaches seminars for university and county programs delivering customized professional development. Kathy has been in education for 20 years and works with teachers at all levels and in groups of varying sizes from one-on-one to entire school districts. She assists administrators and teachers with strategic planning to determine school or district objectives, and presents and collaborates on designing standards-based differentiated curriculum, crafting essential understandings and guiding questions, using compelling instructional strategies that engage all learners, incorporating various effective assessments into curriculum, using six-trait writing instruction and assessment, creating curriculum maps, and more.

In addition to Lesson Design for Differentiated Instruction, Grades 4–9, Kathy has written *Curriculum Mapping: A Step-by-Step Guide to Creating Curriculum Year Overviews* (2007) and *Curriculum Design for Writing Instruction: Creating Standards-Based Lesson Plans and Rubrics* (2005). She is currently coauthoring with Cindy Strickland a professional development guide on *The Parallel Curriculum Model.* In addition, Kathy has served as a reader and reviewer for *Reader's Handbook: A Student Guide for Reading and Learning* (2002) and as a contributing writer and consultant for the Heath Middle Level Literature series (1995).

Originally from Indianapolis, Kathy resides in the San Francisco Bay Area with her supportive husband and two loving and energetic teenagers. She can be reached by phone at 650-366-8122 or through her e-mail at kathy@kathyglassconsulting.com. Her website is www.kathyglassconsult ing.com.

Lin Kuzmich is a consultant, adjunct professor, and author from Loveland, Colorado. She served Thompson School District as the assistant superintendent, executive director of secondary and elementary instruction, director of professional development, assistant director of special education, and as the building principal for nine years. Lin's school was named a 2000 winner of the John R. Irwin Award for Academic Excellence and Improvement. Lin has taught elementary, middle, and high school levels in both regular and special education. Lin earned the Teacher of the Year Award for Denver Public Schools in 1979 and was Northern Colorado Principal of the Year in 2000. In addition, for the past decade, she was involved in staff development through several universities and the Tointon Institute for Educational Change. Currently, Lin is an adjunct professor/instructor at Colorado State University in the Principal Preparation Program. She is a Senior Consultant for the International Center for Leadership in Education. Lin is affiliated with many organizations, including the Association for Supervision and Curriculum Development and the National Association of Secondary Principals, and presents at numerous national conferences. Lin currently works with schools and districts across the country that are struggling to meet the needs of diverse learners, the requirements of state and national laws, and the changing education practices needed for the future success of our students. Lin's work with schools improves achievement results for students and increases the capacity of staff. Lin is passionate about helping educators prepare today's students for a successful future. Lin can be reached at 970-669-2290 or kuzenergy@gmail.com. Her website is www.kcsink.org.

Dr. Mary Slade is a professor in the department of exceptional education at the college of education at James Madison University. Mary received her BS in elementary education with an emphasis in secondary English from Longwood College, and her master's and doctorate degrees from the University of Virginia. Dr. Slade directs the gifted education coursework and the PreK–12 Add-On Gifted Education Endorsement Program at JMU, including the online coursework in this area. Dr. Slade is a member of the JMU chapter of the National Society of Collegiate Scholars.

Dr. Slade has taught in higher education since 1990, teaching in teacher education, special education, and gifted education. Previously she taught in elementary, middle, and high schools as a fourth-grade teacher, gifted education teacher, and English teacher. Dr. Slade is an out-going member of the Board of Directors of the National Association for Gifted Children and won the Early Leader Award from that organization in 1997. Over the past 15 years, Dr. Slade has presented over 200 inservice sessions to educators in preK–12 education, as well as more than 175 professional papers. Dr. Slade has published widely, including more than 40 articles, book chapters, and reports. Dr. Slade is also the co-author of a staff development book in gifted education and co-editor of *Aiming for Excellence: The NAGC PreK–12 Gifted Program Standards*, and the author of a book on consultation and gifted education published from Creative Learning Press.

Dr. Slade's current scholarship includes professional development, advanced studies, differentiation, consultation and collaboration, and web-based distribution of personnel preparation. Dr. Slade consults with individual schools and districts in the areas of consultation and collaboration in gifted education, differentiation, and online learning.

Marilee Sprenger is an experienced classroom teacher at the elementary, middle, high school, and university levels. Marilee's passion is brain-based teaching and best practices using brain research and differentiation. She also consults in the areas of learning styles, using music in the classroom, teaming, multiple intelligences, emotional intelligence, and memory. She speaks internationally, and her interactive and engaging style allows participants the opportunity to make connections to their classrooms and their students. She is affiliated with the American Academy of Neurology and is constantly updated on current research. Marilee is the author of several books, including *Learning and Memory, The Brain in Action, Becoming a Wiz at Brain-Based Teaching, How to Teach So Students Remember, Memory 101 for Educators*, and *The Developing Brain*. She has published numerous articles and contributed to several journals. At her schools, she was always the "brainlady," a nickname she lives up to. Marilee may be reached at 5820 Briarwood Lane, Peoria, IL, 61614; by calling (309) 692-5820; and by e-mail at brainlady@gmail.com. Her website is www.marileesprenger.com.

Donna Walker Tileston is a veteran teacher of three decades, a best-selling and award-winning author, and a full-time consultant. She is the president of Strategic Teaching & Learning, which provides services to schools throughout the United States, Canada, and worldwide. She is the author of more than 20 books, including *What Every Teacher Should Know: The 10-Book Collection* (Corwin, 2004), which won the Association of Educational Publishers' 2004 Distinguished Achievement Award as a Professional Development Handbook. She has also written the following for Corwin: *Closing the Poverty and Culture Gap: Strategies to Reach Every Student* (2009); *Teaching Strategies That Prepare Students for High-Stakes Tests* (2008); *Teaching Strategies for Active Learning: Five Essentials for Your Teaching Plan* (2007); *What Every Parent Should Know About Schools, Standards, and High-Stakes Tests* (2006); *Ten Best Teaching Practices: How Brain Research, Learning Styles, and Standards Define Teaching Competencies, Second Edition* (2005); *Training Manual for What Every Teacher Should Know* (2005); *What Every Teacher Should Know About Learning, Memory, and the Brain* (2004); *What Every Teacher Should Know About Diverse Learners* (2004); *What Every Teacher Should Know About Instructional Planning* (2004); *What Every Teacher Should Know About Effective Teaching Strategies* (2004) ; *What Every Teacher Should Know About Classroom Management and Discipline* (2004); *What Every Teacher Should Know About Student Assessment* (2004); *What Every Teacher Should Know About Special Learners* (2004); *What Every Teacher Should Know About Media and Technology* (2004); *What Every Teacher Should Know About the Profession and Politics of Teaching* (2004); *What Every Teacher Should Know: The 10-Book Collection* (2004); and *Strategies for Teaching Differently: On the Block or Not* (1998).

She received her bachelor's degree from The University of North Texas, her master's from East Texas State University, and her doctorate from Texas A&M University, Commerce. She may be reached at www .wetsk.com.

Carol Ann Tomlinson is the William Clay Parrish Jr. Professor of Educational Leadership, Foundations, and Policy at the University of Virginia's Curry School of Education and the department chair of Leadership, Foundations, and Policy. Prior to joining the University of Virginia's faculty, she was a classroom teacher for twenty-one years, working at the primary, middle, and high school levels. During that time, she also administered district programs for struggling and advanced learners and was recognized as Virginia's Teacher of the Year in 1974. Carol's present work focuses on curriculum and differentiated instruction. She was named outstanding professor at Curry in 2004 and won an all-university teaching award in 2008. Carol is the author of over 200 books, book chapters, articles, and professional development materials—many of them on differentiated instruction.

Anne Udall, vice president of professional development for Northwest Evaluation Association (NWEA), has twenty years of experience in K–12 public education. She has been an aide, teacher, staff developer, program director, and an assistant superintendent with leadership responsibilities for major curriculum, instruction, and professional development initiatives.

Throughout the 1980s, Anne taught in an elementary resource program for learning disabled and gifted students with the Tucson, Arizona Unified School District and provided districtwide training in higher-level thinking skills. In the 1990s, she served in numerous leadership positions for the Charlotte-Mecklenburg Schools, the largest school system in North Carolina, including as assistant superintendent for curriculum and instruction.

She has published numerous articles and has co-authored *Creating the Thoughtful Classroom*. She is an accomplished keynote speaker and presenter.

Prior to joining NWEA, Anne spent nine years as executive director of the Lee Institute, a Charlotte, North Carolina–based nonprofit organization dedicated to encouraging collaboration, problem solving, and strategic planning for individuals, civic organizations, and community efforts.

Anne received her BA in secondary education and her MA in special education from the University of New Mexico and received her PhD in special education from the University of Arizona. She is the co-chair of the Udall Foundation, a federal agency formed in 1996 to honor the work and legacy for her father Morris K. Udall and her uncle Stewart L. Udall.

CREATING A CLIMATE FOR LEARNING 1

Gayle H. Gregory and Carolyn Chapman

CLASSROOMS EVERYWHERE OFFER A DIVERSITY OF FACES AND shapes and sizes, but underneath the diversity, there are fundamental elements that all learners need in order to succeed and to feel positive about their experiences in school.

WHAT DO LEARNERS NEED TO SUCCEED?

For students to succeed, they need to believe that they can learn and that what they are learning is useful, relevant, and meaningful for them. They need to know that they belong in the classroom and that they are responsible for their own learning and behavior. This develops a self-directed learner who is confident in making the information his or her own. This instills *self-efficacy,* which means believing in oneself. In *Education on the Edge of Possibility,* Caine and Caine (1997) state,

> Teachers' beliefs in and about human potential and in the ability of all children to learn and achieve are critical. These aspects of the teachers' mental models have a profound impact on the learning climate and learner states of mind that teachers create. Teachers need to understand students' feelings and attitudes will be involved and will profoundly influence student learning. (p. 124)

Effective teachers believe that all students can learn and be successful. Effective teachers consciously create a climate in which all students feel included. Effective teachers believe that there is potential in each learner and commit to finding the key that will unlock that potential.

CLASSROOM CULTURE AND LEARNING COMMUNITIES

Culture is often referred to as "the way we do things around here." People who live and work in a culture sometimes can't explain or describe it, but they can certainly sense it. Culture may not necessarily be conveyed only through words, but also through actions. Sometimes what we do screams so loudly that we can't hear what is being said. In the words of DePorter, Reardon, and Singer-Nourie (1998), in their book *Quantum Teaching,* "Everything Speaks, Everything Always." They caution teachers that what they do, say, and allude to have an effect on learners and their perceptions of success. According to Gregory and Parry (2006),

> As far as the brain is concerned, actions speak louder than words. Everything that happens in the classroom is monitored by three parts of the brain, two of which have no spoken language but are very adept at reading body language and tone of voice. Every gesture, every inflection, and every invasion of personal space is monitored by the limbic system and evaluated in terms of its threat potential. These skills allowed our ancestors to survive and they are still alive and well in all of us. (p. 13)

Because the brain is a *parallel processor,* it absorbs information on a conscious and an unconscious level. The brain constantly performs many functions at the same time (Ornstein & Thompson, 1984). It therefore can manage to process thoughts, emotions, and perceptions simultaneously.

The brain is also a parallel processor in that it facilitates learning by involving both focused attention and peripheral perception. O'Keefe and Nadel (1978) state that the brain responds to the entire sensory context in which learning takes place. *Peripheral stimuli* include everything in the classroom, from the drab or colorful walls to subtle clues, such as a look or gesture, that conveys meaning and is interpreted by the brain. All sounds and visual signals are full of complex messages. A sarcastic remark can speak volumes to a sensitive learner, and a gesture can convey far more than the spoken word.

In his work with the Mid-continent Research for Education and Learning (McREL) group and with Dimensions of Learning, Robert Marzano (1992) examined the climate for learning, as did Jay McTighe (1990), with the Maryland State Department of Education:

> Closely related to teachers' behavior is the development of a classroom climate conducive to good thinking . . . students cannot think well in a harsh, threatening situation or even in a subtly intimidating environment where group pressure makes independent thinking unlikely. Teachers can make their classrooms more thoughtful places by demonstrating in their actions that they welcome originality and differences of opinion.

Noted researcher Deborah Rozman (1998) remarked that "the neural information the heart sends to the brain can either facilitate or inhibit cortical function, affecting perception, emotional response, learning, and decision making." The heartbeat of another person is perceivable within 3 to 4 feet, because of the electromagnetic field that it projects. The heartbeat of one person registers in the brainwaves of another person. There are intuitive or gut feelings that are picked up by neurons throughout the body. It has often been said, "People need to know you care before they care what you know." And old adages become just that because they are usually true.

As part of his choice theory of motivation, William Glasser (1990, 1998) cites five equally important needs:

- The need to survive and reproduce
- The need to belong and love
- The need to have some power

- The need to have freedom
- The need to have fun

This is also evident in Abraham Maslow's (1968) well-known hierarchy of needs, which includes the following, beginning with the most basic:

- Physiological needs: food, water, air, shelter
- Safety needs: security, freedom from fear, order
- Belongingness and love: friends, spouse, children
- Self-esteem: self-respect, achievement, reputation
- Self-actualization: becoming what the individual has the potential to become

Human beings generally move up the hierarchy from basic to complex needs. As each need has been met, it becomes less of a motivator as the person focuses on the next level.

As we examine motivators, we need to remember that basic needs have to be met first for students. We recognize that all humans have a very strong need to be liked and included. Classrooms everywhere must foster an inclusionary climate. It is essential that students bond with one another and with the teacher to form a positive learning community. Dr. Robert Sapolsky (1998), professor of biological sciences and neuroscience at Stanford University, states that we can minimize the impact of stress by building a supportive environment:

> Put an infant primate through something unpleasant: it gets a stress-response. Put it through the same stressor while in a room full of other primates and . . . it depends. If those primates are strangers, the stress-response gets worse. But if they are friends, the stress-response is decreased. Social support networks—it helps to have a shoulder to cry on, a hand to hold, an ear to listen to you, someone to cradle you and to tell you it will be okay. (p. 215)

Some teachers with their students cooperatively develop classroom "agreements" (Gibbs, 1995), "Trust Statements" (Harmin, 1994), or "rules to live by" to help students feel that they have a voice in the running of the classroom. These rules also help students become more emotionally intelligent and responsible learners. Students in small groups generate statements that they believe the class should live by, for example, "Everyone's ideas count." After the groups share their statements, the class combines, deletes, or adds sentences until consensus is reached and students feel comfortable and can support these rules to live by, which may include the following:

- There is no wrong opinion.
- No put-downs or sarcasm here.
- Everyone must be heard.
- Mistakes are learning points.

If these statements are posted for all students to see and reflect on, students will monitor and honor the rules that they have created.

We also recognize that learning communities foster links between heart and mind. Driscoll (1994) asks us to consider the following:

> Community is the entity in which individuals derive meaning. It is not so much characterized by shared space as it is by shared meanings. Community in this view is not a mere artifact of people living (or working or studying) in the same place, but is rather a rich source of living tradition. (p. 3)

EMOTIONS AND LEARNING

Students living in fear cannot learn. The phenomenon of "downshifting," "the psychophysiological response to threat associated with fatigue or perceived helplessness" (Caine & Caine, 1997, p. 18), suggests that students will not attend to learning if their major concern is safety. This analogy is helpful in planning, so that we challenge students in ways appropriate to their skill levels without overstressing them. Some students may already be so stressed from difficult situations in their personal lives that they are unable to fully attend to lessons, as they are on "high alert" (Gregory & Parry, 2006).

Safety in classrooms means intellectual safety as well as physical safety. During stress, the emotional centers of the brain take control of cognitive functioning, and thus the rational, thinking part of the brain is not as efficient, and this can cause learning to be impeded. If students are living daily with the threat of being ridiculed or bullied, they cannot give their full attention to learning. Students who are challenged beyond their skill levels are more concerned about being embarrassed or laughed at than with the quest for learning. They will not be motivated to attempt the challenge if they aren't able to imagine or perceive success.

In classrooms where the teacher does not adjust the learning to the students' levels of readiness and teaches only to the "middle," some students will be bored from lack of challenge, and others may be placed under undue stress from too great a challenge. Thus, teachers need to consider where their learners are in relation to the learning goal and plan learning experiences just beyond the skill level of each student.

All students are more likely to be engaged in the learning, rise to the challenge, and have a sense of self-confidence as they approach the task if they feel that they have a chance to succeed. Thus, once the levels of readiness have been considered (although it is unrealistic to consider each learner individually), students can often be grouped and experiences designed to accommodate the learners at their levels of understanding.

Teachers need to consider the degree of complexity of learning tasks so that they will be challenging but not overwhelming. This establishes the state of "flow" (Csikszentmihalyi, 1990), the condition that exists when learners are so engaged, excited about learning, challenged, and receiving appropriate feedback that they are oblivious to anything else. Students are at their most productive and most creative in this state:

> People seem to concentrate best when the demands on them are a bit greater than usual, and they are able to give more than usual. If there is too little demand on them, people are bored. If there is too much for them to handle, they get anxious. Flow

occurs in that delicate zone between boredom and anxiety. (Goleman, 1992, as cited in Csikszentmihalyi, 1990, p. 4)

Renate Caine, a well-known pioneer in the field of brain-based education, proposes that there are three basic elements to brain/mind learning and teaching:

- Emotional climate and relationship or relaxed alertness
- Instruction or immersion in complex experience
- Consolidation of learning or active processing

Emotional climate and relationships are important in producing what Kohn (1993) refers to as "relaxed alertness":

> All the methodologies that are used to orchestrate the learning context influence the state of relaxed alertness. It is particularly important for educators to understand the effect of rewards and punishments on student states of mind. Research shows most applications of reward and punishment in the behavioral mode inhibit creativity, interfere with intrinsic motivation, and reduce the likelihood of meaningful learning. (as cited in Caine & Caine, 1997, p. 123)

Rewards and punishments tend to lessen the chances of self-motivation and an appreciation of learning as its own reward. Five practical alternatives to using rewards are the following:

- Eliminating threat
- Creating a strongly positive climate
- Increasing feedback
- Setting goals
- Activating and engaging positive emotions (Jensen, 1998b, p. 68)

It is important, if not imperative, that students feel good, have success, have friends, and celebrate their learning:

> Emotions affect student behavior because they create distinct, mind-body states. A state is a moment composed of a specific posture, breathing rate, and chemical balance in the body. The presence or absence of norepinephrine, vasopressin, testosterone, serotonin, progesterone, dopamine, and dozens of other chemicals dramatically alters your frame of mind and body. How important are states to us? They are all that we have; they are our feelings, desires, memories, and motivations. (Jensen, 1998b, p. 75)

The emotional environment interacts with instruction and influences how information is consolidated. If "downshifting" occurs, the high stress/threat response sabotages connections and thus learning cannot take place. At this point, we are fortunate if even memorization of isolated facts and programmed skills is possible. It is almost impossible for higher-order thinking to take place.

If students think that success isn't possible because the task is too difficult or instructions for a task are ambiguous and not understood, they feel uncertain. These situations cause the learner to form a negative state, and the learner ceases to persevere. Alternately, classrooms that create "eustress" or a state of "flow" create a positive learning environment. Classrooms that embed choices in learning and routines that demonstrate mutual respect are supportive learning environments for students.

EMOTIONAL INTELLIGENCE

Emotional intelligence is a person's ability to use his or her emotions intelligently. It involves maintaining a balance between reason and emotion. Daniel Goleman (1995) organizes emotional intelligence as a set of emotional competencies that occur in five domains.

Self-Awareness

Self-awareness is one's ability to sense and name a feeling when it happens and also to put it into words. Self-aware people can use appropriate strategies to deal with their moods by sharing frustrations with others or seeking support on a bad day. Teachers should encourage students to articulate their feelings and seek and give support. Self-awareness is also being in touch with feelings, not letting feelings become engulfing, and having strategies to cope with moods. In her book *Molecules of Emotion*, Candace B. Pert (1998) suggests, "Feeling low and sluggish? Take a walk. Feeling anxious and jittery? Run!" (p. 293). We all need to find ways to change and manage our moods once we recognize what they are.

Managing Emotions

Managing emotions is an outcome of recognizing and labeling feelings. It is the ability to calm and soothe during anxious moments or to manage and deal with anger. Using "teachable moments" (when an inappropriate emotional response has been given), teachers can help students learn problem-solving skills to generate appropriate alternatives to the feelings. Conflict resolution is easier if students have a repertoire of strategies for dealing with conflict when it erupts.

Self-Motivation

Self-motivation consists of competencies such as persistence, setting one's own goals, and delaying gratification. Many students give up very easily when difficulties occur. Students need to feel hopeful even in the face of setback. The state of "flow" is an integral component of this domain. If students and teachers can create that state of high challenge and low threat, more learning can take place.

Empathy

Empathy is being able to feel for another. Teachers can ask students to "stand in the other person's shoes." These people may be classmates in a situation that calls for empathy. They may be characters in fiction or history with whom students can empathize to understand their emotions. This allows the students to feel how the character or individual might have felt. Understanding another's point of view or perspective is often a standard targeted in many districts. Feeling for others builds tolerance and understanding.

Social Skills

Social skills are the competencies that one uses to "read" other people and manage emotional interactions. People with high levels of social competencies have the ability to handle relationships well and are able to adapt to a variety of social situations. They are said to have "social polish." Teachers modeling these competencies and labeling them when seen in the classroom show the value of emotional intelligence in personal interactions.

The Emotional Intelligence Chart (see Figure 1.1) defines the five domains of emotional intelligence. It also gives suggestions for fostering each intelligence and some strategies for classroom applications.

Figure 1.1   Emotional Intelligence Chart

Intelligence	To Foster	Strategies for Application
Self-awareness: One's ability to sense and name a feeling when it happens	Help students discuss their feelings in different situations.	Reflection Logs and journals
Managing emotions: Recognizing and labeling feelings and responding appropriately	Use "teachable moments" to help students learn to manage emotions.	Deep breathing Counting to 10 Taking time out Physical movement
Self-motivation: Competencies such as persistence, goal setting, and delaying gratification	Help students find a niche. Help them to persist in difficult or challenging situations.	Goal setting Persistence strategies Problem solving
Empathy: Ability to feel for another person	Encourage students to "stand in another's shoes." Think about another person's pain.	Modeling empathy Discussing empathic responses to persons studied
Social skills: Competencies that one uses to "read" and manage emotional interactions	Teach social skills explicitly. Have students practice social skills while doing group tasks.	Modeling social skills Using explicit language to describe behaviors, so students can practice the skills

CLASSROOM CLIMATE

Learning Atmosphere

In a differentiated classroom, all students feel safe and secure enough to take risks and express their understanding or lack of understanding. Many times, the students considered academically gifted feel that they are expected to know all the information. Often these learners pretend to have all the answers in response to the expectations of others. This can cause stress and interfere with learning. A disappointed look or comment can keep the gifted student from expressing a lack of understanding. This student, as well as others, should feel secure in the classroom even when he or she doesn't have all the answers.

The learner who is considered to be at risk or low achieving often lives up to the expectations of the label. Giving a student a look of surprise when he "gets it" shows that he is not expected to get it! Often this puts a cap on potential. Students live up to our expectations.

In a differentiated classroom, the emphasis is on knowledge base and experience rather than IQ and ability. Each student is respected. Learners know that learning is a process and everyone learns differently. Learning includes weeding out what students know with an effective pre-assessment and determining what students need next. This policy establishes a different mind-set of being able to admit mistakes, accept lack of understanding, and celebrate successes and growth in an individual's knowledge base. Each moment of successful improvement makes a positive change for a lifetime.

Physical and Emotional Atmosphere

The climate is influenced by the physical attributes of the classroom. Things such as appropriate lighting, cleanliness, orderliness, and displays of students' work contribute to a positive atmosphere. Plentiful and appropriate resources are necessary to facilitate student success. There could be computers and materials that allow for hands-on manipulation. There should be opportunities for social interaction and intellectual growth.

Enriched environments are created not only by materials but also by the complexity and variety of tasks and challenges and feedback (Caine & Caine, 1997; Jensen, 1998b). Engaging materials and activities help to develop *dendritic growth,* the neural connections that are facilitated by experiences and stimulation (Diamond & Hopson, 1998; Green, Greenough, & Schlumpf, 1983; Healy, 1992). As Dr. Arnold B. Scheibel, professor of neurology at UCLA, suggests,

> On the basis of what we know and have seen from animal experiments, it seems a likely inference that the same phenomenon in rats, mice, cats, and monkeys holds for humans, as well: Increase the level of environmental stimulation and challenge, and you will increase the branching of the dendrites and the thickness of the human cortex. (as cited in Diamond & Hopson, 1998, p. 35)

This growth is stimulated by a variety of complex and intriguing activities, as previously noted by Renate Caine (as cited in Healy, 1992): "If we encourage children to make choices from a selected variety of available challenges, both environmental and intellectual, we are no doubt following the wisest course" (p. 72).

Use of Music

Another component for enhancing classroom climate may be the inclusion of music. Researchers at Strathclyde University have discovered that brainpower soars when students listen to stimulating pop tunes, and they advise that playing the latest hits in classrooms may actually increase student achievement.

This study by Dr. Brian Boyd and Katrina Bowes (*The Brain in the News,* Dana Press, 2001) researched the effects of music after learning about studies in Russia that discovered that medical patients who listened to music recovered faster. In contrast to the belief that only classical music calms the learner, they found that modern music with the same tempo as classical (60 beats per minute) has the same effect and makes the mind more receptive to learning. This music can actually help the brain retain information.

Many teachers who have tried using pop music report higher levels of concentration by their students. Pop music triggers the autonomic nervous system, and we respond by feeling good and tapping our feet to the music. The pupils of the eyes dilate, and endorphin levels and energy rise. Teachers often say that students will learn more in a class if they are enjoying the experience, and music can set the stage for learning. Students will link a known routine with a piece of music and thus be ready for what is to follow. The music can be playful, for example, playing Marvin Gaye's "I Heard It Through the Grapevine" while students are estimating the number of raisins in a small, lunch-size box. Or the music can appeal to the emotions and create a mood, as happens when listening to "When Johnny Comes Marching Home Again" at the beginning of a discussion of World War I or "War," by Bruce Springsteen, in relation to the study of the Vietnam War.

Music energizes people and masks "dead air" when there is a "dip" in the energy level of students. Mozart's music or Baroque music can soothe and calm as well (Campbell, 1998).

Laughter and Celebrating Learning

Laughter is another tool to use in classrooms. It punctuates learning by releasing neuro-chemical transmitters called *endorphins,* and it is said to be the shortest distance between two people. Laughter even helps the immune system to increase the number of type T leukocytes (T cells) in the blood. T cells combat damage and infection, and some researchers have even dubbed them "happiness cells" (Cardoso, 2000). It makes sense to include humor and laughter and to celebrate learning in the classroom. Teachers can encourage students to applaud one another and cheer for each other's successes. Using energizing cheers (Burke, 1993; DePorter et al., 1998), students give rounds of applause, high fives, and other cheers that students can often create for themselves. These cheers also include actions to supplement the aural responses. Kinesthetic actions help energize students by sending more oxygen and glucose to the brain and often result in fun and laughter to raise endorphins.

Celebrating learning is important for students of all ages. A simple way to celebrate any classroom success is to lead an energizing cheer. When an individual or small group has a "lightbulb moment" or presents what has been learned, give a cheer. Besides the emotional boost, these cheers provide a physical boost to the brain. The physical actions send oxygen and glucose to the brain when arms are raised over the head and the body moves.

The following are some examples of cheers that energize and celebrate. Add your own physical movements to punctuate the cheer:

- Yes!
- Triple Yes!!!
- Oh, Yes!
- Ketchup Clap
- Fish Clap
- Table Rap Clap
- Happy Clam Clap
- Wah Hoo
- Awesome
- WOW
- Microwave
- Standing Oh!
- You Did It
- High Five
- Excellent Guitar
- Round of Applause
- You are great and getting greater!

Although each learner in the classroom is very different, everyone needs to feel safe and comfortable. In classrooms, climate and atmosphere play an important part in the learning process. Anything teachers can do to create a risk-free supportive environment where students can feel safe and where they can thrive needs to be considered and implemented in classrooms. Building a community of learners who care for and support one another is essential in a differentiated classroom. Students who know and respect each other are more tolerant of differences and more comfortable when tasks are different. Even though "one size doesn't fit all," learners require all these conditions to succeed.

1. How would you describe your classroom climate?

2. How do you encourage team building throughout the year?

3. What do you do to create an atmosphere where students can take intellectual risks in your classroom?

4. How do you create intellectual safety and prohibit ridicule, put-downs, and
   other negative responses in your classroom?

5. How much wait time do you allow for thinking and answering questions?

6. What steps will you take to create an inclusive atmosphere where students feel safe and included?

7. How is "relaxed alertness" created?

8. How can you create "flow"?

2

Getting to Know Your Students

Learning Strengths

Marilee Sprenger

"I never realized how important different learning environments are. Just understanding those has made a big difference in my classroom. But I know that there is more to it," Janice says as we sit at the lunch table.

"Sit with your students at lunch once in awhile," I offer. "You can learn a lot about them in the cafeteria. See who is sitting with whom. The social hierarchy will really present itself there."

"Margo, I saw your students sitting and working at different activities. What was that about? Don't you worry about what is going on when you can't watch them all at once? I'm so afraid of losing control!" Janice declares.

"If you have them working on something interesting, working together, you've hit their readiness or interest levels, it's not much of a problem," Margo replies. "What you saw were some learning centers that were designed for different learning strengths."

"What kind of learning strengths?"

"Did you ever talk about learning styles or modalities in college?" I ask.

"In one of the classes we talked about that a little bit."

"Well, learning strengths develop as the brain learns. Many of us tend to have a preference for one or more of our senses. I prefer visual information. My friend, Glenn, remembers very little that he reads, but he remembers everything he hears."

Janice looks perplexed, "I thought this was really old stuff. Straight out of the fifties or sixties."

Margo and I look at each other. "Watch out what you call old stuff!" she quips. "Marilee and I are old stuff, and you're asking us for help. This information has been around a while, and recent research is supporting its importance."

I smile. "Janice, this really changed my teaching and made my life easier. Whenever the students are learning and they're happy, the classroom is a great place to be."

We began to fill Janice in on what we were referring to. It doesn't take long to understand some of our students' differences. Margo shared the following story with her.

It is the first day of school. Jeffrey and Elise are both excited about the new school year. At Jeffrey's house, the alarm goes off earlier than usual and he takes great care in dressing, as he wants to look a little extra special for this first day. Jeffrey takes some time in the bathroom fixing his hair. He is eager to see his friends and check out the new students. He has heard that several new girls have entered the district, and some will be in his class.

Elise's mom wakes Elise before she leaves for work. Elise has a brand new outfit, and she is excited about seeing what the other girls will be wearing.

Jeffrey checks over the contents of his book bag before he leaves. Everything appears to be in order: number 2 pencils, three folders, notebook paper, black ink pens, a compass, and a protractor. He zips up the bag and zips out the door.

Elise takes a last minute look at her hair. "Perfect," she thinks as she looks around for her school supplies. The new book bag in forest green looks great! Did she remember to pack those supplies that Mom bought? Oh yes, there's paper, pens, and pencils. That ought to do it until the teachers tell her exactly what they expect. She heads for the bus.

The students mill around in the school yard until the bell rings at 7:45. They then enter the building and head to their homerooms. Jeffrey and Elise are in the same room this year. They've been in school together since first grade. They smile and nod to each other as they head for their seats. Jeffrey sits in the front, while Elise heads to the back corner where she talks to some of her friends.

Mrs. Warmth enters the room. She has been in the hall greeting students. Elise really likes this teacher. She smiles a lot, listens carefully to the kids, and always shares interesting experiences.

Jeffrey wishes he had Mr. Stuff for homeroom. That is one interesting teacher. He has all kinds of things in the room to look at. Mr. Stuff teaches science, and although Jeffrey will have him for one class period later in the day, he would love to be in his homeroom as well.

After Mrs. Warmth takes attendance and lunch count, the bell rings for first hour class. Jeffrey, Elise, and the rest of the students gather their belongings and head for Miss Rigid's language arts class. "All right, boys and girls, you will be sitting alphabetically, so don't get too comfortable." Jeffrey smiles at this. He's in the first part of the alphabet, so he's certain to have a seat up front. He doesn't want to miss anything! Besides, one of the new girls has the last name Adams. He wouldn't mind sitting by her.

Elise rolls her eyes as her name is called. She's sitting in the second row, second seat. All of her friends are in the back of the room. "Why can't I change my last name?" she complains to herself as she settles in the new seat.

The textbooks are on the desks. Jeffrey carefully puts his name in his book and looks through the table of contents as Miss Rigid suggests. Elise opens her book, writes her name, and quickly closes it. "Another year of boring textbooks," she thinks as she turns around to wave to Cheryl.

"Elise!" shouts Miss Rigid. "It's the first day of school; let's not start breaking the rules yet!"

Elise rolls her eyes and turns back around. She figures she'll give this woman 10 minutes. If things don't get active, it will be time to daydream the class period away. There is no way she can sit for 45 minutes listening to a lecture and staring at a book.

Jeffrey sits up eagerly waiting for new information and an assignment. He has his new pen and paper ready.

DIFFERENT LEARNERS/DIFFERENT TEACHERS

Both of these students are eager to start the new year. They want to go to school. Why does Jeffrey eagerly await new information and Elise prepare to daydream her way through class? Does she not care about learning?

The first hour bell rings and Elise jumps! She was thinking about the football game on Friday night. She throws her book and supplies in her bag and lines up at the door with the other students. Jeffrey finishes writing down the assignment and joins her at the door.

"Do we have homework?" Elise asks him.

Jeffrey looks at her and wonders how she got this far. "Call me after school and I'll give you the assignment," he says with a sigh.

They enter Mrs. Precise's math class. The desks that were in the room last year are gone. They have been replaced with modular tables. "Sit wherever you want," Mrs. Precise announces. "We'll be working in groups this year. I've chosen your groups for this first unit. After that, we'll create some special interest groups."

Elise smiles at the possibilities in this classroom. No daydreaming here. From the feel of this setup, she figures she can learn a lot this year in math.

Mrs. Precise interrupts Elise's thoughts. "Okay, the first thing we will do is go to the board. I want to see you work some problems in pairs."

Elise jumps up with glee, grabs Cheryl, and picks a spot right in front of her teacher. She is eager to show off her math ability. Jeffrey slowly rises, nods to one of his friends and goes to the board with him. He can't wait till this part of the class is over. He is also concerned about this group work; he hopes he won't end up doing everyone else's work.

What a difference a class period can make for some students! It is now obvious that both Jeffrey and Elise care about learning. They just learn differently. It is up to their school and its teachers to provide learning opportunities that fit.

> *Learning profiles represent the sum total of strengths and weaknesses that children possess.*

WHAT IS A LEARNING PROFILE?

Learning profiles represent the sum total of strengths and weaknesses that children possess. In order to form such a profile, we need to know how children take in information, in what way they process patterns, their preferred mode of output, and how their attentional system works (Eide & Eide, 2006).

Input, output, and patterning all rely on our senses. The connections that are made to learning are made via visual, auditory, or kinesthetic channels. If a student's input preference is visual, most patterns will be stored as visual ones.

From the short observation of Jeffrey, it looks as though he is a visual learner; that is, his preferential input system is visual. He likes to sit up front, and he enjoys looking at his books. He is also an independent learner. It is uncomfortable for him to work in groups. He is successful at the "school game." He knows how to take in semantic information and probably is very good at giving it back on both teacher-made assessments and standardized tests.

Elise, on the other hand, needs to move and talk. She is a kinesthetic learner who prefers to input information through movement. By working in pairs or groups, Elise has the opportunity to move and to process information through kinesthetic and auditory channels. Auditory learners need to talk as much as they need to listen. That is how learning becomes real to them.

Behavioral psychologist Andrew Meltzoff recommends that teachers use various ways of inputting information (Meltzoff, 2000). All information enters our brains through our senses. Not only are there preferred sensory systems of which educators must be made aware, but it makes perfect "sense" that the more senses that are activated, the more likely it is that information will be encoded. In other words, Elise can take in information visually if she is allowed to move and talk as well. It is understood that we are all capable of using all of our sensory pathways (unless there is a physical problem). Some students are more balanced than others in their ability to take in information in different ways.

Attention

Will students' attentional systems be related to their input systems? It makes sense that they are. If a student prefers visual information, visual stimuli will be appealing to that student. That is not to say that other stimuli that are novel may not also get the student's attention. Marzano (2007) refers to the following stimuli as engaging for most students: high energy, missing information, mild pressure, and mild competition.

Stimuli that are engaging for most students include high energy, missing information, mild pressure, and mild competition.

For high energy, physical movement will get oxygen and blood flowing to the brain. Movement and learning are processed in the same part of the brain! Timing or pacing the learning will have a positive effect on attention and learning. An important area to keep in mind is focus time. Most research suggests that your students' focus time, as measured in minutes, is equal to their age in years. Keep in mind, if you are teaching 10-year-olds, after eight or nine minutes change the activity or your teaching style. Basically, the part of the brain that your students are using for your lesson gets low on chemicals and needs time to regenerate. When you switch to another kind of stimulus, you give the brain the time it needs (Sprenger, 2005). (If you don't change the stimulation, your students will "self-stimulate," as in talking to others, moving, reading comic books, etc.) Finally, Marzano (2007) refers to teacher enthusiasm and energy having a positive effect on attention. If you are excited about the lesson, your excitement will spread.

Missing information offers an opportunity for pattern seeking in the brain. Quiz shows with open-ended questions and other games encourage making connections to prior knowledge. Some teachers put lists of concepts or vocabulary words related to the topic on the overhead or on a slide and ask students to find what is missing or what could be added. Students consider this a challenge and search their brains for missing words. Words or ideas that do not belong stand out, as they do not fit into the network of information that is stored in the brain. An example would be the m & m game. The m's stand for *memory* and *magic*. The students first search their memory to add to the ideas; then they perform the "magic" of making unnecessary information disappear. Some teachers use actual m & m's for each memory recalled and each feat of magic. Figure 2.1 shows an example.

Figure 2.1   Memory and Magic

Look at the following list and determine:

What memory can you recall that needs to be added to the list?

What needs to disappear?

The Planets

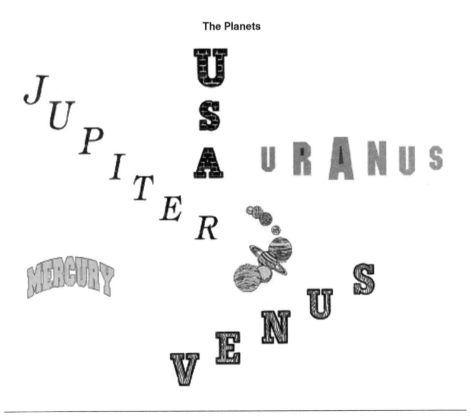

Mild pressure is mild stress. Although bad stress will inhibit learning, good stress helps us to focus. Knowing that they may be quizzed or questioned may keep students attending. Besides the use of focus time, wait time can be used for this purpose. Many students assume that teachers want quick answers and will allow the students who always respond quickly to answer; therefore, they are not required to attend or think. But waiting for students to retrieve information and even expecting that all will raise their hands may provide the mild pressure to pay attention.

> *Although bad stress will inhibit learning, good stress helps us to focus.*

Mild or moderate competition focuses attention for many children. These terms refer to competition that does not cause embarrassment or harassment of any kind. Debate is an example of this kind of competition. Team games or paired games can be fun and interesting for students.

Debra Pickering (2005) offers game ideas that promote fun and learning. At one of her workshops, participants were paired and seated so one partner faced the screen and the other faced away from it. A list of words appeared with a topic at the top. The partner privy to the screen gave definitions or explanations to get the other partner to say the words. The first pair to finish received a small piece of candy. Stickers may be a better alternative for students. The game was fun, and all were attentive. This type of situation actually appeals to all of the aforementioned attention-getters. It is fast paced, there is mild pressure to know your information for your partner's sake, there is missing information, and movement is provided as students move their chairs and sit with their partners.

Patterns

Through our input systems, we store sensory patterns that are our long-term memories. Our brains use those patterns to understand and store new patterns. For instance, if you are introducing the concept of ratio in math or science class, you might ask students if they have ever had a lemonade stand. How did they make the lemonade? Whether it was made from a packaged mix or a frozen concentrate, the instructions provided a ratio for mixing the drink. Students can take this prior knowledge and use this pattern to understand the ratio concept. If you are teaching students who haven't had the lemonade experience, it is easy enough to bring a can to class and demonstrate. Better yet, bring enough for them to each experience pouring the appropriate ratio.

With that said, students have their own preferred patterns for storing memory. They use these patterns in working memory for encoding new information and reflecting upon it. In long-term memory, these patterns are used for filing the information in permanent storage and then retrieving it. After first gaining an understanding of a student's learning style, we can then gain a better understanding of the memory pattern processes that he or she uses.

> *After first gaining an understanding of a student's learning style, we can then gain a better understanding of the memory pattern processes that he or she uses.*

In my classrooms, I find that if I think VAK (visual, auditory, kinesthetic) for every lesson, students not only learn more quickly and easily, they enjoy it. If we want our students to care about learning, they must feel successful in the process.

Mrs. Precise has the concept. She begins her lesson for the kinesthetic learner. First, the students are at the board. Large muscle movement is provided. The students are working in pairs. This provides the auditory learner with input and the opportunity for output. It also helps reduce stress. Those visual learners will soon "see" all kinds of information on that board. But even better yet, this is the way this teacher accesses prior knowledge—a key to learning. Since the brain is a meaning-making organ, making connections with previous learning through different modalities allows each student to make sense of the learning. Once Mrs. Precise has ascertained what her students already know, she can use those hooks for future learning.

WHY SENSORY PATHWAYS?

The brain's system of processing information is summarized in Figure 2.2. Initially, sensory information is sent from our nervous system to the brain stem. From the brain stem it goes to the central filtering station in the middle of the brain called the thalamus. The thalamus sends this information to its designated area of the neocortex. The neocortex is where higher-level thinking takes place. Each sense has a place called an association cortex. For instance, auditory information is sent via the thalamus to the auditory association cortex. The information is examined, and if it is important and should be attended to, another brain structure becomes involved. This is the reticular activating system. Found in the brain stem, this is a powerful structure that can send messages throughout the brain. It "wakes up" the brain to the identified information and helps store patterns in long-term memory (Kittredge, 1990).

Figure 2.2   Information Processing

1. Information enters the brain through the senses. All sensory information except the sense of smell is processed the same way.

2. It goes through the brain stem to the structure called the thalamus.

3. The thalamus sorts the information to send it to the various association areas in the neocortex.

4. Visual information goes to the visual association cortex in the occipital lobe. Auditory information goes to the auditory association cortex in the temporal lobe. Kinesthetic information goes to the motor strip and the cerebellum.

5. If the information requires immediate attention, the reticular activating system in the brain stem releases chemical messages to focus attention.

6. If the information is important and factual, the limbic structure called the hippocampus catalogs it for long-term memory. If the information is important and emotional, the limbic structure called the amygdala catalogs it for long-term memory.

7. The information is then stored in the various areas of the neocortex.

It is in these association areas that patterns are formed. For instance, in the visual center, we have the pattern of a dog. In some cases we have a basic pattern: four legs, a tail, a head, ears, sharp teeth, and fur. We also have specific patterns like a Dalmatian: all of the above characteristics along with a more specific shape of the head and tail as well as a white fur background with black spots. It is through this patterning that we learn to recognize things in our worlds.

All of your senses are always "on." You are bombarded with sensory information every second. It would be impossible to pay attention to all of it. And you wouldn't want to. For instance, until you read the next few words, you are probably not aware of how your chair feels on your bottom. Or how your toes feel in your shoes. This is not important information unless you are extremely uncomfortable in one of these areas. Your brain helps you focus on what is important.

Since all information is received through our five senses, many researchers feel that a preference is developed for a specific sense (Dunn & Dunn, 1987; Grinder, 1991; Markova, 1996; Sprenger, 2007), just as we have two hands and most of us develop a preference for one, which becomes our dominant hand. Well, many people appear to have dominant sensory pathways. Through their experiences, genetics, and brain development, they have found that one of the senses operates better for them than the others. We can designate this sense or modality as their *learning strength*. Since 1971 I have been working with both adults and children and have found that individuals will always learn best if they begin with that strength.

> *Since all information is received through our five senses, many researchers feel that a preference is developed for a specific sense.*

The importance of understanding these sensory approaches to learning will become clearer when we examine how memory works and look at memory problems. According to Barbe and Swassing, sensation, perception, and memory together create a modality (Guild & Garger, 1998). You see, you have visual, auditory, and kinesthetic memory systems. What about the other two senses? Do they have memories? Clearly, we have all been taken back in time by certain smells or tastes. These are usually lumped in with the kinesthetic sense, since they involve "doing" something (Markova & Powell, 1998).

Michael Grinder, author of *Righting the Educational Conveyor Belt* (1991), examines a classroom of 30 students. He says that approximately 22 of these students are very balanced in their ability to retrieve and retain information through all of the sensory pathways. Of the eight remaining, two or three are having a difficult time learning because of problems outside the classroom. Then there are five or six students who have a very difficult time with any sensory pathway other than their strength. He calls these students translators, as they must translate information from the other senses into their preferred style. Translation is difficult at best for many of them. And much can be lost in the translation. These are the students who need more help. We may recognize them as the students whose hands are usually raised after giving some seat work after a lesson.

SENSORY PATHWAYS

There are characteristics that have been identified that may be attributed to sensory preferences. Some of these may be familiar to you. However, if it's been a while, take another look. I think you'll be surprised at what you may have forgotten or what has been more recently discovered. Typically, when observing visual, auditory/verbal, and tactile/kinesthetic learners, one would observe some of the following:

Visual

- Rolls eyes
- Follows you around the room with his/her eyes
- Is distracted by movement
- Loves handouts, work on the board, overheads, and any visual presentations
- Often speaks rapidly
- Will usually retrieve information by looking up and to the left
- Says things like "I see what you mean" or "I get the picture"

Auditory/Verbal

- May answer rhetorical questions
- Talks a lot; may talk to self
- Distracted by sound
- Enjoys cassette tape work and listening to you speak
- Likes to have material read aloud
- Usually speaks distinctly
- Will usually retrieve information by looking from side to side while listening to his/her internal tape recorder
- Says things like "Sounds good to me" or "I hear what you're saying"

Kinesthetic/Tactile

- Sits very comfortably, usually slouched or lots of movement, leans back in chair, taps pencil
- Often speaks very slowly—feeling each word

- Distracted by comfort variations, i.e., temperature, light
- Needs hands-on experiences
- Distracted by movement—often his/her own
- Will usually retrieve information by looking down to feel the movement when he/she learned it
- Says things like "I need a concrete example" or "That feels right"

SENSORY SYSTEMS

We've come so far with brain research, and we still don't have all the answers. There is more information available dealing with how our sensory systems operate. It is this information that can help us understand some of the differences we see in our students. Let's look briefly at information processing. As I stated earlier, information enters our brains through our senses. Each sense has a passageway. The thalamus sorts information and sends it to the top layer of the brain, the neocortex. The neocortex has an area for each type of sensory stimuli. The visual cortex processes visual information, the auditory cortex processes sounds, and the somatic cortex processes touch. The information from each is then sent to the rhinal cortex. This is an area where the senses are put back together into one representation. From the rhinal cortex, the information is sent to the hippocampus. This important memory structure receives information from several convergence zones in the brain. It is here that the information can go from being a simple perception of what is happening to being an abstract concept (LeDoux, 2002).

With this information, we can see how vital our sensory systems are to learning. The concept of having a preferred sensory system has been shared by educators and researchers (DePorter, Reardon, & Nouri, 1999; Grinder, 1991; Markova, 1992; Rose & Nicholl, 1997). When I first learned this information, I thought it was vital that I know the preferred sensory passageway of each of my students. This is interesting information to have, and it is very helpful in working with students who have some difficulties learning. However, it is more important that the students understand their preferences, so they can lead with their strengths.

Visual Memory Preference

The learner who has this preference prefers to see information. It sounds simplistic, but there are at least two types of visual learners. Some are able to easily see and understand graphs and charts, while others are simply print oriented (Kline, 1997). I am a print-oriented visual learner. I often disappoint others because I don't recall the color of their carpet or their new kitchen. I do, however, remember the printed word. When asked a question, if I have read the information, I picture the words, then the page, and finally I can close the book in my mind and state the title. You can generally tell visual learners by the eye contact they will give you. These learners may have some of the characteristics described earlier. They may be happy as clams just to have you say, "Open your books to page 54 and look at . . . ." Learning is real to them if they can see it. Many of these learners have good visualization skills. So, if they have participated in a kinesthetic activity that involved learning a concept, they can conjure up that episode in their mind's eye in order to recall it. Some with this preference will have strong spatial skills and will be able to visualize shapes and sizes with little difficulty. Because they can often easily visualize words or problems, spelling and math may be undemanding for them. Some of these students are very neat, as they are so aware of how things look. Untidiness can be a source of contention for them. Movies, field trips, maps, graphs, charts, and pictures will usually pique their interest.

> *You can generally tell visual learners by the eye contact they will give you.*

Print-oriented learners can become bogged down in the printed word. Most of them are able to learn from the same experiences as other visual learners. They may, however, need to be prodded to do so. This preference also includes writing. Writing information gives these visual learners the opportunity to see how concepts fit together. They may take copious notes, even if they don't have to look at them a second time.

Auditory/Verbal Memory Preference

The auditory preference usually involves both hearing and speaking. The auditory areas and speech areas in the brain are in close proximity. Typically these learners enjoy listening to others as well as listening to themselves talk! Often these students have strong language skills. Their vocabularies are frequently extensive. They enjoy words and speak in a rhythmical fashion. Some of these individuals pick up foreign languages and dialects easily (Markova, 1992). These students may have musical talents. Tone, pitch, rhythm, and rhyme may be appealing to them. At the same time, these students may be sound-sensitive. In other words, certain noises may be annoying to them. As they are learning or concentrating, extraneous noises, such as those emanating from the radiator, may cause them to lose concentration. These are the students who say, "Tell him to stop clicking his pen," or "She's got to stop coughing—it's driving me crazy. I can't think!" I had one student tell me, "He's breathing too loud!" These students usually spell by sounding words out. Perhaps this is why they don't like to write much. Their spelling is often wrong—after all, you can't even spell *phonetically* phonetically!

Many educators believe that those with auditory preferences can listen all day long. That is simply not true. What makes learning real to these students is being able to talk about it. Group work has saved many auditory processors. Working on group or team projects gives these students the opportunity to talk through the material.

Kinesthetic/Tactile Memory Preferences

The kinesthetic/tactile preference includes different types of learners. We often think of these students as simply wigglers and jigglers. My own daughter falls into this category. School was not a happy place for her most of the time. In particular, her teachers who had preferences for visual learning found Marnie's movement a distraction. However, this is not the only characteristic of a child or adult who follows this preference.

There are many different types of kinesthetic learners.

Hands-On Learners

The hands-on tactile-kinesthetic learners need to do something in order to learn it. They usually process best through assembling things, taking things apart, working with textured materials, and manipulating objects. Math manipulatives have really made a difference in the lives of these learners. My husband, Scott, is a hands-on learner. He doesn't read the VCR manual (or any other directions); he plays with the controls until he figures it out.

Whole Body Learners

The whole body tactile-kinesthetic learners need to become what they are learning. This may include role-play, exercise, building, giving live demonstrations, and using whole body movements.

Doodlers

The doodling tactile-kinesthetic learners learn through drawing, coloring, and doodling. Being able to do this at their desks while discussion is going on actually may help them listen. With this learner, I have to remind myself that the doodling is "turning on the brain." Many of these students have good fine and large motor skills. They may be very coordinated and do well in sports. These students are often mislabeled as hyperactive, since sitting still is a major problem for some of them. Often if the teacher stays in close proximity to a mover and shaker, it will make the student calmer. An affirming touch to the shoulder may also calm him or her.

PERCEPTUAL PATTERNS

Dr. Dawna Markova has written several books on the subject of the way we learn. She compares our minds to an orchestra. We are all like different instruments. They are played differently. They sound different. But together they make beautiful music. The trick is to know what instrument you have and how to play it. For many years, I was a teacher playing the trombone. Teaching the trombone to a whole class of students—with very few actually having a trombone! Markova views the sensory approach a little differently. Since we have all five senses, and use all five senses, she categorizes learners into six different patterns (see Figure 2.3). These patterns are one way of grouping students for differentiated instruction.

Figure 2.3   Perceptual Patterns That Can Be Used for Flexible Grouping

Pattern	Preference	Characteristics
Visual-Auditory-Kinesthetic	1. Seeing and Showing 2. Hearing and Saying 3. Experiencing and Doing	Reads and tells stories; good eye contact; can sit still for long periods; shies away from sports
Visual-Kinesthetic-Auditory	1. Seeing and Showing 2. Experiencing and Doing 3. Hearing and Saying	Good eye contact; neat; speaks with hands; shies away from public speaking
Auditory-Kinesthetic-Visual	1. Hearing and Saying 2. Experiencing and Doing 3. Seeing and Showing	Very verbal; high energy; good with language; learns with discussion & lecture; often interrupts; little eye contact
Auditory-Visual-Kinesthetic	1. Hearing and Saying 2. Seeing and Showing 3. Experiencing and Doing	Very verbal; good vocabulary; learns through discussion & lecture; may learn through reading; maintains eye contact
Kinesthetic-Visual-Auditory	1. Experiencing and Doing 2. Seeing and Showing 3. Hearing and Saying	Learns through hands-on; gives eye contact; good at sports; difficulty with oral reading & reports; difficulty with expressing feelings verbally
Kinesthetic-Auditory-Visual	1. Experiencing and Doing 2. Hearing and Saying 3. Seeing and Showing	Learns physically or through hands-on; difficulty sitting still; good at teaching activities; good at sports

If we are looking at the whole child, there are times when understanding these perceptual patterns is helpful. There are some differences, particularly when one looks at the first two sensory preferences. For instance, both my husband and my daughter are kinesthetic learners. Yet, they are different in some obvious ways. Marnie is KAV (kinesthetic-auditory-visual). She moves and then she talks. She wiggles and jiggles. In order to learn, she must be up and moving. Scott, on the other hand, is KVA (kinesthetic-visual-auditory). He learns through doing, doesn't talk much, and finds it very difficult to give formal speeches or read aloud. I believe the awareness of this information can be helpful in dealing with different learners.

THE NEED TO KNOW

There are several ways to identify your students' modalities. Understanding one's sensory preferences is not only part of a learning profile, it is also a step toward metacognition and lifelong learning. The more your students know about themselves, the better learners they will be. Explain the different learning styles to them. Not only will they be fascinated, but you can help them decide which way is best and most comfortable for them to learn and study. Think of this information as a springboard rather than a crutch. Once your students lead with their strengths, they can then explore different ways of learning.

> *The more your students know about themselves,*
> *the better learners they will be.*

The most reliable method of identifying sensory preferences is observation. Between your careful examination and the students' own feelings about it, you can be fairly accurate in determining a preference. I have included an assessment to give your students (see Figure 2.4), but it is limiting. Giving a written test to a student who does not do well on a written test can give false information. I have kept this assessment as simple as possible so that you may use it just to discuss with your students.

After the students have written down their answers, have them count the number of *a*'s, then the number of *b*'s, and finally the number of *c*'s. If they have mostly *a*'s, they favor their visual modality. If they have mostly *b*'s, it appears they favor being auditory. If the *c*'s are their highest, then they lean toward being kinesthetic. You will find many of your students are balanced. This is helpful to them; however, rest assured that in a tough situation they have a preferred modality that they will rely upon.

Figure 2.4   What Kind of Learner Are You?

Answer the following questions by choosing the response that feels the most comfortable to you.

1. When I watch a television show, I most remember
   a. the costumes, scenery, and the actor/actresses.
   b. what the characters say to each other.
   c. the action in the show or how it makes me feel.

2. When I am alone, I like to
   a. read or watch television.
   b. talk on the telephone.
   c. play a game or go outside and play.

3. If I buy my own clothes, I usually buy
   a. light colored clothing in popular styles.
   b. bright colored clothing.
   c. very comfortable clothing.

4. When I remember previous vacations, I remember
   a. the way the places looked.
   b. the sounds and the conversations I had there.
   c. the way it felt to be there and the activities.

5. My favorite way to learn something is to
   a. have someone show me a picture or see it in a book.
   b. have someone tell me how to do it.
   c. do it myself.

6. When I study, I like
   a. to have soft music playing and lots of light.
   b. to have absolute silence and sometimes read aloud.
   c. to be real comfortable - like on a bed or a couch.

7. My favorite kind of class is when the teacher
   a. uses the overhead or chalkboard a lot and I can copy down the information.
   b. tells us the information and I can just listen.
   c. lets us try to do the stuff ourselves.

8. When I spell a word, I
   a. picture the word in my head.
   b. sound out the letters.
   c. write it down and see if it feels right.

9. I
   a. think talking on the phone is okay, but I'd rather see people to talk to them.
   b. love to talk on the phone.
   c. would rather be out doing something than talk on the phone.

10. The most uncomfortable situation for me would be
    a. to not be able to watch television or read.
    b. to not be able to talk.
    c. to not be able to move around.

Never let your learners use their sensory preference as an excuse for inappropriate behavior or failing to finish assignments. This is great information and a wonderful tool. It is no reason for disrupting the class. Rather, this is an awareness of how to work on modifying your teaching and their learning.

Never let your learners use their sensory preference as an excuse for inappropriate behavior or failing to finish assignments.

Jason was an eighth grader who showed an auditory preference. In fact, Jason had to talk about content in order to understand it. I started the year off talking to my students about their brains and their sensory preferences. It had always been obvious that Jason learned best by listening and speaking, and once this was confirmed I found myself less likely to reprimand Jason when he spoke . . . unless he disrupted the class. He started using the new information as an excuse. "But Mrs. Sprenger, I can't help it. I'm an auditory learner." We had a private conversation about how his preference would be honored as long as he didn't disturb others' learning.

Okay, so you think you have a pretty good handle on how your students learn. What should you do about it? As I stress in every class, the first thing to do is to design every lesson as a VAK lesson. Teach your lesson three ways:

1. Use the chalkboard, overhead, hand-outs, PowerPoint, etc.

2. Give students the opportunity to talk about it.

3. Use some kind of movement or activity.

Do not panic over the kinesthetic activity! Usually some simple movements will satisfy your kinesthetic learners. So, try some dyads, triads, or other teamwork. You could simply have them stand up and share. Remember, writing *is* a kinesthetic activity—but don't overuse it. Writing on small chalk boards or dry erase boards sometimes keeps kinesthetic learners on task and up to speed.

RETEACHING

The test of all of this begins the moment you start. After you've taught the lesson, be sure to get them started on a follow-up assignment *in class.* Sit down at your desk, and see who either raises a hand for a question or comes up to your desk. These are the students who missed something.

Students in your classroom who have difficulty encoding information the way that you give it are the translators. What actually is going on in their brains is called a *cross modal transfer.* We all do these transfers at times. For instance, you reach into your pocket and find a small round object. From feeling this object you get the picture in your mind of a coin. From the size, you determine that it is a quarter. These students take your information and translate from your modality to their own. Many people are very good at this transfer; however, information can be lost in the process. It may appear that these students are not paying attention; yet, they may have been working very diligently at the transfer and missed some of the message.

As you find yourself reteaching these students, pay close attention to how they are finally "getting it." Do they need you to literally draw them a picture? Do they need you to explain it again, verbally? Or perhaps, it helps them if they show you how they think it should be and you correct it as they go along? Discover the modality you are reaching the least and plan to hit that one harder in your lessons. Eventually, you will find that very little or *no* reteaching will be necessary. And because you are "speaking the same language" as your students, they will feel they are significant in your class. You will see healthy self-esteem grow in your room.

I have had some great success stories dealing with sensory preferences. These experiences have motivated me to continue researching all of these techniques.

An eighth grader in my homeroom has had some real difficulties all of her life because of her auditory-kinesthetic-visual preference. Erin struggled with her need to hear and feel (externally) that she was succeeding.

I often told Erin to roam around the classroom at different times in order to meet her kinesthetic needs, and frequently sent a group of auditory learners, including Erin, into another room to read stories aloud for literature. During a discussion in class one day, I discovered another area that was a problem for Erin. It started when I asked the question, "How many of you have turned off the radio or an iron and then had to go back and check to see if you had really turned it off?" In checking for this external reinforcer, I had opened a real can of worms!

"Mrs. Sprenger, you wouldn't believe how many times Erin has to go all the way back upstairs to check to see if her curling iron is off!" announced Susan, a close friend of Erin's.

"Oh, yes, Mrs. Sprenger, I've waited for her in the car several times because she has to check and recheck her room," shouted another excited eighth grader.

Erin sat very still, very red-faced, and nodded in agreement. "I just don't trust myself to know that I did it," was her meek response to the barrage of criticism from well-meaning friends who had wanted to complain about this for some time.

As the discussion continued and the topic changed, I took the information about Erin and tucked it away for later study.

The next day I took Erin aside. I told her that I might have some information to help her. I first explained to her that because of her auditory-kinesthetic preferences, looking at the curling iron as she turned it off did not give her a sense of completion. I instructed her to do two things. First of all, I told her that after she turns off the curling iron, she must say aloud to herself, "Yes, Erin!" or "Good job, Erin!" She must use her name and she must say it aloud, at least initially. Second, she must, at the same time she is talking to herself, do something physically to show completion. She could clap her hands or use the hand signal from the movie *Home Alone.*

Erin began using this system that evening. This all took place in November of 1993. As of this writing, Erin no longer has to check to see if the curling iron is off, or the radio, or anything else. After the first two weeks of trying this method, she knew how to complete that success cycle with an appropriate reinforcer.

This carried over into her studying. She now knows when she knows. She gives herself similar reinforcement when she studies for a test and when she is taking a test. She never had the feeling that she was ever really finished answering a question until she discovered how to convince herself. This external convincer eventually became an internal convincer for Erin.

ALL PATHWAYS LEAD TO DIFFERENTIATION

Creating a learning profile is one approach to differentiating the classroom. I feel that it is one of the more important approaches as it relates directly to memory. I am not referring here to memorization.

Memorization within the context of education is often looked upon with distaste. However, memorization is necessary for learning, and I find that most teachers are eager to learn memory strategies to use with their students. By using strategies associated with specific sensory pathways in the brain, teachers can help students make associations and teach them lifelong learning techniques.

DIFFERENT STROKES

1. Playing Simon Sez is a wonderful way to include all senses. Interestingly, those who have a visual preference are most likely to make mistakes. It is a great way to allow students to see the importance of using all of the senses.

2. Mind mapping is another excellent way to utilize VAK. Have students create mind maps for review in their groups. This allows conversation for the auditory preference, movement for the kinesthetic, and plenty of words and symbols for the visual. It's a great review tool!

Exit Card

Describe three things you learned about sensory pathways.

Describe two applications you will make as a result of this chapter.

Describe a translator.

3

Differentiating for Different Learning Styles

Donna Walker Tileston

Help students understand how they learn best. Give them an assessment that helps them discover their multiple intelligences or preferred learning modality. Then show them how to use this information to prevent the difficulty of assignments not matched to their learning style or preferred modality, how to seek help, and how to adapt their studying, note taking, and even the learning task itself to better meet their learning needs.

—R. R. Jackson

We now know that some of the concepts that we held about the brain in the last century were not true. For example, we once believed that intelligence was fixed and could not be changed. Thanks to new and emerging research, we now know that our intelligence changes throughout our lives. True, we are born into this world with about half of our neurological wiring in place. This is one of the reasons we have survived as a species; it is this wiring that allows us to breathe, eat, drink, swallow, learn a language, and take in our world. But as Jensen (2006, pp. 8–9) puts it,

"These connections ensure that the infant can eat, breath and respond to the environment. But they are not fixed; some will die from disuse and others will flourish with constant usage. Brains will produce new neurons, lose neurons, make connections and lose other connections, all based on our experience." Or as Doidge (2007) writes, "Neuroplastic research has shown us that every sustained activity ever mapped—including physical activities, sensory activities, learning, thinking, and imaging—changes the brain as well as the mind" (p. 288). This neurological pruning takes place throughout our lives depending on our interests, health, and willingness to learn.

We know that about 98 percent of all new learning enters the brain through the senses (Jensen, 1997)—primarily through visual, tactile, and auditory experiences. (Taste and smell are also useful avenues for learning but are not often used in the classroom.) Most of us have a preference for how we learn. For example, some of us would rather learn by listening, discussing, and by taking notes. Others need to see the information and learn better when there are visual representations of the learning. Still others would rather learn by doing. These are the students who say, "Just give me the information and let me do it."

The plasticity of the human brain—the way it continues to change in response to different stimuli—is thought to contribute to the development of preferred learning styles. According to Sprenger (2002), these preferences or strengths may have been brought about through positive experiences: "We use the networks of neurons that solve our problems for us in the easiest and fastest way. As we continue to use those same neurons, the connections become stronger. Therefore if an auditory learner gets positive results from listening and dialoguing, he or she will continue to do so as a preference, and that modality will be strengthened through use." As a matter of fact, there is strong evidence that points to the fact that a so-called slow learner must be retaught in the modality most comfortable for him or her if that student is to be successful (Jensen, 1997).

Schools of the past have relied heavily on lecture as a primary teaching method. Lecture assumes that students learn auditorily, yet through brain research we know that the majority does not learn that way. Only about 20 percent of students learn auditorily; the other 80 percent learn either visually or kinesthetically (Sousa, 2006). While lecture has its place in some courses, it should be used only in short segments—15 minutes or fewer, depending on the age of the student. It is unrealistic to believe that students who are constantly stimulated by the multimedia world will sit for hours each day passively listening to lectures, taking notes, and preparing for a pencil-and-paper exam without dropping out mentally. Life is not a spectator sport; it is an exercise in active involvement, and education should reflect that active involvement.

We are born into this world with a tremendous capacity to learn and with the wiring to make it happen. If you had been born in the early part of the last century, your world would have been based largely on listening, reading, and talking. Radio would have been the primary means of gaining national information and entertainment. Reading books was also a way to enlighten and learn—as well as to entertain. If you were privileged, you might have had access to a piano in your home for playing and listening. Your brain became wired to listen, and thus an educational program based on reading and listening was comfortable for you.

Today's students are a part of a multimedia world from birth. They don't just listen; they participate. They don't just sit; they move. Three-year-olds can perform simple computer skills. Why, then, would we think that today's students would be happy learners sitting and listening all day? They aren't restless to make us crazy; their brains are wired to participate. According to Marc Prensky (2006), by the time students today are 21, they will have played more than 10,000 hours of video games, sent and received 250,000 e-mails and text/instant messages, spent 10,000 hours talking on the phone, watched more than 20,000 hours of television, and been exposed to 500,000 commercials. How could we expect them to be actively involved in a classroom without movement and interaction?

In a study led by Marion Diamond (Diamond, Scheibel, Murphy, & Harvey, 1985), baby rats and mature rats were placed in the same cage with rat toys. This is the environment identified by Diamond as enriched and is the environment in which rats in other studies showed brain growth. In this study, the older rats did not allow the baby rats the opportunity to use the rat toys. As a result, the baby rats did not grow dendrites, though the mature rats continued to do so. Diamond concluded that "it isn't enough for students to be in an enriched environment, they need to help create that environment and be active in it."

In order to better understand how learning takes place, we need to examine the modalities through which the majority of our new learning comes. Figure 3.1 identifies the senses or modalities that bring into our brains new learning and new experiences. Note that overall, the brain filters out about 99 percent of incoming stimuli. The upside to that phenomenon is that if we attended to all of the incoming stimuli, we would be phobic. The downside is that some of the information that we had hoped our students would remember is lost.

Figure 3.1   Learning Through the Senses

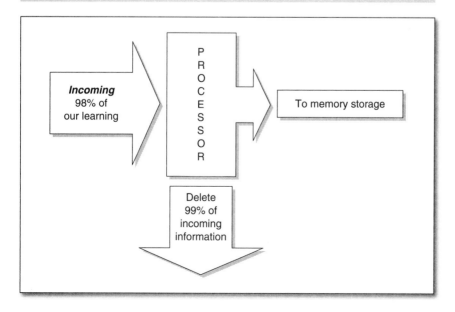

AUDITORY LEARNERS

Auditory learners are those who remember information best when they hear and discuss it. Auditory information is processed and stored in the temporal lobes on the sides of the brain (Jensen, 2006). Auditory students make up about 20 percent of the classroom. They like lecture, adapt well to it, and tend to be successful in our traditional schools. However, in order for the information to have *personal* meaning to auditory learners, it must be discussed or talked through by the learner: Just hearing and taking notes is not enough. In Chapter 1, I discussed the fact that motivation is based in part on the learner's belief that the information has personal meaning. For these learners, that will only occur after they have been given time to talk it through either to themselves or with each other.

Typically, as I've written elsewhere (Tileston 2004b), students who are auditory learners

- like to talk and enjoy activities in which they can talk to their peers or give their opinion,
- encourage people to laugh,
- are good storytellers,
- may show signs of hyperactivity or poor fine-motor coordination,
- usually like listening activities,
- and can memorize easily.

Sprenger (2002) supplies some additional information that can help to identify these students. The auditory learners in your classroom may behave in the following ways:

- They might look out the window while you are talking but be completely aware of what is being said. Such a learner does not need the visual context of looking at the teacher in order to learn.
- They like to talk and discuss. Learning does not have meaning until he or she has had a chance to discuss it either with someone else or with himself or herself. As a matter of fact, an auditory learner may move his or her lips while reading.
- They have difficulty sitting for long periods of time without opportunities for verbalization.

It is important to add that, though these students learn best by hearing, even they grow weary in a straight lecture format. The work of Sousa (2006) and others shows that all of us tend to drop out mentally after 15 or 20 minutes of lecture. In young children, the mental dropout time is significantly less—about 10 minutes. Current indicators are that these numbers may be decreasing slightly for adults and children due to the impact of "instant everything" technology. For example, we once said that we could use a child's age to determine how long he or she could listen at a time: six minutes for a six-year-old. However, indicators point to the fact that this listening span is decreasing as technology has become part of our everyday lives.

Sousa (2006) says that working memory is temporal and deals with information for only a short amount of time before deciding whether or not to discard it. As I stated earlier, the typical time span is about 5 to 10 minutes for preadolescents and 10 to 15 minutes for adolescents. Using this information as a guide, secondary teachers should give information for about 15 minutes and then follow it with activities or discussion to reinforce the learning. Elementary teachers should use four to seven minutes as their guide. Sousa refers to the teaching segments as "prime time." During the first 20 minutes of class, he says, students learn best. New information, information that is of primary importance, should be taught during this time. Figure 3.2 shows how a teacher might use these learning rhythms to enhance student learning.

Figure 3.2   The Rhythm of Teaching

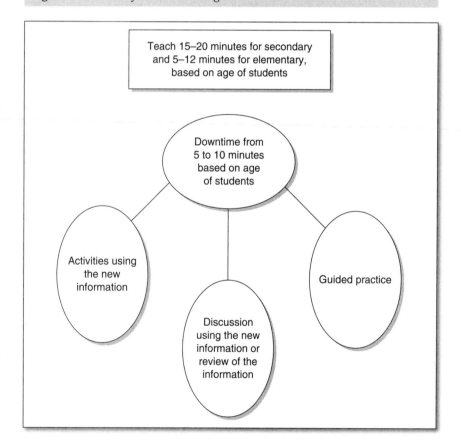

Teaching Auditory Learners

Differentiation does not mean that teachers must teach the same lesson several ways but rather that a variety of techniques should be used. It also means that for students who do not "get it" the first time, a different approach—one more compatible to that student—should be employed the second time. Jensen (1997) says that slow learners will not "get it" until we teach them in the modality most comfortable for them.

Try the following suggestions (Tileston, 2004c) for working with auditory learners:

- Use direct instruction, in which the teacher guides the learning through the application of declarative (what students need to know) and procedural (what students can do with the learning) objectives.
- Employ peer tutoring, in which students help each other practice the learning.
- Plan activities that incorporate music.
- Teach using group discussions, brainstorming, and Socratic seminars.
- Assign specific oral activities.
- Verbalize while learning, including self-talk by the teacher and the learner.
- Use cooperative learning activities that provide for student interaction.

VISUAL LEARNERS

The second type of learning modality is *visual*. Visual information is processed and stored in the occipital lobe at the back of the brain. Visual learners are those who need a mental model that they can see. As I've noted elsewhere (Tileston, 2004c), visual learners are those students who

- have difficulty understanding oral directions,
- may have difficulty remembering names,
- enjoy looking at books or drawing pictures,
- watch the speaker's face,
- like to work puzzles,
- notice small details,
- like for the teacher to use visuals when talking,
- and like to use nonlinguistic organizers.

I am convinced that we could raise math scores immediately all over this country if we could find a way to show kids how math works. Since the majority of learners are visual learners, we need to find ways to show them visually how math works. When I work with audiences, I give them the following problem to solve: if five people shake hands with each other, how many handshakes is that? Now, there is a formula that can be applied to find the answer, and the math people in the audience are quick to work the answer out mathematically. But I like to show the answer visually, because it opens up a new world to people in the audience who need to see how the math works. My visual answer is in Figure 3.3. All that is left is to add up the handshakes: $4 + 3 + 2 + 1 + 0 = 10$ handshakes.

Figure 3.3 A Visual Math Solution

Let's identify the five people as persons A, B, C, D, and E, respectively.

Person A does not shake hands with himself, so he shakes with

A + B

A + C

A + D

A + E

That is 4 handshakes.

Person B already has shaken hands with A and does not shake hands with himself, so

B + C

B + D

B + E

That's 3 more handshakes.

Person C already has shaken hands with Persons A and B and does not shake hands with himself, so

C + D

C + E

That's 2 more handshakes.

Person D already has shaken hands with persons A, B, C, and does not shake hands with himself, so

D + E

That's 1 handshake.

Person E already has shaken hands with persons A, B, C, and D. He does not shake hands with himself, so that is 0 handshakes.

By the way, the formula is

$$(x)(x-1)/2$$

A more complicated version—"One hundred people at the local grocery store shake hands. How many handshakes is that?"—is less threatening once we understand how it works.

Using Nonlinguistic Organizers

One of the most effective tools for visual learners is the nonlinguistic organizer, so called because it relies on structure rather than a lot of words to convey meaning. These organizers help students understand and remember difficult concepts such as sequencing, comparing and contrasting, and classifying. While they are a good teaching strategy for any student, they are important tools for visual students.

The Mid-Continent Regional Education Laboratory (McREL) looked at studies of the most effective teaching practices for the classroom. They set up a control group to test the studies (meta-analysis) to determine whether current strategies had any effect on student learning and, if so, how much of an effect. While this work is ongoing, the meta-analysis studies on the use of nonlinguistic organizers are significant. They found that when nonlinguistic organizers were taught and used appropriately, students on average gained percentile points. For example, if a class average is at the 50th percentile and nonlinguistic organizers are incorporated into the learning, the class average can be moved to the 79th percentile. That is the difference between failure (50) and success (79) (Marzano, 2001b).

Nonlinguistic organizers can be effectively incorporated into classroom learning to achieve many purposes, including the following:

- *To help students connect or relate new information to prior knowledge.* Because these organizers make abstract ideas more visible, they help students understand and remember concepts that are difficult to visualize otherwise. Young students who have difficulty with abstract concepts can be helped by learning to use a set of visual models that makes the abstract concrete. I believe we can raise the scores of students on standardized tests by giving students concrete models to help them perform difficult skills. By taking the information that they know and placing it in a concrete model, students are able to transfer abstract thoughts to concrete ideas more easily. Figure 3.4 is an example of a mind map depicting a student's prior knowledge of a topic before the learning. As new information is added, the mind map will add spokes to connect the new knowledge.

Figure 3.4   Mind Map Using Different Shapes

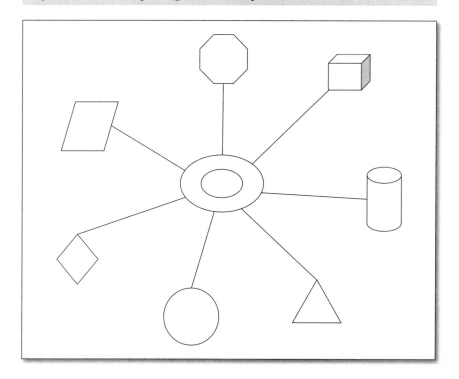

- *To help students create mental models necessary for understanding.* Have you ever read a page in a book and realized at the end of the page that you have no idea what you just read? Perhaps your mind was on something else as your eyes skimmed the page, or maybe the text density was such that it was difficult to make meaning as you read. For struggling students, experiences in the classroom may be much like reading or hearing words that have no meaning. One of the ways that we can help our students make meaning out of the information is by helping them to create mental models of the learning. While there are probably thousands of different organizers on the market today, I have found that they all still fall into general patterns similar to those that Marzano (2001a) describes, such as the following:

  o Descriptive patterns are organizers similar to mind maps that are used to describe or give the critical attributes of something.

  o Sequence patterns are graphic organizers such as might be used for a timeline.

- A process/cause pattern (sometimes called a fishbone) allows the user to determine the causes of something when we already know the outcome. For example, a student might do a fishbone organizer on the causes of World War II.
- Problem/solution patterns provide the problem at the top with possible solutions below the problem.
- A generalization pattern is used when we want to provide information on a principle. Figure 3.5 is an example of this pattern. We are examining the issue of motivation to learn in the example provided.
- *To help students use information.* Nonlinguistic organizers can be used at any time during the learning process, but they are critical in the lesson phase in which the teacher wants the students to use the information in some way. This is a time for clarifying ideas for both the student and the teacher—prior to assessment. This is a great way to teach the real-world application. Ask students to demonstrate understanding by showing a way that the new learning is used in the real world.

Figure 3.5 Generalization Pattern

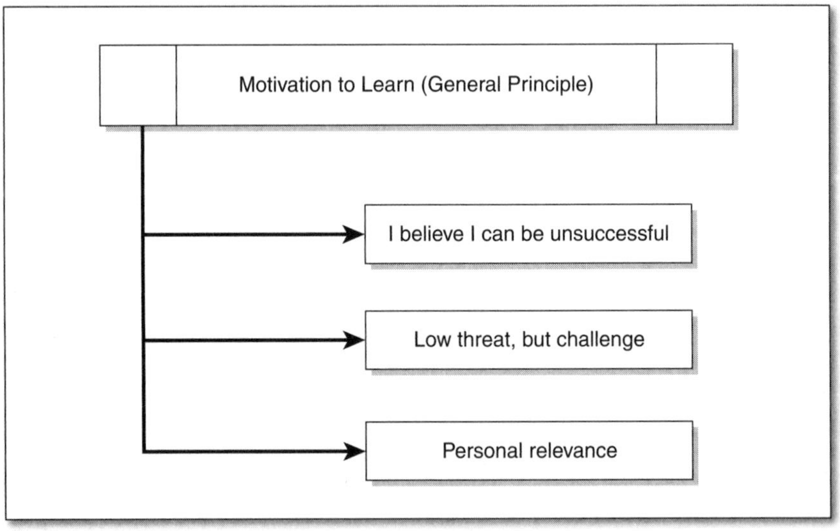

Motivation to Learn (General Principle)

I believe I can be unsuccessful

Low threat, but challenge

Personal relevance

- *To introduce a difficult or abstract concept.* The old adage that a picture is worth a thousand words is absolutely true. Many students have difficulty with logic problems: A matrix is a visual tool that helps make this complex skill more manageable.
- *To assess the learning.* Instead of having students list items from the learning, give them a choice to mind map it. For example, you could give this instruction: "Mind map the key points we discussed in science class today."
- *As part of an individual or group project.* Examples might be mind maps, flow charts, or attribute webs. When these tools are used at the application level or above, they can be important products in student projects.
- *To demonstrate creativity.* Visual students, once they have been exposed to visual models, have little trouble adding creative and elaborative touches to their models.
- *To depict relationships between facts and concepts.* Cause-and-effect, fishbone, and Venn diagrams are examples of mental maps that depict relationships.
- *To generate and organize ideas for writing.* Mind maps and stratification maps are great tools to help students organize their thoughts before writing.
- *To relate new information to prior knowledge.* For a new unit, tap into students' prior knowledge and apply those experiences to the new knowledge they are about to gain. For example, prior to a unit on explorers, ask students if they have ever set a goal and then had difficulty achieving that goal. Have students mind map how they overcame the constraints.
- *To store and retrieve information.* One of my favorite visuals takes vocabulary words—including those in other languages—and draws icons to symbolize the meaning of the words. Students who are visual will see the icons as they retrieve the information from their brains.
- *To assess student thinking and learning.* Ask students to mindmap the key information in a chapter or lesson.
- *To depict relationships between facts and concepts.* Use a matrix to help students make connections from general concepts to determining what are facts and what are not.

Teaching Visual Learners

Some additional ideas for working with visual learners include the following:

- Use visuals when teaching. Remember, these students need to "see" the learning for it to make sense.

- Directly teach students to use visual organizers and provide enough practice so that the process is automatic to the student.
- Show students the patterns in the learning. Remember, the brain likes patterns, and it is the connections that create these patterns that help raise our level of understanding.

Anytime we can help visual learners see the information with visuals, we help them process more efficiently, and we provide a connector so that they can retrieve the information more efficiently from long-term memory. Have you ever had a student say to you on test day, "I know I know the answer; I just can't think of it!" The truth is that it is probably stored in long-term memory, but the student lacks a connector or the language skills (for English language learners) to be able to retrieve it. The semantic memory system that stores factual information is the least reliable of the memory systems and needs a connector to help students retrieve the information. Otherwise, it is much like visiting your local bookstore and finding it has shelved books in random order, and you must search the whole store in hopes of finding the book you need.

KINESTHETIC LEARNERS

The third learning modality is *kinesthetic*. Kinesthetic information is stored at the top of the brain in the motor cortex until permanently learned, and then it is stored in the cerebellum, the area below the occipital lobe (Jensen, 1998). Kinesthetic learners learn best through movement and touching. In the previous handshake exercise (Figure 3.3), kinesthetic learners would solve the problem by physically shaking hands with four other people and counting the handshakes.

As I've written elsewhere (Tileston 2004c), kinesthetic learners may

- need the opportunity to be mobile;
- want to feel, smell, and taste everything;
- want to touch their neighbor as well;
- usually have good motor skills and may be athletic;
- like to take things apart to see how they work;
- may appear immature for their age group;
- and may be hyperactive learners.

Teaching Kinesthetic Learners

Kinesthetic learners, according to Sprenger (2002), are characterized by the following:

- Need hands-on activities. The learning will not have meaning until they have an opportunity to do something with it.

- Respond to physical closeness and physical rewards, such as a pat on the back.
- May become discipline problems in a traditional setting unless they are given the opportunity for movement.
- May slump down in their seats (the comfort of the room is important to them) or may wiggle a great deal in traditional classrooms.

Provide opportunities for your class to go outside, go on field trips, or role-play. In addition, and whenever possible, provide opportunities for them to move around in the classroom, to change groups, or just to stand. The old adage that we think better on our feet is absolutely true. When we stand, we increase the flow of fluids to the brain, and we do learn better. Take advantage of that in the classroom by having students stand to give answers or to discuss with each other.

Providing opportunities for movement in the classroom can make a tremendous difference in the behavior and learning for these students. Try the following suggestions (Tileston, 2004c) for meeting the needs of these students:

- Use a hands-on approach to learning.
- Provide opportunities to move.
- Use simulations when appropriate.
- Bring in music, art, and manipulatives.
- Break up a lecture so that it is in manageable chunks (a good rule is to talk to a student only for the number of minutes equal to his or her age—for a 10-year-old, 10 minutes).
- Use discovery learning when appropriate.
- Use such techniques as discussion groups or cooperative learning so that these students have an opportunity to move about and talk with their peers.

MEASURING SUCCESS

Figure 3.6 shows common indicators of success for teaching effectively to reach all students, regardless of whether they are auditory, visual, or kinesthetic learners.

Figure 3.6 Indicators of a Classroom in Which a Variety of Teaching Strategies Are Used to Address Different Learning Styles

Evaluation Tool	Indicators of Success
Teaching time	Follows the rhythm of the brain, with 15 or fewer minutes of instruction followed by 5–10 minutes, for secondary students, in which the students do something with the learning or, for elementary students, instruction in approximately 10-minute segments followed by opportunities to work with the new learning
Lesson plans	Indicate opportunities for students to stand and move, to go on field trips, and to explore the environment
Lesson plans	Indicate a variety of visual tools are used
Student projects	Indicate choices that include visual, kinesthetic, and auditory learning
Teaching practices	All reteaching is done in the preferred modality of the learner.

CONCLUSION

Although we all record information using all three modalities, most of us have a preference for one over the other two. Sousa (2006) says teachers need to understand that students with different sensory preferences will behave differently during learning and that teachers tend to teach the way they learn. That explains, in part, why so many students have trouble learning from one teacher but may learn easily from another. Behavior interpreted to mean that the student was not interested in the learning or did not want to learn may, in fact, have only been an indication of inappropriate teaching techniques or a classroom where only one modality was valued. The classroom that is enriched with teaching techniques from all three modalities will be a place where quality learning is possible.

4

Curriculum Approaches for Data-Driven Instruction

Gayle H. Gregory and Lin Kuzmich

CURRICULUM MAPPING AND DATA DRIVEN INSTRUCTION

Problem-based math has led to a difficult paradigm shift for many districts. In one Colorado district, teachers at the middle level learned new methods of teaching problem-based math using small groups of students engaged in solving complex problems. Soon after middle-level teachers were trained, high school teachers began learning these methods and curriculum.

Elementary assessment results in math were pretty good, so the curriculum and learning approaches were not adjusted. However, this district noted that at the middle level, around seventh or eighth grade, the scores fell off a cliff and continued downward at the high school level. The district leaders began to question the problem-based math approach even though research supported the path taken by these levels. In addition, district staff was baffled, since the words *problem solving* appear in each of the six Colorado standards, and the released items from the state math assessment were clearly problem based.

Classroom-based data also revealed issues with growth at the secondary level. When the state assessment data were disaggregated by standards and benchmarks, a different conclusion emerged. While the overall results at the elementary level were good, the highest areas of performance were in procedural math and initial numeracy comprehension. Scores for the higher levels of reasoning required in some of the standards, like probability and statistics, were not as good at all levels. The district discovered a compounded effect when the curriculum at the elementary level was not adjusted along with that of the middle and high school levels. Vertical articulation of curricula is a critical component of a standards-based environment, where data helps inform needed adjustments at all levels. This type of adjustment is usually done at the district level rather than the classroom level. We need vertical agreement across levels and horizontal alignment within a level on what it is we are teaching.

Other important components of curriculum mapping are sequence and the developmental difficulty of the expectations for student demonstration of the curriculum. Heidi Hayes Jacobs (1997) has done incredible work in this area.

The problem with curriculum is often the "Dusty Binder Effect." This happens when we create elaborate notebooks full of information about what we should teach. We hand this to new teachers or vaguely refer to the existence of such materials. Jacobs (1997) proposes a much more accessible version of curriculum mapping and even has a very usable electronic version of curriculum mapping, as do several companies now, so that the adjustments can easily be made by district level staff.

Alignment of assessments is another excellent feature of this process. Tying the standards and data analysis results of high-stakes assessments to the curriculum mapping process is essential. Such mapping can be done centrally so that teachers have a starting point for classroom-level planning.

The first level of classroom planning that allows for differentiation is the unit plan. A unit plan can involve a single content area, or it can integrate concepts and skills from several content areas. In this chapter, we have adapted curriculum mapping methods from a variety of sources to a classroom unit-planning method that lends itself to differentiation and adds some components to take into account formative data about students. In Chapter 6 on instructional strategies, we give you differentiated lesson plans that match these unit plans. This method of unit thinking makes further lesson planning easier and decisions about differentiation a habitual part of the planning process.

It is imperative that teachers think in terms of the unit plan before developing any lessons or activities. Unit planning helps teachers align the entire planning process toward student achievement on the final unit assessment. This process also keeps all of the planning congruent with the standards or grade-level benchmarks established by states and districts.

STANDARDS-BASED UNIT PLANNING: SAMPLE MATH UNIT ON DATA ANALYSIS AND PROBABILITY, "THE SURVEY SAYS . . . ," GRADES 3 TO 5

Standards and Benchmarks

Whether or not district curriculum guides and sequences are available, all unit plans start with standards and grade-level expectations. In each state or region, those grade-level or course expectations are called something different. In Ontario, Canada, they are called *expectations* and *indicators;* in Colorado, they are *standards* and *benchmarks;* and in other states, they are *learning expectations.* In this book, we will use the term *standards* for the large overriding or long-term goals set by government agencies, and we will use *benchmarks* or *expectations* to note developmentally (grade or course) specific requirements.

The first task is to decide which of the benchmarks or grade-level targets to hold students accountable for in a given unit. It is best not to use a laundry list but to select benchmarks that reflect what student learning must be at a proficient level. If you are selecting benchmarks or grade-level expectations across standards or content areas, limit the number to those that will be reflected in the final assessment.

For example, the U.S. national standards for math contain four standards for Data Analysis and Probability, and then each standard has one to six expectations for a grade-level range. If a teacher chooses all four standards for third through fifth grade, there are eleven expectations. Which of the expectations are being introduced, and which are recurring and may need to be assessed to a proficient level? Which of these expectations are peripheral to the unit? Teachers need to pick the expectations that will be assessed and be selective about the ones that are introduced in order to establish a true focus for the unit. We will offer specific examples of how to do this in the sample units throughout this chapter.

Unwrapping the Power Standards

Doug Reeves and Larry Ainsworth (Reeves, 2000) have influenced the thinking of many districts by talking about *power standards*. These are the standards that have the greatest impact on proficiency and growth at any given level. Using power standards and then "unwrapping" those standards to build the unit plan and final assessment for the unit are essential steps toward student growth and achievement (Ainsworth, 2003a). These steps in the planning are so critical to a student-centered standards-driven classroom that, without the focus, growth will be compromised. A teacher or group of teachers who merely list fifteen benchmarks or a series of numbers that indicate or stand for the expectations will not get the same result as those who are selective and focused.

Elementary and Secondary Approaches

There is a difference between elementary and secondary approaches to unit planning. Many elementary teachers, especially in the early grades, often list every reading or writing standard for each unit. Unit planning may not be routine at those grades since literacy skills are viewed as continuous progress subjects. However, many excellent primary teachers accelerate learning by choosing a theme or topic in which to embed the expectations for learning and assessment. We know from both brain research and many other fields that relevance and context are critical to higher levels of thought (Parry & Gregory, 2003). At all levels and content areas, it is easier to think about units of study if you review the standards and expectations and then determine a context in which to teach them.

Materials and Activities

We have long been trained to take a published series and use a scope and sequence in a sequential fashion, following teachers' guides. This was (or is) true at every level. These materials then became the de facto curriculum. In a standards-based and data driven world of student learning, this approach will not maximize student growth. A curriculum must be planned on the basis of standards and expectations. Published materials are resources to use in a unit but are not in fact the unit.

Some of us were trained to come up with engaging activities, given motivational issues and learning style concerns. In the initial stages of the standards-based movement, as some folks gave up teachers' guides, we may have overcorrected with what we thought were authentic tasks. However, a series of pleasant activities with or without a rubric does not constitute a unit plan or a meaningful assessment for that plan.

Supporting Differentiation

As we gain a larger body of evidence about student growth, concern grows that our reform efforts may not have the payoff we need, especially for certain populations. There are, however, pockets of growth around the world that can be investigated and replicated. We know that schools with aligned curriculum, careful and frequent assessment, and thoughtful planning and dialogue experience more growth than publisher-driven or activity-based curricula. Now, with a push toward subgroup growth, we must get far better at planning for differentiation as well. Our experience with resources and work with engaging activities will help us if we do some careful "up front" work that is selective with regard to student needs.

Unit planning must take into account district, local, or state expectations of learning for the grade level or course. A district may lay out the curriculum in the history of a country to include certain major events, people, places, government structures, and issues. At the early elementary level in reading, a certain degree of phonemic competency and comprehension may be expected along with knowing the parts of a story or focusing on a particular genre.

To start a unit plan, we need to know what we are expected to include in our plans and assessments. However, we must go back to the standards and benchmarks to truly see how these broad subject area requirements will be filtered. The benchmarks provide a lens that helps us focus the type of skill demonstrations we will need students to display over the course of the unit. We discussed how to create focus and limit the number of benchmarks based on what is required in the final unit assessment. We can talk of other smaller or implied skill demonstrations when we discuss lesson plans (Chapter 7).

Key Concepts

The next step is to determine the key concepts on which to base the demonstrations of learning. These concepts are the big ideas stated or implied in the standards and benchmarks, which answer the following question: What must students know and be able to do?

Let's look at an example in math, linking national standards (Figure 4.1) and key concepts (Figure 4.2). Without a context, we may try to cover all of the concepts listed in Figure 4.2, which is in fact only a partial list. Choosing a theme or context is necessary as the first step to focus a unit. This theme often depends on governmental requirements or the nature of the course. The next step may include marking or starring concepts on your brainstorm list that must be reflected in the final assessment for the unit, as indicated above.

Not all concepts are created equal, just as vocabulary words may differ in complexity. In history, the concepts for freedom, citizenship, and the act of voting are very different. For example,

• A third grade unit may include an awareness of voting as a cycle of events in local government.

• An eighth grade history unit may include an assessment that requires the demonstration or role-play of citizenship in two or more eras of U.S. history.

• A tenth grade unit assessment may have students develop a comparative analysis of the levels of freedom citizens experience across several regions, or they may research freedom as a motivating impulse across history.

Figure 4.1   Math Unit on Data Analysis and Probability, Grades 3 to 5: National Standards

Standard 1. Instructional programs from pre-kindergarten through Grade 12 should enable all students to *formulate questions* that can be addressed with data and collect, organize, and display relevant data to answer them.

Expectations for Grades 3 to 5

- Design investigations to address questions and understand how data collection methods affect the nature of the data set

- Collect data using observations, surveys, and experiments

- Represent data using tables and graphs such as line plots, bar graphs, and line graphs

- Recognize the difference in representing categories and numerical data

Standard 2. Instructional programs from pre-kindergarten through Grade 12 should enable all students to *select and use* appropriate statistical methods to analyze data.

Expectations for Grades 3 to 5

- Describe the shape and important features of a set of data and compare related data sets, with an emphasis on how the data are distributed

- Use measures of center, focusing on the median, and understand what each does and does not indicate about the data set

- Compare different representations of the same data to evaluate how well each representation shows important aspects of the data

Standard 3. Instructional programs from pre-kindergarten through Grade 12 should enable all students to *develop and evaluate* inferences and predictions that are based on data.

Expectations for Grades 3 to 5

- Propose and justify conclusions and predictions that are based on data and design studies to further investigate the conclusions or predictions

Standard 4. Instructional programs from pre-kindergarten through Grade 12 should enable all students to *understand and apply* basic concepts of probability.

Expectations for Grades 3 to 5

- Describe events as likely or unlikely and discuss the degree of likelihood using such words as *certain, equally likely,* and *impossible*

- Predict the probability of outcomes of simple experiments and test the predictions

- Understand that the measure of the likelihood of an event can be represented by a number from 0 to 1

Figure 4.2 Math Unit on Data Analysis and Probability, Grades 3 to 5: Partial List of Key Concepts Linked to National Standards

Standard 1	Standard 2	Standard 3	Standard 4
Data collection • Data relevant experiment survey • Tables • Graphs Line plot Bar graph Line graph Category	Data shape Data features Statistical methods • Analyze Measure Center • Median • Compare importance of data	Predict Infer Conclude Study • Investigate • Justify	Certain Equally likely Impossible Test • Probability • Predict

Concepts can, therefore, be developmental. Another aspect of using key concepts might be the varying difficulties of the words and ideas; this may allow us to differentiate within a single unit. All students in eighth grade may be required to demonstrate analysis of freedom in the United States on the final unit assessment.

Groups may be formed to explore voting and citizenship practices as illustrations of freedom in certain countries or through specific eras and events:

1. The group working on voting may demonstrate less sophisticated analysis skills.

2. The group working on citizenship may be able to combine factors in an analysis.

3. Both groups are working on aspects of a bigger, more complex concept like freedom.

4. They can share information or use what they know from these smaller groups to complete the final assessment task.

When selecting key concepts, it is important to understand the level of complexity. More difficult concepts may provide the framework and categories for the simpler concepts. The challenging and thought-provoking concepts may help us create the final assessment, and simpler concepts may help build understanding throughout the chunks of learning within a unit.

Figure 4.3 Math Unit on Data Analysis and Probability, Grades 3 to 5: Developing Unit Skills Based on Key Concepts and National Standards

Key Concepts: What must students remember and be able to use, even after this unit?

Standard 1	Standard 2	Standard 3	Standard 4
• Data Tables • Graphs Line plot Bar graph Line graph	• Analyze • Median • Compare	• Investigate • Justify	• Probability • Predict

Unit Skills: How will students demonstrate they can use what they learned in a meaningful way?

Standard/Benchmark 1	Standard/Benchmark 2
1. Students will design investigations to address a question 2. Students will decide which data methods will give them the needed information	3. Students will represent data in two or more ways to help others understand and compare the data 4. Students will demonstrate the use of *median* and *mean* to understand and analyze data
Standard/Benchmark 3	Standard/Benchmark 4
5. Students will propose and justify a prediction based on data collection and interpretation	6. Students will predict the probability of a result and test the accuracy of that prediction

Unit Skills

When we plan a standards-based unit, skills are the demonstrations of student learning necessary to provide the rehearsal and learning for the final assessment, since most state and national standards are written at higher levels of critical thinking. Skills should contain verbs found in the expectations or benchmarks for the standards as well as verbs that allow learning demonstrations at initial stages of understanding.

Figure 4.3 offers an illustration of how we can take key concepts and embed them into the demonstration of skills for a unit on predicting preferences in fellow students. We have determined a context; we will limit the standard and grade range expectations through a focused approach to the concepts and assessment. The skills help us describe the level at which students will need to demonstrate these concepts.

Skills are not statements or objectives that denote the work of a single day. Skill statements help us divide the learning into chunks or unwrap the standard. Lesson plans can be created from one or more of these demonstrations of learning (Chapter 7). Instead of prescribing activities day by day, lesson plans give the amount of time or days needed to develop the background and rehearsal needed to demonstrate the skills. All of these skills will be needed for the final assessment in some form and to some degree. Now we need to develop that final assessment.

States and regional standards are often confusing to use in planning concepts and skill statements if you do not have them filtered by district curriculum mapping. In a state like Ohio, where each expectation is broken into numerous very small pieces of learning, we would take a different approach. The small pieces of learning may lend themselves to the lesson plan and the larger headings to the skills. Remember to base the skills on the long-term standards and midrange portion of the standard for learning in a unit plan. Shorter-range goals, indicators of learning, or benchmarks are best suited to lesson plans that are built around chunks of learning in a unit.

Relevance

Students need a personal connection to new learning. It helps them form complex schema and develop good skills in generalizing what they are learning for use with other applications. We need learning systems that are "driven by realistic problems and questions" (Silver, Strong, & Perini, 2000, p. 70). When we studied Madeline Hunter and Carol Cummings and the elements of effective instruction in the 1970s and beyond, we discovered that relevance is a powerful motivator. In addition, setting the stage for realistic connections helps to get students' minds more ready to accept new learning.

While we understand the need to build authenticity into assessment and learning practices, we must plan for this in the units. Figure 4.4 shows an example of relevance for our sample unit in math.

Establishing relevance can be as simple as using a school-to-life orientation with careers. It can also be done by using a prompt or activity that helps students show their application of skills in daily life. An excellent way to establish relevance is through the questions we ask and encourage students to ask as we engage in meaningful dialogue. Internet searches on almost any topic or set of skills to be taught yield many good ideas. Another source is the national website for a particular content area. Using literature and quotes also helps us establish relevance when we encourage imagination or help students see others engaging in the

Figure 4.4   Math Unit on Data Analysis and Probability, Grades 3 to 5: Establishing Relevance

---

Why must students learn this and what need is there for this learning across time and applications?

Students will need to know how to use, understand, and represent data in science, math, social studies, and economics. These are important technology literacy skills for the 21st century and certainly useful career skills. Students may understand the relevance by having to review data representations from various sections of the newspaper and from magazines. A few graphs on viewership from a television station's website may also provide relevancy. It is important that students see the everyday application of what they are about to learn. This review of graphs could provide an engaging small-group introduction to the unit.

---

concepts being taught. Meaningful learning is respectful and invites students to see the possibilities. Establishing relevance helps engage students in a bigger picture of the world and relates upcoming learning to their personal lives.

Unit Assessments

There are many books and articles on how to create authentic performance-based assessments. These are the best types for unit-level final assessments. Most of the literature on creating final assessments includes

- A well-written prompt and set of directions
- A rubric form of scoring
- Models or templates to assist the student in proficient performance

Wiggins and McTighe (1998), Stiggins (1997), Reeves (2000, 2003), and others describe in detail how to create standards-based final assessments. For our purposes on differentiation and data use, we have focused more on formative assessment since other resources exist for performance assessments.

The next step in unit planning is to create a simple description of the final assessment for your unit plan (see Figure 4.5). This will guide and focus your work regardless of the method of performance assessment you choose (Chapter 3). The final assessment will ask: What does the demonstration of learning for this unit look like? Following the assessment description, we will develop a prompt (Figure 4.6) and a rubric (Figure 4.7) that allows the demonstration of our standards-based skills and concepts.

When creating a final assessment, examples or models can be collected or developed. Remember to base your left-hand column on concepts, not

Figure 4.5 Math Unit on Data Analysis and Probability, Grades 3 to 5: Final Unit Assessment Description

Final Unit Assessment Description

Unit Title: The Survey Says . . .

Students will investigate the entertainment preferences of peers and staff. During this process, students will analyze and report the results of an investigation that is supported with data and select a method of reporting that demonstrates their use of data, prediction, and analysis. A rubric and set of directions will support student learning and assessment. *See rubric and directions for final assessments.*

Figure 4.6 Math Unit on Data Analysis and Probability, Grades 3 to 5: Final Unit Assessment Prompt

Final Unit Assessment Prompt

Unit Title: The Survey Says . . .

We are going to investigate what forms of entertainment students and staff prefer during their free time. You can choose what to survey about preferences people like. Please follow these steps:

1. Create a question that you will ask to gather information about preferences

2. Survey at least twenty-five students from several grades

3. Create a table and a graph to show your results

4. Summarize your results using median and mean to help your audience understand the results and these mathematical terms

5. Create a prediction about how the next twenty-five students may answer (use the same number of students from each grade as you used in your first survey)

6. Create another set of data displays

7. Now compare the results from both surveys and decide how accurate your Step 5 prediction was

8. Choose a method of sharing your data displays, prediction, and analysis. Make certain you use data to support your conclusions

9. Use the rubric to help you plan and think about your work

   Remember:
   - Use of correct grammar, usage, punctuation, and spelling is required in all parts of your work
   - You can use the computer to create your tables and graphs or you can neatly write and draw them

Figure 4.7 Math Unit on Data Analysis and Probability, Grades 3 to 5: Rubric

Key Concepts	Advanced	Proficient	Partially Proficient
1. Data in graphs and tables	Tables and graphs are easy to interpret and contain labels and data that clearly answer the question	Tables and graphs are accurate and labeled and clearly display important data	Tables and graphs have a title and are easy to read, and accurate
2. Median and Mean	Students use the median and mean to help them draw conclusions and make predictions	Students explain the median and mean result in their data interpretation	Students report the median and mean
3. Investigation process and questions	Students can explain the process they used and can develop interview questions that help them to create the analysis	Steps were followed and the interview questions developed helped students collect data	Steps were followed, and the interview questions make sense given the assignment
4. Predict and Justify	Students make predictions based on data and can justify their prediction using the first data collection step	Predictions make sense given the first data collection step	Predictions include elements (words) from the first set of data
5. Analysis and Sharing	Students describe why the data sets are similar or dissimilar and what may have caused that result Students share their conclusions such that peers use the mean and median to draw similar conclusions	Students compare the two sets of data and describe the accuracy of their prediction Students share this information such that peers draw a similar conclusion	Students describe the final data collection and whether or not it matched the prediction Students share this information clearly. Students share tables and graphs such that peers can check the accuracy of the data.

directions for the unit assessment or parts of the assessment. Examples of prompts and rubrics may be complex or simple depending on the grade level of your students. It is possible to differentiate the assessment without differentiating the rubric. This will help teachers stay aligned to grade-level or course expectations.

CRITICAL QUESTIONS FOR UNIT PLANNING

Critical Questions and Higher-Level Thinking

Questions are the cornerstone of increasing higher-level thinking. Linda Elder and Richard Paul (2002) indicate, "It is not possible to be a good thinker and a poor questioner" (p. 3). Questioning is a key component for both the teacher and the students in a standards-based, differentiated classroom. A two- or three-year-old drives a parent crazy with a multitude of questions, and the rate at which the questions are asked and the type of questions are in direct proportion to the knowledge the child acquires. Good readers actively construct meaning through unconscious questions they continually ask themselves (Healy, 1990). Creating a classroom where questioning is the routine method of learning is essential, given the challenging nature of most state and regional standards, let alone the lifelong impact of this positive habit of inquiry.

Rich and meaningful questions to guide a unit of learning create conditions for thinking that pervade the unit. Students will want to do more thinking when these strategies are used. Modeling this as a regular component of lessons and units tells students that such expectations are acceptable and encouraged. Rules for learning that make sense for adult and child learners (Kuzmich, 2002) include

1. What teachers ask is what they get.

2. What teachers choose to model is what they get.

3. What teachers spend time doing in class gets done.

4. What dialogue and discourse occurs in a classroom directly influences learning.

Critical questions differ from essential questions in only one way, and that is through the three key issues that they highlight for teachers. Unit plans are driven and focused through standards and final assessment, so the critical questions we ask about our unit planning (Figure 4.8) help us to determine if we have created effective essential questions for the unit's final assessment. This type of critical questioning formation distinguishes these questions from those that may guide formative learning in portions of the unit lessons. If districts or schools already use the term *essential questions,* that is fine. Just remember the three indicators for successful unit planning and critical questions detailed in Figure 4.8.

The composition of critical questions can be focused around key concepts, levels of thinking, and indicators of the skill, process, or demonstration of learning for the final assessment. These questions are not the prompt for the final assessment since prompts require far more detail to be effective.

Figure 4.8 Critical Questions About Effective Unit Planning

Yes	No	Are the unit questions at the deeper levels of thinking needed to truly demonstrate the standard?
Yes	No	Are the answers to the questions crucial to the demonstration of proficient learning in the unit?
Yes	No	Do students demonstrate the answers to the critical questions for the unit as a part of the final assessment?

Critical Questions and Brain Research

This approach to critical unit questions lends itself to differentiation throughout the unit and closely follows what we know from brain research and learning.

Chunks of skills from the unit plan can be introduced to the learning, which allows students to rehearse and demonstrate aspects and uses for the concepts in preparation for the final assessment or in the construction of portions of the unit. These chunks of learning should always be related back to the critical questions. Establishing a clear connection to the critical questions allows learners to make parts-to-whole relationships throughout the unit. Brain research from a variety of sources underscores the need to detect patterns in neuron development and to build the complex schema necessary for higher level thinking (Hart, 1993).

In addition, split-brain research tells us that we have an innate capacity to deal with parts and wholes simultaneously; only then can the brain make connections and interpretations necessary to learning and future utilization of that learning (Caine & Caine, 1991). "Good training and education recognize this, for instance by introducing natural 'global' projects and ideas from the beginning" (Caine & Caine, 1997, p. 106). For example, a kindergarten teacher may develop a critical question for a unit on retelling stories and understanding sequence in stories. How can you retell a story with a beginning, middle, and end? The teacher can chunk the unit into three or four parts such as retelling beginning, middle, and ending. When the teacher introduces the work on the concept of beginning, the teacher may say the following to a class or group: "Our question for the unit is, How can you retell a story with a beginning, middle, and end? Today, we are going to learn two ways to remember the beginning of the story. These tricks will help you when you retell the whole story."

Teachers need to help students see the connections to the whole at each step of the learning or invite students to make those connections themselves throughout the learning. Students must have time to reflect on and integrate these parts-to-whole relationships. This can be done through dialogue, written reflection, demonstrations of learning, and numerous other methods of reflective thinking.

Critical Questions and Differentiation

Critical questions should engage the learner. When students look only for the correct answer rather than for interesting questions, they are condemned to "live inside other men's discoveries" (Vail, 1989). Critical questions should also set forth possibilities and options. This allows learners to use new learning and rehearse with multiple strategies and interest pathways.

These types of questions allow us to build unit plans that include the flexibility of adjusting for learner readiness and needs, yet still help us hold all students accountable for the standards. It is not acceptable to modify and differentiate the standards unless the student has a special education or English as a second language plan that legally allows us to differentiate and accommodate the standards for an individual learner. The rest of the class must be held accountable for the same standard, concepts, and demonstrations of final learning. How we get there, with what resources, at what rate, and with what guidance and tools is another matter. Building in choices is also an integral part of unit planning and differentiation. Changing the standard is not an option, especially in a world of high-stakes assessments and subgroup growth.

Critical Questions, Standards, and Benchmarks

Some teachers find that it is easier to start with goal-type statements since it helps them move from daily objectives to using longer-term goals to enhance student thinking and learning. While this is a great step, it is helpful to move into creating meaningful and challenging questions to help define the final standards-based demonstration for the unit. "A critical thinker is often described as a person who can evaluate the quality of thinking used to solve problems" (Fogarty & Bellanca, 1993, p. 226).

Teachers in some districts and schools have been told by their principal or evaluator that they must tell the students what standard or benchmarks are the basis for the unit or lesson. While that is a practice that makes supervisors happy, it is not the best approach with students. In our story-retelling example, should the teacher have told the five-year-olds the standard: "Students will read and write for a variety of purposes" (Colorado Department of Education website)? Would sixteen-year-olds really benefit

Figure 4.9   Math Unit on Data Analysis and Probability, Grades 3 to 5: Critical Unit Questions

---

> **What questions will the students answer, if they are successful on the final assessment?**
>
> 1. How can we use data to predict how people think about and choose preferences?
>
> 2. How does the collection and analysis of data increase the accuracy of our predictions?

from knowing we are working on benchmarks 5.6 through 5.22? A compromise may include posting the standards and benchmarks and finding ways to use them in communicating with parents and students in newsletters and unit plan summaries that could go home. These could help parents and supervisors know you are holding the students accountable for standards-based learning. Worthy questions, written at a developmentally appropriate level, will do far more for student growth.

In Figure 4.9, we offer some possible examples of critical questions for our sample math unit. Note that the words or ideas used in the critical questions should be easy to trace back to the standards and benchmarks, the key concepts, and the skill statements.

Another way to use this type of questioning when you are introducing the unit is to engage learners in developing questions of their own. This is an important feature of this process if we use a constructivist approach in the unit design. Students could compare their questions to the ones the teacher developed, and the rich reflection that could occur as a result would certainly be impressive. There are numerous ways to activate learning through the carefully crafted use of critical questions and student formation of questions; these will be discussed in Chapters 5 and 6.

PRE-ASSESSING THE LEARNING GAP FOR UNIT PLANNING

It is imperative to define what we know about our learners and what the target for this unit looks like. Then we can determine what we don't know about learners and pre-assess that gap in information. In a learning environment where performance assessments are the rule for unit planning, a simple Form A and Form B for pre-assessment will not work well. We need information about our learners so that we can create the right differentiation opportunities in the unit. We can gather this information in a variety

Figure 4.10   Math Unit on Data Analysis and Probability, Grades 3 to 5: Pre-Assessment Design

---

Part One: What do we already know about our math students?

We will have information about their written reflection in math, calculation accuracy, and ability to estimate and some idea of their ability to create simple graphs or tables.

Part Two: What do we need to know to get students to grow from where they are to the final assessment?

We need to know student understanding and interpretation of data and student ability to communicate at an analysis level using the language of math accurately.

A Way to Pre-Assess the Gap

Students will be given a table and graph that represent the same data. Partners will discuss the data and decide what conclusions they can draw from the information. Teacher will listen for

1. Understanding of the visual representations of data

2. Logical conclusions given the data

Students will "Quick Write" about their conclusions. (Quick Write in Math: topic sentence is the big understanding, next two to three sentences are the supporting detail for the big understanding, and last sentence is the rationale or why the conclusion makes sense.)

Teachers will not grade these paragraphs. Instead they will note whether the writing

1. Is logical given the prompt and supports the conclusion

2. Demonstrates the ability to express analysis through writing about math

Teachers will be able to teach the concepts as expressed, but adjust their coaching, time, order, difficulty level, and supporting resources to address these results.

---

of informal ways. Pre-assessment methods and diagnostic thinking are addressed extensively in Chapter 3. We need to learn to take what we discover and differentiate learning opportunities, timing, and materials to better and more accurately meet the needs of diverse learners. The diagnostic thinking that teachers employ to make continuous course corrections in a unit is essential to the success of learners. These course corrections or opportunities provide a great place in the unit for differentiation. The first opportunity comes early in the unit as we determine what we know about learners and what we need to know to get more of them to demonstrate proficient performance on the final assessment.

Figure 4.10 offers one example, but many more possibilities would work. Also, check out other ideas at the back of this chapter and throughout the remaining chapters. Remember to focus your gap analysis on concepts, thinking skills, and the type of demonstration of learning students will need to be successful on the final assessment. You can use your analysis of this data to create differentiation opportunities in grouping, teaching methods, and learning methods.

CHUNKING THE LEARNING

Chunking learning is not a new concept. Brain research and the psychology of learning have talked about the need to chunk new ideas to integrate, remember, and use these concepts (Healy, 1990). The ability to chunk learning more effectively for student growth is a skill that teachers will need to advance as they approach the type of standardized and data driven curriculum planning that is needed to accelerate student growth. We must move beyond the remedial thinking of older models for Title I, reading, and special education groups. Chunking learning by critical thinking level and skill load will help us maximize the limited amount of time we have with students.

Chunking a unit means to divide a topic of study into logical portions of learning that may be longer than one day or one period in time. To chunk a unit, we need to understand the necessary sequence and layering of learning that would best assist a learner to get ready for or perform proficiently on the final assessment.

Chunking a unit into ever increasing levels of meaning and usefulness works better to advance learning than daily lesson plans. A day or a period is an arbitrary unit of time. Learning, especially learning that may need to be differentiated, does not occur quite as conveniently as daily lesson planning would lead us to believe.

Chunking affects how we plan lessons to differentiate. Planning day by day is frequently inefficient and ineffective. It is better to plan standards-based units and then to plan by chunking the learning into key concepts and combinations of concepts that need to be taught. Determining the optimal sequence of these concepts is also essential. Performance and thinking can then be verified through ongoing formative assessment during and at the end of each chunk of learning in a unit. Some chunks will take only one day. However, if concepts are grouped and timed well, most chunks of a unit will take multiple days or even longer.

We need to establish the background needed for the early learning of what the concept means and how to use it; then we need to provide rehearsal opportunities that allow us to approximate what is needed for the final performance assessment. The last step in the plan should be a formative assessment that tells us whether the student has reached the desired level of critical thinking and use of the concept. If your final assessment is unwrapped and forms the chunks of your unit plan, this formative rehearsal can take various forms before you plan for the final

Figure 4.11   Math Unit on Data Analysis and Probability, Grades 3 to 5: Chunking or Outlining the Unit

---

How will teachers break up the unit into chunks of learning that represent various degrees of growing skill and thinking?

1. Activating learning for the total unit and developing a survey question

2. Learning about visual representations of data

3. Summarizing using median and mean

4. Predicting with data

5. Analyzing data results and sharing

---

demonstration of this segment of the unit (Ainsworth, 2003b). The formative data we collect in either method of unit planning lets us plan for further differentiation of the unit based on the student's level of thinking and use of the concepts and skills taught (Kuzmich, 1998).

One excellent benefit of unit chunking is that in a three-week unit, only five lessons may be needed, each lasting multiple days. For example, Figure 4.11 shows how we might chunk our sample math unit for its thinking and skill load of key concepts. While this form of unit planning takes getting used to and does take time, this method also reduces teacher preparation by changing daily lesson plans into multiday plans around a set of concepts. This may affect teacher evaluation and supervision expectations, so principals and district staff will need to adjust any teacher evaluation system that requires daily lesson plans. This method of planning is well worth it in terms of increased student achievement. Numerous examples of this type of chunking rather than just daily lesson planning are given in Chapter 7.

SUMMARY

This type of unit-based planning is a highly effective way of keeping the focus on standards and student achievement. This method allows teachers to take a curriculum and turn it into meaningful connections and critical thinking and use of concepts and skills. Planning for data collection right away also allows teachers to plan for differentiation to better meet the needs of learners. It also takes the old lesson planning to a new level and reduces the amount of daily paperwork needed. Using this type of approach to curriculum makes differentiation a natural part of thinking when planning and adjusting for diverse learners.

OTHER SAMPLE UNIT PLANS

THE WEATHER REPORTER, GRADES K TO 2

Standards/Benchmarks: Earth and Space Science—Weather

What must students learn?

(Please note that while science standards are listed, this unit could easily be integrated with reading, writing, math, and even arts standards.)

Standard 1 (Colorado/national). Students understand the processes of scientific investigation and design; conduct, communicate about, and evaluate such investigations.

Standard 4 (Colorado/national). Students know and understand the processes and interactions of Earth's systems and the structure and dynamics of Earth and other objects in space.

Standard 5 (Colorado/national). Students know and understand interrelationships among science, technology, and human activity and how they can affect the world.

Standard 6 (Colorado/national). Students understand that science involves a particular way of knowing and understand common connections among scientific disciplines.

Benchmarks

> 1b Select and use simple devices to gather data related to an investigation.
>
> 1c Use data based on observations.
>
> 1d Communicate about investigations and explanations.
>
> 4.2a Recognize that the sun is a principal source of Earth's heat and light.
>
> 4.2b Recognize how our daily activities are affected by the weather.
>
> 4.2c Describe existing weather conditions by collecting and recording weather data.

4.4c Recognize the characteristics of seasons.

5d Identify careers that use science and technology.

6c Identify observable patterns.

Key Concepts

What must students remember and be able to use, even after this unit?

Standard/Benchmark 1b, c, d	Standard/Benchmark 4.2 and 4.4
Thermometer Degrees Temperature	Sun Sunny Shady Daytime Nighttime Heat

Standard/Benchmark 5	Standard/Benchmark 6
Weather reporter	Seasons

Skills

How will students demonstrate they can utilize what they learned in a meaningful way?

Standard/Benchmark 1	Standard/Benchmark 4
1. Students use a digital thermometer and are able to "read" the temperature using the word *degrees*	3. Students compare the temperatures in sunny and shady places as well as daytime and nighttime temperatures
2. Students tell whether a temperature is cold or hot	4. Students explain why it is usually warmer during the day and identify the sun as the main source of heat and light

Standard/Benchmark 5	Standard/Benchmark 6
5. Students report the weather	6. Students describe the type of weather characteristics for each season

Relevance

Why must students learn this, and what need
is there for this learning across time and applications?

Students need to begin to see that we are part of many systems. Weather is a great way to do that in the early years of elementary school. Students can create personal connections to what they already know and learn new ways to describe the physical systems of the Earth and solar system in relationship to weather.

Give students the job of predicting tomorrow's weather. Ask them to watch the weather on TV tonight and see if their prediction matches the weather reported. Write down and draw what they know about the weather the next day. How well did they predict the weather? Describe ways they will learn to make more accurate predictions during this unit.

Final Assessment Description

What does the demonstration of learning for this unit look like?

Students use what they know about weather and seasons to create a way to report about the weather for each season.

Critical Unit Questions

What questions will the students answer if
they are successful on the final assessment?

1. Can you tell what the weather will be like during the winter, spring, summer, and fall?

2. Can you report how hot or cold it is today?

Pre-Assessment Design

Part One: What do we already know about our science students?

Students know and can describe what the weather is today in general terms. Students have some information about the seasons. Many students know that if the teacher says that it is 72 degrees outside, that is the temperature.

Part Two: What do we need to know to get students to
grow from where they are to the final assessment?

Do students know why temperatures and seasons change? Can students characterize the weather and what they would need to do in each season?

Ways to Pre-Assess the Gap

1. Discuss these two questions with students and note responses.

2. Read a book about the seasons as a class and make predictions about the weather.

Chunking or Outlining the Unit

How will teachers break up the unit into chunks of
learning that represent various degrees of growing skill and thinking?

1. Temperature and thermometers

2. The sun and heat-shade contrasts and sunny places

3. What do we need to do when the weather changes?

4. Reporting the weather

5. The seasons in our area and the weather

Final Assessment: The Weather Reporter

1. Students will choose a way to report about the weather and seasons.

Some examples:

- Use a verbal report or newscast with notes and pictures.
- Create a computer-assisted report.
- Write with pictures.
- Make a game.
- Create a song.

2. Students will use what they know about temperature and weather for each season.

3. Students will need to use correct spelling, grammar, punctuation, and capitalization.

4. Students will need to describe or show how the sun affects weather in each season.

5. Students describe or show how they need to be prepared (dress, walk, activities) for each season.

Key Concepts	Advanced	Proficient	Partially Proficient
1. Thermometer, degree, temperature	Students can use a thermometer and write the temperature in degrees, creating a chart to tell the degree of hot or cold	Students read a thermometer and create a chart or graph to tell whether it is hot or cold	Students can tell if a temperature is hot or cold
2. Sun and heat, temperature changes	Students can describe how the sun helps make it warm or cold depending on the time of day and the amount of sunlight	Students can describe the difference in temperature between sunny and shady places and daytime and night-time temperatures	Students can tell if it is warm or cold depending on time of day and amount of sun
3. Weather reporting	Students report the weather using temperature descriptions and the sun to describe characteristics of the seasons	Students report the weather for each season using descriptions of the weather	Students report the weather for each season using pictures to show how the major weather looks
4. Seasons	Students can describe how to dress and what activities are special for each season	Students can tell how they need to dress or act in each season	Students can tell how they need to dress for each season

Student Checklist (in student language)

- ❏ I can use a thermometer to tell temperature.
- ❏ I know about the sun and how it gets hot and cold.
- ❏ I can tell what kind of weather we have in the winter, spring, summer, and fall.
- ❏ I can tell what we should wear and do in winter, spring, summer, and fall.

DO YOU KNOW YOUR RIGHTS?
GRADES 5 TO 8

Standards/Benchmarks

What must students learn?

(Please note that while history and civics standards are listed, this unit could easily be integrated with reading and writing standards as well as the arts.)

History Standard 5 from Colorado State Standards

Standard 5. Students understand political institutions and theories that have developed over time.

Standard 5.1. Students understand how democratic ideas and institutions in the United States have developed, changed, and/or been maintained.

Benchmarks for Grades 5 to 8

> a. Explain the historical development of democratic governmental principles and institutions.
> b. Describe the basic ideas set forth in the Declaration of Independence, Articles of Confederation, Constitution, and Bill of Rights.
> c. Give examples of extensions of political and civil rights in U.S. history.

Key Concepts

What must students remember and be able to use, even after this unit?

Standard 5–5.1	*Benchmark b*
Democracy	Bill of Rights
Freedom	Constitution

Benchmark a	*Benchmark c*
Historical context	Rights
Amendments	Personal rights
Citizenship	Restriction or violation of rights

Skills

*How will students demonstrate they can
use what they learned in a meaningful way?*

Standard 5–5.1	Benchmark b
1. Students will compare governments with freedom as a core belief with those that are not based on democracy	4. Students will describe the rights granted in the Bill of Rights and describe the impact on their families

Benchmark a	Benchmark c
2. Students will explain the reasons for the Bill of Rights and how this critical document has changed over time	5. Students will give examples of the consequences and rationale of rights that are denied
3. Students will explain the implications for participating as citizens in the United States, given the Bill of Rights	6. Students will understand current events with relationship to the Bill of Rights and give examples of applications of the Bill of Rights today

Relevance

*Why must students learn this and what need
is there for this learning across time and applications?*

Since it is important for students to form a personal connection with the Bill of Rights, they first need to see the relevance of this critical document in everyday dealings and various aspects of our lives as U.S. citizens.

One way for a teacher to set the stage for this unit is to bring in the following:

- A school district job application or college application with a nondiscrimination clause
- A copy of the Miranda rights (from the local police)
- A copy of a blank tax form
- A newspaper
- A ballot
- A church bulletin or notice

Students are given a summary copy of the Bill of Rights and split into small groups. Ask students to explain to the whole group which right corresponds to a particular document. In addition, ask if they can think of any other examples.

Final Assessment Description

What does the demonstration of learning for this unit look like?

Students will investigate the current relevance of the Bill of Rights using newspapers and other periodicals. Students will focus on civil rights as a major historical and current theme, events related to the Bill of Rights, and its interpretations for citizens of the United States. Students will write an essay to summarize their findings on a particular aspect of civil rights. Students will also have a choice of ways to present this learning using ideas from multiple intelligences.

Critical Unit Questions

What questions will the students answer
if they are successful on the final assessment?

1. How will you compare the reasons the Bill of Rights was drafted and the reasons it is still a powerful and influential document today?

2. Can you design a summary and examples of one of the rights in the Bill of Rights and describe the role of a particular historical movement or issue that played a role in development of those rights?

Pre-Assessment Design

Part One: What do we already know about our history students?

We have information from the previous unit on the Constitution, which includes an initial understanding of historical and governmental documents that are important today. We know they can write and look up information and comprehend the main idea in historical texts. They also have an initial understanding of legislation and its impact on their lives.

Part Two: What do we need to know to
get students to grow from where they are to the
final assessment so that more students reach proficiency?

We need to know what informal information students have about the Bill of Rights. We also need to know if they can understand examples of citizens' rights.

A Way to Pre-Assess the Gap

1. Students will brainstorm a list of what they know about the Bill of Rights independently (done on the first day of the unit). Teachers will

determine the degree of prior knowledge to judge how much time to spend on the introductory portions of the unit and determine methods for teaching background information.

2. Students will use a newspaper article and the Bill of Rights to see if they understand the current application of a right (done as a first assignment after an introduction to the unit).

3. Teachers will judge what rehearsal may be necessary in comparing rights to current interpretations and to what degree writing summaries of information will need to be included in the unit lessons.

Chunking or Outlining the Unit

*How will teachers break up the unit into chunks of
learning that represent various degrees of growing skill and thinking?*

1. The unit is activated through relevance and application to students' lives.

2. A sense of historical background and context is developed, including the concepts of freedom and citizenship. What were some of the influences that led to the Preamble and the first ten amendments?

3. Examples are used to explain current application of rights, including personal application.

4. How has the Bill of Rights changed over time and why? What is the past and current relationship of the Bill of Rights to the U.S. Constitution (tying current unit to previous unit)? What were some of the movements and violations of rights that led to amendments eleven through twenty-seven?

5. Students will explore documents from nondemocratic countries and compare them to the Bill of Rights, creating a visual framework of citizenship.

6. Groups of students will research an aspect of a movement or historical period to describe how and why the Bill of Rights changed and the impact of that change today.

7. Students will work on sharing what they have learned about the rights of citizens in the United States.

Final Assessment: Do You Know Your Rights?

Students will be able to answer the critical questions for this unit through a series of tasks that demonstrate their ability to interpret and apply the Bill of Rights. You are going to investigate and research one of the rights in the Bill of Rights.

Directions

1. Look up two or three rights that interest you on the Internet sites listed, and then choose one of the rights on which to focus your research. You may work with a partner or two or by yourself on the research phase of this assessment.

2. Research that right, how it came to be a part of the Bill of Rights and what meaning it has today.

    a. Why did you choose this right? How is it meaningful to you?
    b. What was the historical background?
    c. Who was involved in the events or issues that led to this right being added to the Bill of Rights and why was it added?
    d. What rights were violated or misused? Was the freedom of a set of citizens compromised and if so, how?
    e. What evidence is there that this right is still important to you and your family today? Give examples, please.
    f. What do you see as the most important aspect of this right and how should we keep from violating this right?

3. Individually write a paper that answers the questions in Step 2. Please include a title page and references. Remember that the writing standards apply to all written work in this class. Be certain to edit your work before turning it in. You may ask a friend to help you edit and review your work. Review the models posted and the checklist for good research-based writing.

4. Complete the self-evaluation form for your paper.

5. Decide how you will share your conclusions and the information that you discovered. You may work with others who researched the same right, or you may work alone. Use the multiple intelligences suggestion chart to help you choose an interesting way to describe what your right means to citizens today and what it means to you.

6. Check the rubric below to help you with your performance on this assessment.

Self and Peer Assessment Checklist for Research Paper on Rights

❑ Title page
❑ References listed properly

❏ Answered each question

❏ Edited

❏ Checked model

❏ Double-check your work by rating yourself on the rubric

Rubric for Final Assessment: Do You Know Your Rights?

Key Concepts	Advanced	Proficient	Partially Proficient
Using examples of application to student and other citizens today	Students describe in detail and give personal examples of why this right is essential today	Students describe and give examples of why this right is important today	Students describe the importance of this right
Understanding what influenced the history of a right becoming part of the Bill of Rights	Students describe what was going on in the country when the right was added to the Constitution in the Bill of Rights, and give examples of rights that were violated	Students give examples of violations of rights that led to the creation of or an addition to the Bill of Rights	Students tell why a right became part of the Bill of Rights
Protecting our rights today as citizens of the United States	Students use examples from current publications and government documents to explain how we protect this right today	Students use news-based examples to explain how courts, law enforcement, and other agencies protect this right of citizens today	Students use examples from the newspaper or Internet news sources to explain how this right is protected today
Describing the role of important leaders in creating change in our country	Students describe the actions and thinking of key leaders in a movement toward creating change or protecting rights in our country	Students describe the role of key leaders toward protecting citizens' freedoms	Students describe a key leader or author of a right
Sharing what you learned and how it affects you	Students help the audience to understand what the right means to them and to other citizens today	Students help the audience to understand what the right means to them today	Students help the audience understand the right

Peer and Teacher Checklist for Sharing Your Right

1. I understand that this right is important today because:

2. This right is important to me because:

3. This right is important to others because:

PERSUASIVE WRITING— CONVINCE ME! GRADES 9 TO 12

Standards/Benchmarks: Language Arts 9 to 12, Persuasive Writing

What must students learn?

Standard 2. Students write and speak for a variety of purposes and audiences.

2a Write a variety of genres such as essays that persuade

2b Organize writing so that it has an inviting introduction, a logical progression of ideas, and a purposeful conclusion

2c Use vivid and precise language appropriate to audience and purpose

2d Plan, draft, revise, and edit for a legible final copy

2e Write in format and voice appropriate to purpose and audience

2f Vary sentence structure and length to enhance meaning and fluency

2g Develop ideas and content with significant details, examples, and/or reasons to address a prompt

Standard 3. Students write and speak using conventional grammar, usage, sentence structure, punctuation, capitalization, and spelling.

3c Write in complete sentences

3d Use conventions correctly

3e Use conventional spelling

3f Use paragraphing correctly so that each paragraph is differentiated by indenting or blocking and includes one major, focused idea

Key Concepts

What must students remember and be able to use, even after this unit?

Standard 2	*Standard 3*
Persuade	Conventions
Voice	Format
Claim or position	Self-edit
Rationale	Peer edit
Sentence variety	
Word choice	

Skills

*How will students demonstrate they
can use what they learned in a meaningful way?*

Standard 2	Standard 3
1. Students will demonstrate effective persuasive writing in paragraphs and letters	4. Students will edit and improve their work using a rubric and models
2. Students will choose and research evidence as a point of view on a controversial issue	5. Students will use peer editing to gain an additional point of view about their work
3. Students will write in a compelling manner to persuade a specific audience	

Relevance

*Why must students learn this and what need
is there for this learning across time and applications?*

The teacher can pique interest in this unit by describing persuasive writing as a key trait that adults need. Students will be given a recent county tax brochure with directions on how to persuade county officials to lower property taxes from the estimated value. Students will brainstorm how they would go about making a persuasive argument to county officials. Students will be given an appraisal form and a comparables report from a realtor so that they can refine their ideas around evidence. Students will also discuss other circumstances in which adults use persuasive writing to get something done.

Final Assessment Description

What does the demonstration of learning for this unit look like?

Choose an issue you feel strongly about from a newspaper or magazine article, a news report, or other current events sources and write a persuasive researched paper to express your point of view. Be certain to add enough researched details to clarify your point of view and also point out issues for other points of view. Make certain that your sentence variety and word choice is compelling, so that your readers want to understand what you are saying and want to finish reading your letter. Also, make certain that readers see a clear connection between the evidence you presented and your conclusion. See the rubric and models to help you write this paper.

Critical Questions

What questions will the students answer
if they are successful on the final assessment?

1. How can I research and write to persuade others that I have a valid point of view?

2. How can I make my persuasive writing more compelling to my intended audience?

Pre-Assessment Design

Part One: What do we already know about our English students?

We have samples of writing from other units that indicate some degree of editing, word choice, and voice. We have no current examples of writing to persuade. Sentence fluency and variety appear limited for most of the class.

Part Two: What do we need to know to get students to
grow from where they are to proficient performance on the final assessment?

We need to know the students' ability to research and clearly communicate a point of view.

A Way to Pre-Assess the Gap

Students in your class also take history and have already written a short research-based paper. Check with the history teacher and other teachers about their impressions of student research ability. Another way to assess this is to use a beginning assignment in the unit to fine-tune your coaching around research. (See "Chunking the Unit".)

To check on initial persuasive writing skills, have students write a single paragraph to convince you to cancel tonight's homework assignment. Make certain to give students two to three minutes before turning this in for final editing. This will give you information on how much time to spend on various aspects of persuasive writing with this class and how much coaching is needed for various individuals.

Chunking or Outlining the Unit

How will teachers break up the unit into chunks
of learning that represent various degrees of growing skill and thinking?

1. Introduction to persuasive writing: Why do we need it? See relevance above

2. Reviewing the model and rubric

3. Learning the pieces of good persuasive writing and practicing the pieces

    a. Compelling introductions and conclusions, adding background

    b. Using evidence for and against a claim

    c. Occasion/position statements and other ways to state your point of view

    d. Voice, sentence variety, and word choice that help the reader

4. Choosing an issue and researching your point of view

5. Time for research and use of graphic organizer

6. Final assessment

Final Assessment: Convince Me!

Choose a current event or issue that portrays a controversial topic of interest to you personally. This could be a topic or issue about which you take a side, feel strongly, or are outraged by current events. Prepare a persuasive paper arguing for and against your point of view. Use primary and secondary source research techniques and cite your sources within your letter. Use the rubric on page 113 and models you received in class to help you edit and improve your letter.

Steps

1. Review the rubric and model as well as the tip sheets you received throughout this unit.

2. Use the advanced organizer for the assessment. Get approval from the teacher after completing the topic. Be prepared to share why this is a critical or important issue for you.

3. Briefly state your point of view.

4. Complete your research and list points you want to make for and against the claim. Keep a list of sources. Use quotation marks in wording to note exact quotation if you use the original wording of the author or source.

5. What is your conclusion? Does it match your original point of view? Have you changed your mind or confirmed your opinion?

6. What solutions do you see?

7. Review the rubric and models and then begin writing your letter.

8. Use self and peer editing prior to turning in your work.

Persuasive Writing Template

Student Name: Block/Period: Date:

```
State Your Topic in Terms of a Question:




```

⬇

State Your Point of View:

⬇   ⬇

List evidence for your point of view and the sources for the evidence:	List the evidence against your point of view and the sources for the evidence:

⬇   ⬇

Which evidence was the most persuasive for you?

Given the evidence you collected, what conclusion makes the most sense to you?

Rubric for Convince Me!

Key Concepts	Advanced	Proficient	Partially Proficient
Claim or point of view	Claim indicates what is controversial about this topic or issues and why it is critical to this student	Claim indicates why this issue is important to student	Claim is stated and issue is identified
Reasons for and against the claim	Claim uses researched information to support the claim and identify other points of view	Claim is well supported by the reasons for and reasons against; brings up other points of view	Reasons for and against are listed and related to the claim although a direct connection may not be apparent
Organization	Writing has a compelling and interesting introduction and conclusion that are clearly supported by evidence	Writing has a clear introduction and a logical conclusion that are supported by evidence	Writing has a beginning, a logical middle, and a conclusion such that the reader can infer the author's point of view
Word choice	Word choice convinces the reader of the emotions of the writer	Word choice is varied and suited to the theme	Word choice is suited to the theme.
Voice	Writing is compelling and seeks to influence a specific reader or audience	Writing is clearly geared to a specific audience or reader	Writing includes the author's point of view, but the reader or audience may be unclear
Sentence variety	Questions, sentences, and quotes support a convincing letter	Sentences are varied in length and type to add interest to the letter	Sentences are varied in length and type and may or may not add interest
Conventions and editing	Not applicable	Error-free writing is submitted	There are few errors, and they do not interfere with the meaning or readability of the letter
Research use and sources cited	Primary and secondary sources are used and quoted in the letter to help make a point clearer or more convincing	Primary and secondary sources are used and quoted in the letter	Primary and secondary sources are used and referred to in the letter

Unit Planning Grid

Unit Plan for: Subject: Grade:

Standards/Benchmarks: What should students know and be able to do?
Key Concepts: What must students remember and be able to use, even after this unit?
Skills: How will students demonstrate they can utilize what they learned in a meaningful way?
Relevance: Why must students learn this and what need is there for this learning across time and applications?
Final Assessment Description: What does the demonstration of learning for this unit look like?
Critical Unit Questions: The students will answer what questions, if they are successful on the final assessment?
Pre-Assessment Design: What do we already know about our science students? What do we need to know to get student growth from where they are to the final assessment?
Chunking or Outlining the Unit: How will teachers break up the unit into chunks of learning that represent various degrees of growing skill and thinking?
Next steps to finish unit planning: • Create the final Assessment Prompt and Rubric. Collect or create models. • Create Student self-assessment tool or checklist • Use a "Planning Grid" for each unit chunk after you pre-assess.

5

Differentiated Instruction and Strategies

Kathy Tuchman Glass

This book focuses on creating differentiated lessons and not entire units of study. It is imperative that teachers understand not only the overarching goals of a given lesson but also the broader unit of study before diving in and teaching. The backward design model emphasizes beginning with the end in mind. In their book *Integrating Differentiated Instruction + Understanding by Design*, authors Carol Tomlinson and Jay McTighe (2006) write: "The concept of planning backward from desired results is not new. In 1949, Ralph Tyler described this approach as an effective process for focusing instruction. More recently, Stephen Covey (1989) in the best-selling book *Seven Habits of Highly Effective People*, reports that effective people in various fields are goal oriented and plan with the end in mind. Although not a new idea, we have found that the deliberate use of backward design for planning courses, units, and individual lessons results in more clearly defined goals, more appropriate assessments, and more purposeful teaching." Typically, we think of applying backward design to comprehensive units of study. But since the notion of this design process is essentially a sequence for curriculum, employing backward design to each lesson is prudent so teachers know what direction a lesson is headed by looking at the final goal first. One way to do this is by creating guiding questions that emanate from standards to use as a guidepost in devising lessons. Using these questions allows teachers to be more effective in teaching by focusing a lesson on standards and concepts so students can grasp the overarching goals.

In this book, teachers will find a multitude of differentiated lessons tied to a curriculum for fourth- to ninth-grade students. Each lesson includes the tenets of backward design in that they begin with clearly articulated standards and guiding questions. Subsequently, I include details to execute lessons including student groupings, strategies, assessments, resources, student handouts, suggestions for differentiation, and more.

DIFFERENTIATED INSTRUCTION

The term *differentiation* and its use in the classroom are familiar to many educators. There are innumerable books, articles, websites, and other resources dedicated to differentiation. Extensive lists of authors who are experts in this area abound; many are listed in the References and Further Reading section of this book. Even those who are unaware of differentiation realize that in a classroom of students, there are those who are more advanced learners and those who are far below grade-level expectations. There are students who have a proclivity for the arts and others who have a tendency to favor the sciences. Some students are content sitting for most of the day at a desk, whereas others are clamoring for time to move about the room or school campus. The list of ways that contribute to student diversity is an extensive one. Students are also keenly aware of the fact that there are differences among them. Just as students know that on a given sports team, not all players are experts in every position, so do students realize that their classmates possess a variety of expertise and interest in areas relating to school work and learning styles. Teachers who employ differentiation are aware of student differences and capitalize on opportunities to challenge students to their abilities, taking into account learner interests, readiness, and learning styles. These teachers' mission is to seek out and learn ways to meet their students' needs. In turn, students appreciate teachers who understand and respond to differences.

DEFINITION: CONTENT, PROCESS, PRODUCT

Carol Ann Tomlinson, a leading author in this field, crystallizes the definition of differentiation in this way: "In a differentiated classroom, the teacher proactively plans and carries out varied approaches to content, process, and product in anticipation of and response to student difference in readiness, interest, and learning needs" (Tomlinson, 2001). Below is a cursory definition of the major components of differentiation; throughout the book, specific examples are provided.

Content

The *content* is the essential knowledge, understandings, and skills of a unit of study or lesson. To identify the content, teachers refer to content standards from the district, state, or school in addition to accessing textbooks, curriculum, and other guides and deferring to teacher expertise.

This combination of sources will most likely be needed for teachers to clearly identify the content—what students should know, understand, and be able to do. Some refer to the content as the *input* since teachers are filling up students' brains with new information.

Teachers introduce students to content in a variety of ways. The traditional way is through a textbook or lecture. Other ways include a performance, a video, computer software, a website, a field trip, an audio recording, a guest speaker, a summary, an article, and so forth. As teachers come to know their students through formal and informal assessments, they can present content in a differentiated way. For example, content-area teachers can have several biographies available on various individuals and at different levels of readability. The teacher then assigns students appropriate biographies based on students' reading levels and takes into account their interests in a particular noteworthy figure. Or a social studies teacher can arrange students in groups according to their interests on a particular topic, such as a country. Each group then reads various resources centered on the country of choice. Alternatively, the teacher can arrange groups homogeneously by ability and assign more difficult reading to high-achieving students and more accessible text to those who are struggling.

Teachers do not necessarily have to differentiate content for each lesson all the time. They can present the whole class with a resource, such as a video, and then differentiate subsequent activities by instructing groups of students who are arranged by ability level or interest to explore further. For example, if students are studying slavery, a teacher might present an excerpt from a video of Alex Haley's *Roots* to the entire class to expose them to specific content. For further acquisition of this content, the teacher can divide students into readiness-based groups and assign various reading material at an appropriately challenging level for each group. This might mean using a more advanced textbook for the most able readers and providing an excerpt from a grade-level text for other students. Struggling students might be challenged through a brief summary that exposes key ideas.

Process

Process is the method used to make sense of the content. In other words, *process* is the sense-making part of a lesson when teachers call upon students to assimilate and apply the information presented in the content. Typically, this is done through classroom activities and lessons that teachers conduct, although homework assignments are also part of the process.

One frequently used differentiated strategy for teaching or reteaching is through mini-workshops or small-group instruction. In this strategy, students are preassessed to determine their understanding of a particular skill, concept, or topic—for example, their ability to use complex sentences, define *mitosis*, or identify the main idea of a reading selection. Based on this information, teachers might pull a small group of students who need additional support to hone this learning and conduct a mini-workshop to assist them. Or an alternative method is when teachers create and assign several versions of an assignment to appeal to different ability levels. The preassessment will provide information about which assignment is best suited for each student or groups of students. These previous examples highlight differentiation for readiness level, but teachers can also preassess students in terms of learning style or interest and provide assignment choices so students can work within their preferred learning mode or area of interest.

Another common differentiation practice for process is questioning. Teachers can differentiate questions that appeal to students' interests and also that consider students' readiness. In the latter, questions for advanced learners are those that contain more depth and complexity; however, all learners are given questions that address the overarching concepts of a given lesson or unit. Developing various learning centers, journal prompts, lab experiments, and project choices are just some of the many other ways to differentiate for process.

Any activity or lesson that teachers conduct in the process stage constitutes practice so students have the opportunity to use the content and construct clear understandings. Throughout this critical time of teaching, it is prudent to continually assess how well students are doing and adjust lessons or activities as appropriate. Teachers will feel the need to formulate their own system of accountability; however, they should not overgrade these types of assessments as the emphasis is on practice. A tangible formative assessment for an activity might be a journal-writing response, a math-problem-of-the-week write-up, or an outline. A less concrete albeit critical indicator of how students are faring in their understanding is through observing their participation in small-group tasks and whole-group discussion. When teachers consistently and consciously employ formative (or ongoing) assessment throughout the entire course of a unit, they are able to offer learning that best meets students' needs by, for example, pulling small groups to reteach, revising a lesson, or varying the pace of instruction.

Formative assessment yields valuable information about the effectiveness of curriculum and instruction. During lessons and activities (process), teachers rely on formative assessments to get a pulse on students' understanding of a targeted skill or concept. As Douglas Fisher and Nancy Frey (2007) state in *Checking for Understanding: Formative Assessment Techniques for Your Classroom*, the purpose is "to improve instruction and provide student feedback." It gives teachers the ability to redirect and strengthen teaching that can have an immediate impact on learners. Chapter 4 includes a number of formative assessment examples and ideas.

Product

As evidence of learning after a considerable unit of study, teachers then issue a culminating product (or summative assessment) to demonstrate students' understanding of a unit's content and process. Since content is what students should know, understand, and be able to do, the product should be designed in a way that allows students to demonstrate this learning and to do so with clear and appropriate criteria for success. Some teachers issue a test after a given segment of learning, which signifies just one type of product. But products also come in other forms. Teachers should consider issuing both a final exam and a different type of product for a comprehensive assessment of what students have come to know, understand, and be able to do.

In a language arts classroom, products can include a performance, a poster project, an interview, or a formal writing assignment (e.g., response to literature, persuasive, summary). In a science class, a summative assessment could be writing a lab report or building a kite in a physics unit. Differentiating products is a powerful and valuable means of allowing students to exhibit what they have learned. Teachers should present the summative assessment to students at the beginning of the unit so they are well aware of expectations and have specific goals in mind as they work to accomplish each task that leads to the final product.

STUDENT CHARACTERISTICS: READINESS, INTEREST, LEARNING PROFILE

Teachers differentiate content, process, and/or product as they take into account students' readiness, interest, and learning profile. If teachers differentiate by pairing student characteristics with the curriculum and instruction, powerful learning is the result. Teachers can address one or a combination of characteristics, such as readiness and interest, when planning differentiated lessons or units. Following is a brief explanation of these three key types of student characteristics; there are a multitude of resources on each facet presented here, especially on learning profile. The References and Further Reading section provides a partial list of books, but teachers are encouraged to search for their own resources to foster their students' learning in any of these areas.

Readiness

Through pre- and ongoing (or formative) assessments, teachers can glean information regarding what students know, understand, and can do so they can gauge their *readiness*. Readiness varies from student to student, and teachers need to differentiate to appropriately challenge each student at his or her ability level. If students receive material way too demanding for them, they will feel defeated and frustrated. On the other hand, if they are given work that is far below their ability, they are insulted or are turned off completely. Moderately challenging students just above what they are capable of performing is necessary for learning. When teachers differentiate content based on readiness level, they might gather materials across a spectrum of readability and assign students reading selections accordingly. A tiered activity in which teachers modify and extend a particular assignment so that it has various versions at varying levels of difficulty is one example of differentiation by readiness. Other brief examples are given in the list below and throughout this book.

- In a core classroom of language arts/social studies, assign students to read one of three different books that are chosen specifically by readability. The advanced group reads selections by Frederick Douglass, the grade-level group reads *The Slave Dancer* by Paula Fox, and the struggling group reads *Nightjohn* by Gary Paulsen. During the reading, students at all levels from struggling to high achieving complete various tasks individually and in small groups related to the guiding question: *How does the historical setting affect individuals?* As an extension, the high-achieving group might investigate answers to more complex questions, which might require additional reading, such as: *How does social or political oppression lead to conflict or revolution? How do the physical and emotional results of conflict create lasting change for members of society?*

- During a research project, teachers provide a list of topic choices based on the level of difficulty of the topic. Then, teachers assign high-achieving students a list of more sophisticated topics that require more extensive or introspective research.

- In math, assign different math prompts for students to complete that are at various levels of difficulty with high achievers solving more complex problems than struggling students. Students can even create problems for one another to solve.

- Divide science students into groups based on ability levels. Instruct each group to complete one of three lab experiments that are designed to challenge each group appropriately. For students approaching grade level, scaffold the lab so it is accessible to them by providing more concrete directions with examples and adult assistance. Or, expect all students to complete the same lab but provide extension learning opportunities for high achievers, such as posing more challenging problems, creating prediction scenarios, or connecting the work to professions in the world.

Interest

When teachers take into account students' likes and dislikes, they differentiate according to *interest*. Differentiating this way is powerful in that students are more apt to be engaged in learning when it taps into what appeals to them, and there are specific instances where this type of differentiation might apply. Even if a state standard dictates that students write in a particular genre, there still can be the opportunity to consider student interest. For example, students might be expected to write a biography, but teachers can allow each student to choose his or her own subject as the basis for writing. Similarly, teachers who give students the freedom to choose a topic for a persuasive writing assignment from a comprehensive student-generated list or a research topic from a current unit of study are thus engaging in interest-based differentiation. Selecting a novel as the basis of a literature circle or independent reading is another such example.

Learning Profile

Learning profile encompasses a broad range of areas that involve how students learn best. It most commonly includes learning style and intelligence preferences. Teachers who present content in the same way repeatedly to all students and expect the entire class to demonstrate their learning through only written means do not vary learning styles but rather expect students to work in one modality. Conversely, teachers who selectively present content to groups of students through a variety of ways—video, taped recording, reading selection, hands-on experiment, field trip—are conscious of learning profiles. There are several ways to assign activities that are appropriate for students' learning profiles too. And students can choose products in their preferred modality, such as an interview, storyboard, performance, or written composition—one that best suits their learning style and demonstrates their understanding of the concepts and skills presented in a lesson or unit. Teachers know that students do not always operate in the same learning style for all discipline areas.

Rita Dunn and Ken Dunn (1987) developed a widely accepted learning-style model that includes five classifications of learning styles as summarized in Figure 5.1.

Another commonly known learning profile is *multiple intelligences,* which was conceived by Howard Gardner (1983). He identifies eight different ways to demonstrate intellectual ability, as shown in Figure 5.2, along with suggestions for planning differentiated curriculum opportunities.

Equally noteworthy is Robert Sternberg's (1996) model of intelligence that includes three skill areas: analytical, creative, and practical. Analytical intelligence encompasses those skills most taught in school and represents linear thinking. It involves comparing and contrasting, making judgments, and defining cause-and-effect relationships. Creative thinkers are innovators who have original approaches and ideas and are good at problem solving. The practical thinkers are "street smart" and have the need to know why and how things work within a context in the greater world.

Linking Interest- and Readiness-Based Differentiation

Designing differentiated opportunities that address both interest and readiness is a challenging task, with the goal being to maximize learning.

Learning Styles

Learning Style	Description
Auditory learners	Students who are auditory learn best through listening. They prefer listening to a lecture or book rather than receiving the information from reading. They like to engage in discussions so they can talk and listen to their classmates about content, ideas, and opinions. Furthermore, they glean much information from speaking strategies, such as pitch, intonation, pacing, and gestures. To appeal to the learning style of auditory learners, teachers might suggest that these students read text aloud and use a tape recorder.
Visual learners	As the term indicates, visual learners learn best through seeing. This means they prefer to read along when a teacher is reading or will need to display the information they hear visually by taking notes or developing graphic organizers. Teachers can assist visual learners by making sure information that is presented is also shown on PowerPoint slides, transparencies, a document camera, handouts, pictures, or videos so they can better assimilate the information. When someone is presenting, it is important to these students that they are able to see the person talking so they can read facial cues and body language. Therefore, an unobstructed view to the teacher or featured speaker is important.
Tactile learners	Students who are tactile like working with their hands. They learn best through touching, so provide math manipulatives, drawing devices, science apparatus, or other materials that they can use for hands-on learning.
Kinesthetic learners	Kinesthetic learners learn best by being physically active in the learning process. They like doing and moving so they can assimilate and connect the information presented so that it is meaningful to them. These students find it difficult to sit and would rather move around the classroom.
Tactile/kinesthetic learners	Tactile/kinesthetic learners learn through moving, doing, and touching. These students want to be physically involved in a hands-on way. Since they have a need to be active and explore, they cannot sit still for long periods of time. Simulations and role-playing are appropriate strategies for these students.

FIGURE 5.1

There are several ways to connect interest and readiness in any classroom. One such example is the strategy of literature circles (Daniels, 1994) in which students are organized in groups with others who have selected the same reading text. Typically, all the students focus on the same genre (e.g., biography, autobiography, classic literature, or historical fiction), author, or a consistent theme such as alienation, coming of age, or conflict.

Multiple Intelligences

Multiple Intelligence	Summary of Each Intelligence	Differentiated Curriculum Suggestions
Verbal/ linguistic	Reading, writing, listening, speaking	• Use storytelling to . . . • Write a poem, myth, legend, short play, or news article about . . . • Lead a class discussion on . . . • Create a radio program about . . . • Invent slogans for . . . • Conduct an interview of . . . on . . .
Logical/ mathematical	Working with numbers and abstract patterns	• Create story problems for . . . • Translate . . . into a formula for. . . • Create a timeline of . . . • Invent a strategy game that . . . • Make up analogies to explain . . .
Visual/spatial	Working with images, mind mapping, visualizing, drawing	• Chart, map, cluster, or graph . . . • Create a slide show, videotape, or photo album of . . . • Design a poster, bulletin board, or mural of . . . • Create advertisements for . . . • Vary the size and shape of . . . • Color-code the process of . . .
Musical/ rhythmic	Using rhythm, melody, patterned sound, song, rap, dance	• Give a presentation with a musical accompaniment on . . . • Sing a rap song that explains . . . • Indicate the rhythmical patterns in . . . • Explain how a piece of music is similar to . . . • Use music to enhance learning . . . • Create a musical collage to depict . . .
Bodily/ kinesthetic	Processing information through touch, movement, dramatics	• Role-play or simulate . . . • Choreograph a dance of . . . • Invent a board or floor game of . . . • Build or construct a . . . • Devise a scavenger hunt to . . . • Design a product for . . .
Interpersonal	Sharing, cooperating, interviewing, relating	• Conduct a meeting to . . . • Act out diverse perspectives on . . . • Intentionally use . . . social skills to learn about . . .

FIGURE 5.2 *(Continued)*

Multiple Intelligence	Summary of Each Intelligence	Differentiated Curriculum Suggestions
		• Teach someone else about ... • Collaboratively plan rules or procedures to ... • Give and receive feedback on ...
Intrapersonal	Working alone, self-paced instruction, individualized projects	• Set and pursue a goal to ... • Describe how you feel about ... • Describe your personal values about ... • Write a journal entry on ... • Do a project of your choice on ... • Self-assess your work in ...
Naturalist	Spending time outdoors, sorting, classifying, noticing patterns	• Collect and categorize data on ... • Keep a journal of observations about ... • Explain how a plant or animal species resembles ... • Make a taxonomy of ... • Specify the characteristics of ... • Attend an outdoor field trip to ...

FIGURE 5.2

Source: The multiple intelligence summaries are from *Differentiated Instructional Strategies: One Size Doesn't Fit All*, 2nd edition, by G. Gregory and C. Chapman. Thousand Oaks, CA: Corwin, 2007, pp. 33–34. The differentiated curriculum suggestions are from *Multiple Intelligences and Student Achievement: Success Stories From Six Schools* by Bruce Campbell and Linda Campbell. Alexandria, VA: Association for Supervision and Curriculum Development, 1999, p. 69.

Teachers usually conduct literature circles during language arts, but they are certainly suitable for other subject areas too. For example, a social studies teacher can offer a variety of historical fiction as the basis for literature circles, or science teachers can provide a selection of biographies on various scientists.

Each student is responsible for a prescribed role that has specific expectations, and each role is rotated. Daniels (1994) offers a list of roles, although teachers tend to expand on them. For example, one student is the "Discussion Director" whose responsibility it is to generate questions and facilitate a group discussion around these questions. Another student assumes the role of "Capable Connector," sharing and facilitating a conversation about connections with characters and themes in other selections or with the real world. Eventually, students internalize the roles and are able to discuss them in depth without the aid of prescriptive jobs and their directions.

Although it is important in literature circles for students to choose a reading selection from a list of choices that interest them, it is equally important that the text is not too advanced or effortless for each student's reading ability, but rather presents an appropriate challenge. To arrange this proper balance, teachers provide controlled choice by preparing a list of reading selections that represent all different levels of readability. Students choose three books from this list that interest them. Then, teachers review each student's three selections and purposefully assign just the right book for each pupil. A teacher can satisfy the needs of a struggling student who has selected as his first choice a book too challenging by assigning him his third choice, a book more appropriate for his reading level. In this scenario, students read selections of interest to them while the teacher assists with making sure the readability level and content of the texts are appropriately challenging. This combination of interest and readiness can yield meaningful learning opportunities.

Linking Learning Style and Readiness-Based Differentiation

Teachers can also differentiate by linking learning style and readiness. For example, students can choose a culminating project from among a teacher-generated list that addresses their learning style, for example, an interview (for more outgoing students), a short story (for those who like to write), a PowerPoint presentation (for the technology-minded student), a detailed illustration (for the artistically inclined), a musical composition (for the musician), and so forth. To include the element of readiness, teachers can allow students to choose the project type but direct the content. The content on which the project is based could be the result of reading text at different levels of challenge (e.g., articles, textbook chapters, picture books), focusing the project on topics that span levels of difficulty, or analyzing different laboratory outcomes and basing the project on the findings.

DIFFERENTIATED STRATEGY SUGGESTIONS

Figure 5.3 includes several strategies along with suggestions for differentiating instruction. A brief overview and example of how each strategy can be used is included along with identification of content, process, and/or product and whether it applies to readiness, interest, or learning profile. More thorough applications and explanations of some strategies are located throughout this book. With the pervasive nature of this topic, however, one book cannot possibly provide all the necessary information about differentiation. Therefore, refer to the References and Further Reading section for a list of books that serve to improve teachers' awareness, understanding, and implementation of differentiation.

Differentiating Instruction

What Is the Strategy?	How Do I Use It?
Various texts, resources, supplemental materials	*Content for Readiness:* Teachers can make available a wide array of reading materials at various levels of readability, for example, textbook excerpts from different grade-level texts (and not just the text from the current grade taught), supplemental materials from publishers, various articles, pictures books, and so forth. Teachers assign different groups or individuals appropriately challenging text based on students' reading abilities.
	Content for Interest: In a readiness-based situation, students are assigned reading materials that are appropriately challenging. In an interest-based model, students choose the texts, resources, and materials that involve topics of interest to them.
	Process for Readiness: Similar to providing a wide array of reading material for students to acquire content knowledge, teachers can make available a multitude of resource material at varying levels of difficulty so students can process this content. High-achieving students can read materials that are more complex and advanced. Struggling readers will be assigned less complicated material. Additionally, teachers can employ other differentiated strategies for these students, such as reading partners and using classmates' notes to guide or supplement reading.
	Process for Learning Profile: Teachers consider students' learning styles when providing various kinds of resource materials for students to assimilate content, for example, interviews, demonstrations, computer software, videotapes, or reading excerpts.
Organizing ideas through graphic organizers (or other methods)	*Content or Process for Readiness:* As students read various-leveled texts or materials or listen to a lecture, teachers may assign different graphic organizers based on readiness with some more challenging and that ask for more complex understanding than others. Although the organizers vary in design and complexity, all students are expected to acquire conceptual understanding of overarching themes. Teachers might also copy and share completed organizers from students who could benefit from classmates' notes. Teachers can also issue different organizers to students to use as a prewriting tool. These brainstorming sheets are modified or more complex, and each mirrors the differentiated writing rubrics students address.
	Content or Process for Learning Profile: Some students organize information through outlining to better understand and assimilate the information; some students prefer writing a brief summary. Teachers who allow students to choose an organizational method that best suits individual learning styles are assisting students in grasping the information. Besides outlining and summarizing, students might create or select a web, chart, diagram, storyboard, and so forth to organize thoughts in a way suitable for individual learning characteristics. There are many websites that feature graphic organizers: • http://www.eduplace.com/graphicorganizer/ • http://www.edhelper.com/teachers/graphic_organizers.htm • http://www.nvo.com/ecnewletter/graphicorganizers/ • http://www.region15.org/curriculum/graphicorg.html

FIGURE 5.3 *(Continued)*

What Is the Strategy?	How Do I Use It?
Reading buddies or partners/ reciprocal teaching (Palincsar, 1985, 1986)	*Content for Readiness:* Pair students to read material to supplement concepts presented. Students read material silently and then aloud to each other and discuss the material presented. To differentiate by readiness, teachers pair students of comparable reading abilities. Teachers may also choose to employ the reciprocal teaching strategy so partners have a prescribed method of discussing and understanding materials read through predicting, questioning, summarizing, and clarifying, which represent the hallmark of the Reciprocal Teaching strategy.
Varied computer programs	*Content for Readiness:* Just as teachers assign students designated material to read based on students' levels of reading and comprehension, so can teachers assign students to work on a software program geared to a certain level of difficulty matched to each learner.
Tape-recorded materials	*Content for Readiness/Learning Profile:* Some students are better able to assimilate and understand material if they hear it tape-recorded. Allow those students who are struggling readers or those who are highly auditory to listen to tape-recorded material in lieu of reading an excerpt, to follow along with a reading excerpt, or to supplement the reading with an additional tape-recorded piece. Here are some options: • Kurzweil 3000 (www.kurzweiledu.com) is a program designed to help low-performing students and those with some learning disabilities read and write and be independent learners. Students can scan in a teacher's handout or an article, and the Kurzweil will read the article out loud. There are options to read slower or faster, to take notes, and to highlight text. • Microsoft Word has a tape-recording feature that can help students read. • Teachers can also tape-record a lecture and allow students to listen to the lecture again and read a copy of accompanying lecture notes. • If a story is not currently available on tape or CD, invite students who read with strong inflection and modulation to tape-record stories to share with students who could benefit from listening. Students can also download novels onto their iPods from iTunes, but this source is limited. • Recording for the Blind & Dyslexic (RFB&D), a national nonprofit and volunteer organization, has produced accessible educational materials for students with disabilities (e.g., visual impairment or dyslexia) that make reading standard print difficult or impossible. Their digitally recorded textbooks and novels are available in every subject area and grade level from kindergarten through graduate studies. Those interested can become members, and it operates similarly to a lending library (www.rfbd.org). • LibriVox (www.librivox.org) provides free audiobooks from the public domain. Volunteers record chapters of books in the public domain and release the audio files back onto the Net. Their catalog includes more than 1,500 works from which to choose.
Videotapes	*Content for Readiness/Learning Profile:* Assign students to watch videotapes to supplement an explanation or a lecture.

FIGURE 5.3 *(Continued)*

What Is the Strategy?	How Do I Use It?
Visual, auditory, tactile, kinesthetic modes	*Content for Learning Profile:* To maximize learning opportunities for all students, teachers can present content that addresses their varied learning styles. For example, teachers can accompany lectures (auditory) by showing graphic organizers or notes (visual) on an overhead, a document camera, or a PowerPoint slide. Or teachers can set up math stations with manipulatives (tactile) or assign students to act out a part of a play (kinesthetic).
Jigsaw (Aronson, 1978; Clarke, 1994; Clarke, Widerman, & Eadie, 1990; Slavin, 1994)	*Content and Process for Readiness/Interest:* The jigsaw strategy involves groups of students reading different material based on readiness or their interests. Students then teach each other what they have learned. *Group configuration #1:* Students are arranged in initial groups and assigned or choose a subtopic of a greater topic of study. Students read, discuss, and clarify information about the subtopic to become experts. *Group configuration #2:* Students form a different group comprised of one individual from the first group, who have become experts on a subtopic. Each student's job is to teach others in his or her group about what she or he has learned from the first group. Students may ask questions for clarification and take notes on the subtopic a classmate has explained. At the end of the exercise, students will have learned information about several subtopics. *Extension:* Teachers extend the jigsaw with additional activities to further students' understanding of the reading, plus they can issue an assessment.
Curriculum compacting (Reis, Burns, & Renzulli, 1992)	*Content, Process, or Product for Readiness/Interest/Learning Profile:* According to Reis, Burns, and Renzulli (1992), "the term *curriculum compacting* refers to a process in which a teacher preassesses above-average-ability students' skills or knowledge about content prior to instruction and uses this information to modify curriculum." This strategy is used for students who can master information at a faster pace. Although the authors present eight specific steps, there are three basic phases to curriculum compacting: (1) identify learning objectives or standards of the curriculum to be taught; (2) preassess students on what they know, understand, and are able to do in a given unit; and (3) plan and provide curriculum enrichment for students who have mastered learning objectives based on preassessment results. Although readiness drives curriculum compacting, teachers should collaborate with students to consider interest and learning style preferences as well.
Learning contracts (Tomlinson, 2001; Winebrenner, 2001)	*Content, Process, or Product for Readiness/Interest/Learning Profile:* A learning contract is an agreement between the teacher and student about independent work that the student will accomplish with teacher guidance. It can be part of the curriculum compacting plan or not. The contract can take many forms and can be used for individuals or groups of students. For example, a student who has shown mastery of certain skills and concepts from a preassessment can work on a learning contract while the class works on teacher-directed learning. During some lessons, these students work independently on the contract, but other times they join the class for whole-group activities or lessons with content matter they need to learn. Students with learning contracts must abide by working conditions and rules set forth by the teacher and agreed to by the student(s), such as working quietly, not disturbing the teacher when she or he is teaching, following activity directions, maintaining a log of work accomplished, abiding by time lines, etc. Criteria for performance (or scoring guide) are necessary to focus students as they work on projects.

FIGURE 5.3 (*Continued*)

What Is the Strategy?	How Do I Use It?
Learning centers	*Process for Readiness:* Teachers can teach, extend, and reinforce the skills and concepts of a particular unit through learning centers. In this strategy, teachers create several meaningful activities and organize/arrange the materials and directions of these activities throughout the classroom—on the floor, at a back table, on a cluster of desks pulled together. Students are then directed to certain activities—or learning centers—to acquire readiness-based competencies they need to learn. For example, teachers will dictate that some students visit Centers #1 and #2, and go to other centers only if time allows. Other students are designated to visit Centers #3 and #4. Students show evidence of the work completed at each center through a visible recordkeeping device set up in the classroom or by housing work in a folder.
Interest centers	*Process for Interest:* Similar to learning centers, interest centers are set up throughout the classroom or housed in folders or boxes that can be worked on at students' desks. Interest centers are meant to allow students to explore a topic in further depth based on their interests. This interest-based motivation is what differentiates interest centers from learning centers, which focus more on mastery. The topics for interest centers can be related to a current unit of study or another topic outside the unit.
Games to practice mastery of information and skills	*Process for Readiness:* Teachers can arrange for students to play a variety of games to review and master skills and information. Teachers or students can prepare game cards by level of difficulty and assign students to answer selected questions. Teachers can make game cards based on popular games (e.g., Jeopardy, Bingo) or make their own generic game board and create clues based on unit content. Clue and answer cards can be color-coded based on difficulty level. Students can act out differentiated concepts or vocabulary words/terms for others to guess. Instead of creating their own, teachers can find various games at conferences where vendors sell their wares, at teacher supply houses, or by searching online; or they can even alter popular games to meet the needs of students.
Anchor activities	*Process for Readiness/Interest:* Because students work at different paces, in a differentiated classroom students are given a choice of activities (called anchor activities) to work on independently when they finish work early. As students work on these activities that extend the concepts and skills of a lesson or unit, teachers have the opportunity to pull individuals or small groups of students for assessment or further instruction.
Mini-workshops	*Process for Readiness:* To teach or reteach a skill, concept, or topic, teachers can conduct mini-workshops and invite selected students who are in need of honing targeted learning to participate. Through pre- and ongoing assessments, teachers can detect which students are in need of additional instruction. Teachers would then invite those students to attend a mini-workshop on this skill, topic, or concept as an adjunct to whole-group instruction. Other names for mini-workshops are (1) small-group instruction or (2) flexible-skills grouping if the work of the group focuses on skill building only. Teachers can conduct mini-workshops for a small group while others are working on anchor activities.

FIGURE 5.3 *(Continued)*

What Is the Strategy?	How Do I Use It?
Homework assignments	*Process for Readiness:* Teachers assign homework at varying difficulty levels to students based on readiness. Differentiating homework assignments serves to further elucidate and challenge students' understanding of a given concept, skill, or topic. For example, teachers can assign different levels of writing or math prompts; in language arts, teachers can assign short stories at different levels of complexity; in science, teachers can offer different challenge levels of science articles for students to read and summarize.
Multiple levels of questioning (California Department of Education, 1994)	*Process for Readiness:* Questioning is an effective strategy used in classrooms, but in a differentiated classroom specific questions can be purposefully devised to challenge groups of students at varying levels of difficulty and complexity. All questions, though, emanate from the overarching concepts the class is studying. It would behoove teachers to explore the research of Dr. Sandra Kaplan from Southern California's Rossier School of Education when devising differentiated questions. Drawing from her work, key vocabulary is used as the impetus to enrich content knowledge through depth within a discipline and complexity across disciplines. Key words and phrases to foster questioning include *patterns, rules, trends, vocabulary, ethics, traits,* and *purposes.*
Exit cards	*Process for Readiness:* Teachers prepare prompts that they issue to students during the last 3 to 5 minutes of class. The prompts relate to the day's lesson, and students respond to them as a way for teachers to check for understanding and progress and for students to reflect upon key learning. Students can respond on index cards or scraps of paper. Students put their names on their exit cards and the teacher collects them. Afterwards, teachers sort the cards into three piles according to students' understanding: (1) students who are on target and clearly understand what is taught, (2) students who kind of "get it," and (3) students who are clearly floundering and need additional support. With this information, teachers can differentiate instruction by modifying or extending the subsequent lessons. Exit cards can be used on an ongoing basis as part of a teacher's routine, or they can be used on a periodic basis as a teacher deems necessary. Some teachers call exit cards "tickets to leave" since the students hand teachers their cards before leaving the classroom.
Literature circles (Daniels, 1994)	*Process for Readiness/Interest:* Teachers present a collection of books at varying reading levels and topics of interest to students. In groups, students read the same book and are each assigned a specific role that rotates among students. The roles are intended to illuminate the reading by providing a structured way to delve into the complexities of a work of literature. Once students are well versed in the roles, the structured aspect of each job is suspended so spontaneity will emerge. This same model can be used with nonfiction text, as well.
Think-Pair-Share (Lyman, 1981, 1992)	*Process for Readiness/Interest:* To facilitate answering questions and factoring in "wait time," teachers can conduct the Think-Pair-Share (T-P-S) strategy to encourage student participation. To use T-P-S: (1) Teachers pose a thoughtful question, (2) students individually think of or write a response, (3) students pair with another and discuss possible answers, and (4) pairs then share their

FIGURE 5.3 *(Continued)*

What Is the Strategy?	How Do I Use It?
	responses with the whole group and continue with discussion. This strategy can be differentiated in many ways, such as pairing students by readiness or by posing an interest-based question for different groups.
Varied journal prompts	*Process for Readiness/Interest:* Teachers can create a list of prompts to issue throughout a unit of study. Students can respond to those prompts of interest or teachers can assign groups of students specific prompts based on level of complexity. To apply to both interest and readiness, teachers can provide a list of interest-based prompt choices among a span of ability levels.
Group work preferences	*Process or Product for Learning Profile:* Some students work best alone, while others excel within a group. Teachers who allow students to choose to work independently, in pairs, or in small groups on activities or products are differentiating according to students' learning profiles.
WebQuest (Kelly, 2000)	*Process or Product for Readiness/Interest:* A WebQuest is a short- or long-term/individual or small-group project. The model was developed by Bernie Dodge at San Diego State University in February 1995 with early input from SDSU/Pacific Bell Fellow Tom March, the Educational Technology staff at San Diego Unified School District, and waves of participants each summer at the Teach the Teachers Consortium. Its focus is inquiry oriented as students research information on teacher preselected websites to investigate a research question. Students read and analyze the resources from the websites and produce a product showing evidence of understanding. The nature of the activity or project and the associated websites can be differentiated by either readiness or interest level or both.
Independent study	*Process or Product for Interest/Readiness:* In an independent study, students discuss with teachers a topic that forms the basis for a project. The focus can be problem based or an exploration of a topic that is of interest to the student. Both teacher and student collaborate to determine the steps in the process to product completion, time line of each step, the form the product will take, and criteria for success. Independent study is also based on readiness as some students may not be prepared to assume the responsibility of independence in completing the product. Students can work independently, in pairs, or in small groups.
Complex instruction (Cohen, 1994)	*Process or Product for Learning Profile:* Teachers emphasize each student's talents and contributions in a cooperative group by creating and assigning specific challenging and complex learning tasks geared to each student's intellectual strength. A significant goal is for students to appreciate each other's intellectual strengths as they work collaboratively to produce a meaningful product. For example, students work together on creating a fictitious island. Tasks within the project include creating a brochure, drawing a detailed map with a legend, orating the political views of the island, and so on.
RAFT (Santa, 1988)	*Process or Product for Readiness/Interest:* RAFT is an acronym for role, audience, format, and topic. Students work on an assignment that takes into account four components: (1) Role: *From whose point of view is the piece written? What role should the student assume?* (2) Audience: *Who is the audience? Who will see, read,*

FIGURE 5.3 *(Continued)*

What Is the Strategy?	How Do I Use It?
	or use this? (3) Format: *What is the more effective and meaningful product format to show understanding?* (4) Topic: *What is the topic focus for the product or assignment?* Teachers can differentiate for readiness by making more challenging RAFT choices than others or by interest so students can choose the RAFT that most appeals to them. Examples:

American Revolution

Role	Audience	Format	Topic
George Washington	Mother of wounded soldier	Personal letter	How she feels
King George	Sons of Liberty	Document	Why independence is a bad idea
Patrick Henry	Tories or Neutralists	Propaganda	Why fighting for independence is essential

Money

Role	Audience	Format	Topic
Store owner	Customers	Advertisement	All items 10% or 15% off
Baker	Customers	Window sign	Advertising 35% off on some baked goods and 25% off on others
Restaurant owner	Dining customers who are senior citizens	Discounted menu	Entrees 20% off

What Is the Strategy?	How Do I Use It?
Group investigation (Sharon & Sharon, 1992)	*Process or Product for Interest/Learning Profile:* In groups, students select and explore specific subtopics of interest within a general problem area. Students plan and execute investigation relying on multiple sources as they gather, organize, and analyze the information. Groups present their information in a variety of forms that are appropriate for learning styles; classmates and the teacher evaluate the presentations.
Tiered activities, labs, products (Tomlinson, 1999)	*Process or Product for Readiness:* Teachers create various interesting and thought-provoking versions of an activity or culminating product in a range of difficulty levels. Students are then assigned activities or products at an appropriate level of challenge. Even though they vary in the level of complexity, all tiered work focuses on what all students should know, understand, and be able to do. Students can work in pairs or small groups with learners of similar readiness profiles or work independently. If students work in groups, the number of each group will not necessarily be equal given the ability levels of students in a given classroom. For example, there might be one group of four high achievers and

FIGURE 5.3 (*Continued*)

What Is the Strategy?	How Do I Use It?
	two of struggling students. The rest of the groups are comprised of at-grade-level students. Commonly, activities or products are tiered so that there are three varying levels of complexity, but there can also be two or five levels. *Example:* In a poetry unit, one particular assignment can be tiered in which advanced students identify and analyze a poet's use of metaphor, symbolism, and imagery in a sophisticated and complex published poem; at grade level, students identify and analyze the use of metaphor in a less complex poem; struggling learners find two similes in a poem at an appropriate level for them and discuss in a teacher-led group the purpose of the similes used in the piece.
Tic-tac-toe (variations by Winebrenner, 2001; and Tomlinson, 2001)	*Process or Product for Readiness/Learning Profile:* Teachers create a variety of learning-style product choices (e.g., produce a skit, create a song, write a short story or poem) and place them in a tic-tac-toe grid. Students choose which assignments or products they want to complete so that they win a game of tic-tac-toe. Specifically, students choose three assignments that are in a row horizontally, vertically, or diagonally. Teachers can intentionally design the board to apply to readiness by fashioning tasks in appropriate rows based on level of difficulty. Or teachers can create three different tic-tac-toe boards each geared to an ability level. In this way, the tic-tac-toe boards serve as a tiered product for both learning style and readiness.
Portfolios	*Product for Interest:* Teachers can assign students to collect a sampling of their best work in a portfolio. To guide collection, teachers can make a list of the contents of the portfolios and allow for student choice. Within the portfolio, students write a self-reflection answering such questions as: *Which piece is your favorite and why? Which piece might you revise? Which piece shows your best work? Which piece was the most challenging one and why?*
Grade-level and individual student learning rubrics	*Product for Readiness:* Rubrics, or scoring guides, delineate how students will be assessed or evaluated for a given product. It guides both students and teachers in identifying quality work. Sometimes teachers find or create a rubric that represents the key criteria for assessment. They can create rubrics for the different levels of learners in a classroom being mindful of satisfying standards. Other times, teachers and students collaborate to create a rubric that is appropriately challenging to use as a guide for goal-setting when working on a project. The columns represent performance factors (e.g., emergent or approaching grade level, capable, developing, advanced or numbered 1 to 4, 5, or 6). The rows indicate the criteria being assessed.
I-Search (Joyce & Tallman, 1997; Macrorie, 1988) or research project	*Product for Interest:* In an I-Search paper, students actively engage in the research process by exploring answers to interest-based questions that they generate. The research involves four steps from formulating the research question to representing knowledge gained. For a traditional research paper, students can choose a topic of interest within a greater unit of study.

FIGURE 5.3 *(Continued)*

What Is the Strategy?	How Do I Use It?
Community mentorships to guide product	*Product for Interest:* Teachers can assist students in arranging mentorships with employees in the community to complete a product. For example, students who are working on independent study or an I-Search paper might choose a topic related to the environment. To research information for this product, students can spend time working with environmentalists to better understand what qualifications are required in the job, what problems these employees face, how to participate in an environmental study, and so forth.
Community service projects	*Product for Interest:* Students can determine a need in the community and create a service-learning project that reaches out to the community. This appeals to many students because it allows them to do real-world work in an area of interest. For example, students could start a recycling program at a school, organize a tutoring program to benefit struggling students, visit a senior center regularly and read to the seniors or play games with them, or coach younger children in a sport at a local recreation center that is in need of such a program.
Product format choices	*Product for Readiness/Interest/Learning Profile:* Teachers can allow students to show their understanding of what they have learned by choosing a product to complete from a teacher- or student-generated list of choices. Offering several product choices is important when considering each student's learning profile. For example, teachers can list a variety of choices such as interview, short story, project cube, game board, song, PowerPoint presentation, and so on. To design products for readiness and interest, provide a wide array of topic choices that are more challenging and complex for advanced learners and less so for struggling learners. Ensure that all choices are interesting and thoughtful and also allow students to show evidence of conceptual and "big idea" learning. A criterion (rubric) for performance is necessary to guide students as they work on products.
Modify performance assessments	*Product for Readiness/Learning style:* Teachers can assist students in showing what they have learned through modifications of assessments and teacher support. For example, students who have difficulty showing what they know through a written essay that a teacher issues can be asked to tape-record their responses to the essay questions instead. Or students who have fine-motor issues can keyboard their responses. Other ways to support success include (1) extending the due date of products, (2) providing checkpoints along the way with a calendar for students to track and complete work in chunks, and/or (3) submitting sections of a product and assessing them in pieces.

FIGURE 5.3

SUMMARY

Differentiation does not mean that every single lesson or unit includes a differentiated content, process, and product for each and every student's interest, readiness level, and learning profile. As Carol Tomlinson (1999) states in her book *The Differentiated Classroom: Responding to the Needs of All Learners*: "Teachers may adapt one or more of the curricular elements (content, process, product) based on one or more of the student characteristics (readiness, interest, learning profile) at any point in a lesson or unit."

Teachers will instruct students as a whole class in many points throughout the unit and then find it in alignment with the goals of the unit to divide students into differentiated groups for certain activities. Essentially, differentiation is woven in and out of a unit as appropriate; there is no prescribed way that each lesson or unit is to be conducted every time. And it certainly does not mean giving more work to the high achievers and drill practice to lower-level learners. The way and extent to which teachers differentiate depend on the learning goals and the students. But most importantly, it depends on a teacher's willingness to do what is best in the name of education to service students in the more effective way for growth and enlightenment.

Differentiation can be achieved in many different ways. Two teachers who conduct the same lesson or unit can each effectively employ differentiation, although using different techniques, as long as they are clear-sighted about the goals of a given lesson or unit. When teachers are guided by standards and have a firm understanding of the end in mind, they can devise thoughtful curriculum that accounts for the ability levels, learning styles, and interests of their student-clients. This chapter lists a variety of differentiation opportunities (see recap in Figure 5.4). In the following chapters, teachers will receive specific examples and additional support to make differentiation a reality in their classrooms on a consistent basis.

Differentiating Instruction: Recap

Strategy	Readiness	Interest	Learning Profile
CONTENT			
Various texts, resources, supplemental materials	X	X	
Organizing ideas through graphic organizers	X		X
Reading buddies or partner/reciprocal teaching	X		
Varied computer programs	X		
Tape-recorded materials	X		X
Videotapes	X		X
Visual, auditory, tactile, kinesthetic modes			X
Jigsaw	X	X	
Curriculum compacting	X	X	X
Learning contracts	X	X	X

FIGURE 5.4 *(Continued)*

Strategy	Readiness	Interest	Learning Profile
PROCESS			
Various texts, resources, supplemental materials	X		X
Organizing ideas through graphic organizers (or other methods)	X		X
Jigsaw	X	X	
Curriculum compacting	X	X	X
Learning contracts	X	X	X
Learning centers	X		
Interest centers		X	
Games to practice mastery of information and skills	X		
Anchor activities	X	X	
Mini-workshops	X		
Homework assignments	X		
Multiple levels of questioning	X		
Exit cards	X		
Literature circles	X	X	
Think-Pair-Share	X	X	
Varied journal prompts	X	X	
Group work preferences			X
WebQuests	X	X	
Independent study	X	X	
Complex instruction			X
RAFT	X	X	
Group investigation		X	X
Tiered activities, labs, products	X		
Tic-tac-toe	X		X

FIGURE 5.4 *(Continued)*

Strategy	Readiness	Interest	Learning Profile
PRODUCT			
Curriculum compacting	X	X	X
Learning contracts	X	X	X
Group work preferences			X
WebQuests	X	X	
Independent study	X	X	
Complex instruction			X
RAFT	X	X	
Group investigation		X	X
Tiered activities, labs, products	X		
Tic-tac-toe	X		X
Portfolios		X	
Grade-level and individual student learning rubrics	X		
I-Search or research project		X	
Community mentorships		X	
Community service projects		X	
Product format choices	X	X	X
Modify performance assessments	X		X

FIGURE 5.4

6

Graphic Organizers

Tools to Promote Differentiation

Patti Drapeau

Cognitive graphic organizers are one of the more powerful tools we have to support differentiated instruction. Many teachers, however, use these graphic organizers as whole class activities. Although this may be effective teaching practice, whole class lessons can sometimes be limiting because they only address some of the learner's needs some of the time. The versatility of the graphic organizers makes them perfect tools for differentiation. If teachers think about why they differentiate, then they can figure out how to use the graphic organizers to address students' interests, styles, and abilities.

Below, I have listed ten principles of differentiated instruction (adapted from Tomlinson, 1999; Tomlinson & McTighe, 2006), and paired these principles with the ways in which graphic organizers can be used to support them (see Figure 6.1 and the discussion that follows). These principles are not listed in a prioritized fashion. They are all important and they often interrelate.

1. *Addressing readiness, interests, and styles.* A high-level thinking graphic organizer can be used as soon as students are ready to think about content at a sophisticated level (Drapeau, 2004; Howard & Fogarty, 2003; Jensen, 2006; Tomlinson & Edison, 2003). Students who are not ready to apply information at this level may receive the graphic organizer a few days later than other students. In this way, they will have extra time to review basic content with other instructional strategies before they are expected to apply the information at a high level of complexity. We know that some students are more interested in certain topics within a subject area (Gregory & Chapman, 2002; Tomlinson & Edison, 2003). Students use different graphic organizers to tailor their work to their areas of interest. We also know that most of our students prefer a visual style of learning. "Research conducted by 3M Corporation in 2001 found the brain processes visuals 60,000 times faster than text, and visual aids in the classroom have been found to improve learning up to 400 percent" (Gangwer, 2005, p. 24). Gangwer recommends the use of color, graphs, tables, and pictures for visual learners. When memorizing information, visual learners are often the ones who write information over and over before it is encoded and stored in their long-term memory. Visual learners who are not usually successful with high-level thinking have more of a chance for success with the visual format of graphic organizers.

Figure 6.1   How Graphic Organizers Support Differentiated Instruction

Principles of Differentiation	Graphic Organizer Application
1. Modify the content, thinking process, and/or product when addressing student readiness, interests, and styles.	1. Use high-level thinking graphic organizers with different students at different times.
2. Adjust pace of instruction to accommodate rate of learning.	2. Students who use graphic organizers may work faster because of their increased learning rate or slower because of delays in processing information.
3. Provide different levels of assistance.	3. The graphic organizer itself provides a level of assistance because it directs the learning process.
4. Offer controlled choice as much as possible.	4. Open choice is great, but no choice is OK, too. Control the choice by offering just two or three graphic organizers when necessary.
5. Foster active learning through varied grouping practices and different types of instructional strategies.	5. Formats provide a guide for small group and paired discussions.
6. Provide feedback and different types of assessment.	6. The graphic organizer lets the teacher see how the student is thinking. Rating scales and rubrics provide feedback guides.
7. Allow for resource variety and text modifications.	7. Based on expanded resources or limited resources, organizers are useful tools.
8. Modify assignments by length, time, and complexity.	8. Simplify the organizer, allow more time to fill it out, integrate different levels of content complexity.
9. Provide a supportive classroom environment that fosters individual differences and promotes individual successes.	9. Honor both critical and creative thinking, offer choice, and allow for modifications.
10. Devise management strategies for both teachers and students.	10. Use file folders to store graphic organizers and use spreadsheets to keep track of student choices.

2. *Adjusting the pace of instruction.* We know that some students take longer to learn things than others. It takes a gifted and talented learner a shorter amount of practice time than other learners to know, understand, apply, and remember information. It takes an average student seven to fourteen meaningful exposures to a word before it becomes part of his or her working vocabulary (Beers, 2003). Graphic organizers can be used to help students through areas of the curriculum where they are stuck or slower.

3. *Providing different levels of assistance.* The graphic formats and the accompanying language presented in the organizers in this book can serve as a support for students. Not only do students do their work more efficiently, they also require less help from the teacher. The cognitive graphic organizers walk students through thinking processes, so that students are provided with cues to move from

step to step. Students who have difficulty writing responses or young students with minimal writing skills, however, will still need teacher or peer support to make their thoughts known.

4. *Offering controlled choice.* Choice enhances engagement (Howard & Fogarty, 2003; Jensen, 2006) and motivation (Glasser, 1999; Sprenger, 2005). It's important, whenever possible, to foster critical and creative thinking by offering students a choice of graphic organizers that will promote deep learning. Because students feel empowered when they have choice, we can expect it to increase student motivation. Choice, however, doesn't mean giving over total control of the learning process. Teachers can offer students a limited choice between two or three graphic organizers.

5. *Fostering active learning through grouping practices and instructional strategies.* Each group may address the same content, and they may use a different graphic organizer. The use of the graphic organizer format provides a structure that promotes productive small group discussion. The group doesn't have to figure out how they will structure their responses. They have a tool that does this for them.

Without a basic structure to get the group going, some groups don't get going! Whether students work in pairs or individually, the graphic organizer helps keep learners on task. In some cases, students modify the organizer to create space for their responses. Each group successfully reports out to the whole class, and their responses are discussed with the other groups.

6. *Providing feedback and different types of assessment.* The cognitive graphic organizers presented in this book allow for specific feedback because the structure of the organizers provides a window into the students' reasoning. The framework lets both you and the student see how the student is thinking (Burke, 1994). The teacher is able to see just where the student needs help in coming up with a more complete or better answer. Wiggins (1998, quoted in Tomlinson and McTighe, 2006, p. 77) suggests "the use of real feedback in allowing the student to make self-adjustments." The rating systems and rubrics that are used with the graphic organizers give teachers tools to demonstrate to students how to check to see if their answers are logical, rational, and/or creative. Because the tool provides shared language, students more readily understand feedback.

7. *Allowing for resource variety and text modifications.* Some students may need resource variety and text modifications (Forsten, Grant, & Hollas, 2003). For high-end learners, this means they utilize information from many and varied resources, and organize and synthesize it. For struggling learners, this might mean they read only key passages. In both instances, graphic organizers help learners think more deeply about content at their ability level.

8. *Modifying assignments by length, time, and complexity.* This might mean shortening or altering the graphic organizer, instructing students to use some but not all of the steps on the organizer. Too many steps are just too much for some students!

Some students, however, like to break information down into detailed steps. Some students may need more "think time" to complete the graphic organizer. Students who use critical and creative thinking may need more time to answer a prompt than when they're answering factual questions.

9. *Providing a supportive classroom environment that fosters individual differences and successes.* The best graphic organizer is not going to work in an environment

where students are afraid to express their ideas. Teachers connect with students by showing that they care and can express emotions (Intrator, 2004, p. 23). Because graphic organizers lend themselves to more than one correct answer, students need to trust their teacher. They need to understand that the teacher is asking them to think about the content and then state their own ideas, which is different from stating the one right answer.

In a supportive classroom environment, you will need to model critical and creative thinking. "Of all the instructional strategies, modeling is by far the most effective" (Fogarty, 1994, p. xiv). One way to honor individual differences is to accept both critical and creative reasoning. Both types of thinking are important and necessary. Cognitive graphic organizers help teachers demonstrate to students that they value all kinds of thinking.

10. *Devising management strategies.* It's important to make sure that differentiation does not overwhelm teachers or students. Graphic organizers can easily be managed in a file folder system (Drapeau, 2004) and kept in a particular area of the classroom. Students can access the folders when they need a new graphic organizer. If you offer a lot of choice, you have to watch out for students choosing the same type of graphic organizer again and again. Although a particular thinking skill might be the student's preferred thinking style, it's still important to make sure that students experience a variety of thinking skills.

A simple spreadsheet with student names or numbers down one side and verbs across the top can help you keep track of who is choosing what type of graphic organizer. On a master list, older students can check off the type of graphic organizer they choose. With younger students, teachers will need to do the record keeping. In order to promote variety, you might make up rules, for example, students may not use the same graphic organizer more than three times in a row or more than five times a semester. Rules may not apply in your situation but are something to consider.

Another issue is managing the paperwork. In other words, it takes a lot longer to grade a variety of papers than it does if everyone uses the same graphic organizer. Do what works for you. If you feel you can correct only one or two organizers at a time, then offer limited choice. Try to offer one organizer based on critical thinking and a second based on creative thinking. In this way, you are offering different cognitive style choices.

Also remember that not everything has to be graded (Wormelli, 2006). This especially holds true if graphic organizers are used to review for a test, as tools for discussion, as part of a rough draft, or to organize information for a culminating activity.

SIX WAYS TO DIFFERENTIATE USING GRAPHIC ORGANIZERS

I have identified six ways to differentiate using graphic organizers. Five of these focus on modifying the organizer itself, the prompt, and/or the resources based on the needs of your students. A sixth way to differentiate involves creating your own graphic organizer, when existing ones just won't work in a situation. Both teachers and students can use the steps to create their own formats. Let's take a look at the advantages and disadvantages of these six ways to differentiate.

> ### The Open-Ended Prompt
>
> - All students use the same high-level thinking graphic organizer.
> - All students hear the same prompt.
> - All students use the same resources.
>
> *Note:* Students are able to respond at their own level of understanding.

The first way to differentiate involves an *open-ended prompt*. A prompt is a directive that students respond to on a graphic organizer. The prompt usually is in statement form but can include a question. For example, the teacher asks students to "use the Framed Puzzle graphic organizer to analyze Stanley's actions in the beginning and middle of the story." Such prompts allow teachers to use the same graphic organizer, the same prompt, and the same resources with the whole class. The graphic organizer provides an open-ended structure that allows for a basic level of differentiation. The teacher expects student responses to reflect their level of understanding of the character's actions. This is differentiated because students are able to respond at their own level of understanding. All students, not just those with stronger abilities, should be encouraged to think deeply.

Using open-ended prompts works well for teachers who are just beginning to differentiate in their classrooms and are comfortable with whole class instruction. When teachers ask an essential question, they often want all students to respond at the same time. They can then use the responses to build a class discussion, so that all students gain a comprehensive understanding of the answers to the question. This is only fair, however, when all students have the knowledge to respond to the prompt and the activity is equally challenging for all. Since it is difficult to create a prompt that is equally challenging for all students, this option should be used with caution.

This basic level of differentiation, however, is an easy way for teachers to get used to using new graphic organizers. Teachers may feel awkward at first addressing the verb, and the students might wonder why the teacher is spending time going over what the verb means. It is good teaching practice to discuss the verbs with your students, show them how to fill out the graphic organizer, show them how to use the rating scale or rubric, and model a sample lesson. They can fill out an organizer as a whole class, and the teacher can record responses on the board, overhead, or flip chart. When the students understand how the format works and the expectations are clear, then, in most cases, the students are ready to use an organizer on their own.

The advantages of using a graphic organizer when students receive the same organizer, hear the same prompt, and use the same resources are many (see Figure 6.2). First of all, students have access to the same activity. Teachers do not have to worry about students' perception of fairness. Students often think if their assignments differ from those of classmates, that other students have it easier or are having more fun. Another advantage is that students may experience success because they can work with others if they need or want to, because everyone is doing the same task based on the same information. Therefore, there is more opportunity for help if they need it. Students also like to work together for the social aspect of learning, which leads to greater success. Finally, it is important for all students to experience high-level thinking.

A major drawback to this way of differentiating is that we don't always get the level of response we're looking for. Have you ever felt a student could have answered a question more completely or with more detail? Perhaps you ask the student to revise her answer. In all fairness to the student, she did answer the question correctly. Some students don't even know how to make the answer more complete. They may feel they disappointed you because their answer wasn't good enough. For these reasons, it may be better to differentiate the prompt.

Figure 6.2   Advantages and Disadvantages of Using the "Open-Ended Prompt"

Pros	Cons
1. All students have access to the same activity.	1. The teacher does not always get the level of response that she wants from the student!
2. All students have the potential for success.	
3. Provides an opportunity for grouping arrangements.	
4. All students are exposed to high-level thinking with content.	

The Directed Prompt

- All students use the same high-level thinking graphic organizer.
- Students receive differentiated prompts.
- All students use the same resources.

Note: Students' responses are focused and specific.

In the next differentiation scenario, the *directed prompt*, only one graphic organizer is used, which means all students are using the same high-level verb, and all students read or interact with the same resources. All students read the same chapter or hear the same lecture or watch the same video. They might be reacting to the same assignment or the same Internet research materials. This time, however, the prompts are different for different students. For example, all students in science class are required to read a chapter on the respiratory system. But some students might be asked to analyze how the lungs function while other students are asked to analyze the respiratory system. The first prompt demands a comprehensive understanding of the chapter information. The second is appropriate for students who are ready to deal with more complex information because they are able to analyze the chapter content information and fit it in with prior knowledge of the respiratory system as a whole. This is not to say that the student who answers the first question will never answer the second question. It will just happen at a different time, perhaps one or two days later, or in a different way, such as through a lesson in which students listen to other students present information and then they talk about it.

The prompt provides the set-up for the student response. When providing two different prompts, check each one to make sure it asks what you want it to ask. The first thing to check is the content-specific language used in the prompts. Although specialized language helps make the prompt clear, you may be assuming the student has an understanding of a vocabulary word that she does not have. If she does not, the student is unable to respond to the prompt. Therefore, it's important to make sure all students understand the vocabulary before using it in prompts.

Even some of our most common words mean different things when used in different content areas. In looking at the math content area, a study conducted by Kathryn Sullivan (1982, cited in Kenney et al., 2005) showed that even a brief, three-week program centered on helping students distinguish the mathematical usage of small words can significantly improve student mathematics computation scores. Students need to understand that even small words can take on different meanings in different content areas. For example, "add" in math does not always result in an increase. Therefore, make sure all students understand what the words in the prompt mean.

Be aware also that students may not even be able to read the vocabulary word. The NASSP Bulletin (Barton, 1997, cited in Jacobs, 2006) reported 35 percent of all achievement test errors were fundamentally reading errors, in that many of the words were not part of the student's day-to-day language. Even if they can read the words, students may not use verbs such as "infer" or "analyze" often enough to actually remember what they mean. They do not say to their mother, "I need to analyze what to bring on my field trip tomorrow." Yet we expect students to conduct these processes and respond to question prompts using such verbs. Students need to learn and use "school language."

I recommend using key words and phrases to help you create directed prompts. These words inserted into an existing prompt can make it even more specific. Richard Paul's (1999) concepts can be particularly helpful to teachers who like to have a list of prompts to bump up content. Paul identifies eight elements of reasoning (see the first column of Figure 6.3) that drive understanding and promote depth of learning in a meaningful way. In this figure, you can also compare the difference between the open-ended prompt and the directed prompt.

Let's take a closer look at how Paul's elements are used as key words to direct the prompt. Take the first row in the figure: When we ask students to analyze the different forms of government, as in the third column, we are asking them to compare the different forms and describe their relationships to one another. But if we ask students to analyze the *purpose* of having different forms of government, then we move the content to a more conceptual level of knowing (Anderson & Krathwohl, 2001). By adding the word "purpose" to the prompt, we make it more specific and conceptual. This may be appropriate for students who need more challenge.

Another element of reasoning is to target questions, solve problems, and resolve issues. If you want to move the prompt from a basic level to a more complex level, change the prompt to include one or more of these concepts. For example, a more difficult and more specific prompt would ask students to "analyze the problems the character has in the story and how these problems create issues." If you want to keep the prompt simple and more open ended, the prompt might ask students to "analyze the character in the story." In both cases, students could use the same "analyze" graphic organizer, but one group focuses on the character in general while the other group focuses on the character's problems.

Figure 6.3   Using Key Words

Element of Reasoning (Adapted from Paul, 1999)	Directed Prompt	Open-Ended Prompt
Purpose (goals, objectives)	Analyze the purposes of having different kinds of government.	Analyze the different forms of government.
Issues or problems	Analyze the problems the character has in the story and explain how these problems create issues in the story.	Analyze the character in the story.
Information (facts, observations, experiences)	What might you infer from the animals' experiences regarding the pros and cons of zoos to draw conclusions about zoo effectiveness?	What inferences can you make after reading this article on the pros and cons of zoos?
Interpretation or inference (including conclusions and solutions)	How might we analyze different interpretations of Seurat's paintings?	Analyze Seurat's paintings.
Concepts	Elaborate on the different theories of dinosaur extinction.	Elaborate on why you think the dinosaurs died out.
Assumptions (that which we take for granted)	Judge the assumptions the character makes and how they help drive the action.	Judge the character's actions in the story.
Implications/consequences	Prioritize the implications or consequences of the character's action in the story.	Prioritize the events in the story.
Point of view (frame of reference, perspective, orientation)	Brain-write: How do the lungs function from the point of view of a surgeon, and from the point of view of an asthmatic?	Brain-write: How do the lungs function?

Sandra Kaplan (2005) is another who advocates the use of key words and phrases to promote complexity and depth. Her words and phrases can also be used to differentiate a prompt.

- Define over time.
- Note patterns.
- State trends.
- State ethical considerations.
- Define unanswered questions.
- View different perspectives.
- Identify rules.
- Recognize multiple points of view.
- State generalizations, principles, or big ideas.

Not all of your students will be ready for this level of abstraction. Such language can be eliminated for your struggling learners. They can still be successful thinking at a high level, if the content is addressed at a basic level. For advanced learners, when a prompt does not include such language, it is helpful to have the key words by Paul (1999) and Kaplan (2005) readily available to help you differentiate. It is easier to complexify a prompt when you have a word list to refer to than to create something from nothing.

There are advantages and disadvantages in differentiating with directed prompts (see Figure 6.4). First, every student uses the same graphic organizer. Because students can follow the step-by-step procedure on the graphic organizer, they have more chances to be successful when responding to the question. The biggest advantage I see with using this type of differentiation is that all students are challenged, because they all use critical or creative thinking. Just by tweaking the question with one or two words, the teacher creates harder and easier questions. This is also important because, in some cases, teachers are required to use the same text with all students. Teachers can easily differentiate textbook questions or questions in a teacher's manual by tailoring the prompt. All students will be challenged to think beyond the literal information to one degree or another.

Of course, some students do not want to be challenged. This becomes a disadvantage because it is sometimes difficult for the teacher to convince a student to work to her potential. By using familiar formats and providing support through shared language and commonly used procedures, the reluctant learner may find she has the tools to engage comfortably at the challenge level.

Another negative aspect of the second way to differentiate is that it takes longer to correct responses from graphic organizers with different prompts. As Nunley (2006) acknowledges in her list of general teacher complaints, the paperwork can be overwhelming. In addition, there is no answer key. Teachers have to take the time to determine what an acceptable level of response is and create their own answer keys. Because teachers do like the organizers but find them difficult to correct, they often use them as tools to generate discussion and do not correct them. This is unfortunate because students benefit from specific feedback.

A final drawback is it takes time and hard work to come up with differentiated prompts, particularly more difficult prompts. That is why I like the key words by Paul (1999) and Kaplan (2005) in which one or two words can easily change the level of complexity.

Figure 6.4   Advantages and Disadvantages of Using the "Directed Prompt"

Pros	Cons
1. All students have access to the same activity.	1. Some students do not want the challenge.
2. All students have the potential for success.	2. Teachers complain this type of activity takes too long to correct.
3. All students experience high-level thinking with content.	3. Teachers complain it's too hard to come up with challenging prompts.
4. All students are challenged!	

> **Different But the Same**
>
> - Students use different graphic organizers.
> - Students receive differentiated prompts.
> - All students use the same resources.
>
> *Note:* Students may have to read the same material but responses to the material can target more or less depth of understanding at a particular point in time.

A third way to differentiate using high-level thinking graphic organizers is to use different graphic organizers with different prompts, even though students use the same resources (Figure 6.5). I call this type of differentiation *different but the same.* This works well when teachers are using a prescribed reading series or textbook and are required by the district to follow the published materials. Teachers in this situation often feel there is little time for students to do additional readings, and the teachers often do direct teaching in a whole class setting. Once the teacher has presented or reviewed the content, however, the teacher may be willing to differentiate the follow-up activities by providing students with different prompts on different graphic organizers. Teachers can either assign different graphic organizers or let students choose the ones they would like to use.

Given a choice, students most often choose graphic organizers that match their cognitive style. Robert Sternberg (1996), professor of psychology and education at Yale University, calls analytical thinkers "school smart." They are the students that do school well. They are the learners that will choose graphic organizers based on critical thinking. They like to make judgments and evaluate, as well as to compare and contrast things. Sternberg's research indicates that people still need to be taught, even in their areas of strength, to become better within their cognitive thinking disposition. Therefore, whether teachers allow students to choose a graphic organizer and they choose to stay in their comfort zone, or whether the teacher assigns particular graphic organizers, students will benefit from explicit instruction either way.

Figure 6.5   Advantages and Disadvantages of Using "Different But the Same"

Pros	Cons
1. Differentiation is hidden.	1. Teacher has to prepare more than one organizer.
2. May allow for student choice.	2. Teacher has to keep track of who does which one.
3. Allows for variety in the classroom.	3. May take different amounts of time for students to finish.
4. All students are challenged!	

One wonderful advantage in differentiating with different but the same is that students expect to be doing different graphic organizers. It becomes the class norm and it's fair. Rather than have one group of students working on graphic organizers and another group doing something else, all students are doing the same type of activity. Teachers can assign different organizers or allow student choice. Of course if you allow choice, students may choose the organizer with an easier prompt. Preadolescent and adolescent learners may choose only the formats that their friends choose, *but that's OK because they get their work done.* All learners like to work with their friends, and we know that social learning helps change our stress level, our confidence, and even our content knowledge (Jensen, 2006).

Whenever you're unsure about allowing students choice in working together, err on the side of choice. Remember—choice empowers students and gives them control over their learning. For some students, this may be the only sense of control they have over their lives. Do not, however, sacrifice learning in the name of choice. This sounds obvious, but you might be surprised that teachers, in their efforts to differentiate, offer choice when this may not be the best way for students to learn. Remember, you can control choice. That is, give students a choice between two graphic organizers that are geared for their levels of understanding rather than total free choice.

Similar to the directed prompt, the different but the same approach also requires the teacher to make up more than one question to go on more than one graphic organizer. Even though this is more work for the teacher, you will likely see that the payoff is worth it. The students will be more engaged and student achievement will increase. It's also more work if the teacher has to keep track of the graphic organizers that the students choose; but this will eliminate the possibility of the student doing the same type of graphic organizer over and over again. Once a student finds a formula for success, it's tempting to keep repeating the same type of thinking. Teachers should discourage this. Look at the example of the simple spreadsheet (Figure 2.6) with students noted by number down one side of the page and the different thinking skills across the top. This allows the teacher to keep track of the students' choices. When students choose a graphic organizer, put the date in the cell next to their number, and watch for patterns of choice. This will minimize redundancy.

Figure 6.6   Sample Spreadsheet for Tracking Use of Graphic Organizers

	Assume	Infer	Analyze	Prioritize	Judge	Brainstorm	Connect	Create	Elaborate
1	3/12	3/09		3/10	3/07				
2						3/12, 3/07	3/09		3/10
3	3/12			3/09		3/10	3/07		
4		3/12			3/09		3/10		3/07
5	3/12	3/09		3/10	3/07				
6		3/12			3/09	3/10	3/07		
7			3/12	3/09	3/10	3/07			

After looking at the chart, the teacher makes sure that Student 1 does some creative thinking activities next time. Student 2 will be required to do some critical thinking activities, and perhaps Students 1 and 5 will not work together next time. I wouldn't want to pair Student 1 with Student 2 for the next few activities because I know the one who prefers to think in a particular manner might take over the lesson and do all the work. This would undermine the teacher's attempt to make sure all students do different types of thinking at least some of the time.

A final concern for teachers with the different but the same way to differentiate is that students finish filling in the graphic organizer at different times. This is actually a problem with any type of differentiation. Make sure students who finish earlier know what to do while they are waiting for others to finish. Asking them to fill out another graphic organizer is NOT A GOOD IDEA. Students will soon learn that if they finish early, the teacher will just ask them to do more of the same. Watch how quickly your students slow down so that they don't finish before the others. Instead, let them move on to the next activity or give them time to look at extension materials.

Resources Make the Difference

- All students use the same graphic organizer.
- All students receive the same prompt.
- Students use different resources.

Note: Students respond at their level based on their engagement with different material.

In this fourth way to differentiate, *resources make the difference,* all students use the same graphic organizer with the same prompt, but they use different resources This is a great approach if you want everyone to focus on the same content, but you need to modify the print material for students who are struggling readers or extend the print material for advanced learners. This is also most effective when the teacher pretests students and finds out the student's prior knowledge. Differentiation entails finding entry and exit points to learning (Gardner, 1999; Heacox, 2002). If the pre-assessment indicates that no students have prior knowledge, then the teacher can focus on whole group instruction with students doing different follow-up readings.

Some students may need to read the content information at a lower level than the one being used by most of the students in a classroom. In the average third-grade classroom, ten reading levels exist. At the high school level, "A textbook with a 10th grade readability level means that 50% of 10th graders can read and comprehend this textbook with teacher assistance" (Nunley, 2006, p. 117). This does not take into account students who can read the material, but who do not understand or remember what they read.

This is a particular problem for teachers who use a required reading or math series, or a required textbook. They may not be allowed to use alternative print material. In this case, adjustments will need to be made for some students to successfully deal with the content. Teachers might minimize the passages that struggling students read, or they may buddy them up with a more advanced partner so they can work together.

Figure 6.7 Advantages and Disadvantages of Using "Resources Make the Difference"

Pros	Cons
1. Whole class can discuss the process.	1. Teacher has to collect a variety of reading materials.
2. Easy for teacher to correct.	2. Teacher modifies materials.
3. Students use materials commensurate with their abilities.	3. May take different amounts of time for students to finish.
4. Teacher does not have to keep track of who is doing what.	4. Students may see this as unfair.

There are actually many advantages to the resources make the difference way of differentiating. The whole class is doing the same lesson, so students can process information and discuss ideas as a whole group. Those students who read more sophisticated material can add information that others might not have read. In this way, struggling students gain additional information without actually having to read the material. The graphic organizers are easy to correct because everyone is using the same format. Students are also reading materials at their ability level, which enables them to be more successful. Teachers really do not have to keep track of who is doing what because everyone is doing the same graphic organizer with the same prompt.

The biggest drawback to this way of differentiating is the teacher needs to find many different resources or reading materials. As we all know, doing an Internet search on a topic can also mean hours of looking at layers and layers of materials at different websites. However, once the teacher takes the time to compile a list of resources that students can use, she won't have to do this again or will only have to modify the search the next time. Collecting resources for a particular unit is usually a one-time investment if the teacher teaches the same content year after year.

Even when teachers find articles on the Internet, they may still need to modify the information because they might not want students spending a great deal of time on one article. There might be only a portion of the article that applies to the content. In this situation, copy the article, cut it into sections, and throw away the parts that don't relate to the assignment. In some cases, teachers might actually have to highlight important information for the students. This helps the struggling reader a great deal. The average- and high-ability reader should be able to tackle the whole article and sort through relevant and irrelevant information without the teacher's assistance.

It is important to consider whether the objective of the lesson is for the student to apply the content information or to discern important information. The objectives in a science or social studies lesson are usually content-specific, whereas discerning important information is a specific skill area. If your lesson objectives do not include the specific skill area, then help out your struggling readers by doing this for them. It is not the intent of the lesson to have them bogged down in the skill area. There may be other lessons to practice discerning important information.

Another drawback, as I mentioned before, is that students may take varying amounts of time to finish. By modifying the resources, however, teachers can anticipate how long it will take students to read the materials. Most often, instead of the struggling learners taking a longer time than others to get through print material, now all students take a similar amount of time to process differentiated print information.

Finally, if the fairness issue surfaces—Why does one student only have to read an article and another an entire chapter?—I recommend being honest with your students. Tell them that students are reading what they can handle at that time. This isn't really news. Students know who can read smoothly and who struggles. If you're matter of fact about it, students will accept this as the norm. Help them to understand that by modifying resources or providing different resources, some learners may not have such a hard time keeping up with other learners. High school teachers, in particular, often feel this backfires in the classroom and affects the struggling learner's self-esteem. The danger of changing resources in the content areas is not only that the struggling learner is jealous and wants to read the harder material, but that the proficient reader doesn't want to work that hard and would prefer to coast. This is minimized if all the print materials "look" age appropriate. Then the different levels of reading are not so obvious.

Variety Plus

- Students use different graphic organizers.
- Students receive different prompts.
- Students use different resources.

Note: Students' needs are met in a variety of ways.

I call the fifth way of differentiating—using critical and creative thinking graphic organizers—*variety plus,* because it offers the most variety. Students use different graphic organizers with different prompts as well as different resources. The teacher can assign a type of graphic organizer or the students can choose, although this may not involve unlimited choice. The teacher provides different prompts for each graphic organizer in use. Finally, students may be reading from different sources, or may have modified reading passages from a text. The key factor here is that every element is targeted to meet individual needs.

In practice, this fifth form of differentiation is not as complicated as it sounds and its benefits can be numerous. Imagine a language arts class that is studying the fairy tale genre—specifically, the many different versions of Cinderella and how it translates in various cultures. Some students read *The Salmon Princess: An Alaskan Cinderella Story* by Mindy Dwyer. Other students read *The Golden Sandal: A Middle Eastern Cinderella Story* by Rebecca Hickox. Another group reads *Ella's Big Chance: A Jazz Age Cinderella* by Shirley Hughes.

The students who read *An Alaskan Cinderella Story* use the Paint Jars graphic organizer to create inferences about the main character's life in Alaska. The students who read *A Middle Eastern Cinderella Story* make "assumptions" about the main character based on their knowledge of the basic story line and Middle Eastern culture. The third group that read *A Jazz Age Cinderella* uses the "create" graphic organizer to design the shop that Ella and Buttons will have when they live happily ever after.

Notice that not every person is using a different resource. The whole class is broken down into three groups that use different resources, have different prompts, and complete different organizers. Eventually, they come back together as a whole class, summarize their stories for the other students, and share their graphic organizers. Ideally, the whole class discussion will entice at least some students to read the other versions of the story that classmates read!

The variety plus way of differentiating can be extremely motivating when teachers allow students to choose their own reading material and graphic organizer. For example, a boy might choose a modern-day fairy tale that targets his interest or at least has a boy as a main character. Another way to use the variety plus method with older students is to place the learning objective on the white board or overhead. Ask the students to choose a graphic organizer and create a question that uses the verb on the organizer and addresses the objective. Students are more invested in their learning when they come up with their own questions. It's quite difficult, however, for students to create their own questions based on the learning objective; so, make sure you are available to help students or else they may just sit there and waste time.

The variety plus approach hides differentiation because many students are doing different things. It allows for student choice and variety. It is important, however, for the teacher to introduce the verb, explain the procedural steps used to process the verb, and show students how to use the graphic organizer. Before students can work independently, the teacher should model lessons and demonstrate just what the expectation is.

The variety plus approach allows for different levels of challenge, because all aspects of the lesson can be geared specifically to the individual student. Teachers can reach all learners, because the graphic organizer activity is matched to what each student needs. If some students need to be motivated, teachers can target different materials and perhaps use one of the creative thinking graphic organizers. If some students need to review information, you can modify required readings and choose a graphic organizer like "adding details." This activity will reinforce the learning and build on the lesson's vocabulary and concepts. Some students who can read sophisticated material may like to analyze the information. All students are working on the same standard or objective but at different levels. The different levels are targeted through the learning activities, which are adjusted by all three elements—the graphic organizer, the prompt, and the resource.

The negative aspects of this type of differentiation include having to prepare more than one graphic organizer and coming up with many different prompts. This can be tedious even for the most dedicated teacher. So that you do not feel overwhelmed, begin by taking the standard or objective and changing the verb to one of the graphic organizer

Figure 6.8   Advantages and Disadvantages of Using "Variety Plus"

Pros	Cons
1. Differentiation is hidden.	1. Teacher has to prepare more than one organizer.
2. May allow for student choice.	2. Teacher has to keep track of who does which one.
3. Allows for variety in the classroom.	3. May take different amounts of time for students to finish.
4. Allows for different levels of challenge.	4. Students can fall through the cracks.
5. Reaches all learners.	5. Difficult to grade.

verbs. Turn this into a question or prompt and make sure it makes sense. Then, check to make sure the question maintains the content elements. If it loses the content thread, the question should not be used. The content connected to the standard must be an integral part of the newly revised question. Continue to substitute the different graphic organizer verbs to see which organizers will work. Then offer these as choices. With practice, you can quickly tweak the questions to use with various graphic organizers.

Of course, when students use different graphic organizers it does, again, create the problem of keeping track of who does what, and some students finishing earlier than others. Handling these issues has been discussed previously. The greatest danger with the variety plus approach, however, is that some students can slip through the cracks. They appear to be busy but do not accomplish much. They're quiet and do not draw attention to themselves. If you grade graphic organizers, then it becomes apparent who is not finishing their work. If you do not grade papers, give feedback, or at the very least check off who is doing what, these students may stay under the radar and do very little.

This brings us to a final problem, which is that it may be difficult to grade the graphic organizers when using a variety plus approach. This is true for many reasons. One graphic organizer appears easier than another; therefore, is an A on the easier graphic organizer worth the same as an A on the harder graphic organizer? If there's a rating scale or rubric that guides the scoring, then that gives you a place to start. If not, then the teacher scores each paper in terms of the responses. If the organizers are not graded, some teachers feel their students will either not do the work or not take them seriously.

Effort is always a factor. Did the student really think about the responses or just fill in the graphic organizer to complete the assignment? One student's answers may be basic, but could be a big improvement when compared to prior work as opposed to being compared to another student's work. Grading is a philosophical issue and most of us, whether we agree with our district's guidelines or not, grade according to the school's philosophy.

Regardless of what grading system you use, students need to know what the rules are. In the book, *Fair Isn't Always Equal: Assessing and Grading in the Differentiated Classroom,* Rick Wormelli (2006) describes effective assessment and grading practices. He suggests giving feedback on practice papers and only grading summative work.

Most of the time, the graphic organizers in this book are not used as truly summative work. I think of summative work as being more encompassing than responses on graphic organizers. Therefore, my intent in providing you with rubrics and rating scales in Chapters 3–11 is to give you tools you can use to provide students feedback so that their work with graphic organizers can lead to higher achievement and enhance their ability to use critical and creative thinking.

Create Your Own Organizer

- Create a graphic organizer when no graphic organizer exists to meet your needs.
- Target the critical and/or creative thinking verb.

Note: Teachers create graphic organizers to focus on a specific thinking skill area. Students create graphic organizers as a metacognitive skill to show how they think about what they know.

Perhaps the ultimate way to differentiate using high-level thinking graphic organizers is to create your own, to better suit your students' needs. You might adjust a graphic organizer with little difficulty, but find the idea of creating your own overwhelming. Creating your own graphic organizer is really not that hard! First of all, unless you are a graphic artist or a computer whiz, let go of the idea that it has to look great. As long as it works and is neat, students can use it. Here are some recommended steps that will help you create your own tool:

1. Identify the verb around which you want to create an organizer. Let's use the verb "predict" as an example.

2. Search through graphic organizer books to see if a "predict" graphic organizer exists. If one does exist, decide whether you need to modify it for the whole class or for some students. If one is not available, then move on to the next step.

3. Do an Internet search or book search to find out if others have identified a process for "predict" that you are comfortable with. These processes may be in language form and not yet in graphic organizer form. For example, Nancy Polette, in her book *The ABCs of Books and Thinking Skills: A Literature-Based Thinking Skills Program K–8* (1987, p. 109), identifies four steps for prediction: "Clarify what is to be predicted; analyze data to find a basis for predicting; make a tentative predication; and consider related data and modify predictions as necessary." Barry Beyer, in *Teaching Thinking Skills: A Handbook for Elementary School Teachers* (1991) and *Teaching Thinking Skills: A Handbook for Secondary School Teachers* (1991), defines the process in seven steps. Other books that delineate thinking skill procedures are *Thinking Skills Resource Book* (1990) by Lorene Reid and *Assessing Student Outcomes: Performance Assessment Using the Dimensions of Learning Model* (1993) by Marzano, Pickering, and McTighe. If you find useful material identified with the verb you are researching, choose which process you like best for your students or come up with your own process. If you have to come up with your own language to help students process the thinking skill, move on to the next step.

4. Think about what you do when you make a prediction. It's best to work with a colleague on this because you'll be able to bounce ideas off each other. Whether you're working alone or with a colleague, write down the process that you expect your students to use. Here is an example of the procedure that I might use:

Step 1. Write the prediction statement.

Step 2. Give reasons for your prediction based on the information presented in the text.

Step 3. Give reasons to support your prediction from information that exists outside of the information presented in the text.

Step 4. Consider other possible predictions and modify your prediction if necessary.

Step 5. Determine the likelihood that your prediction will occur.

For instance, let's say I'm a language arts teacher teaching a fairy tale unit to my fourth graders, and the students are reading *Cinderella*. I might ask them to predict her chances for long-term happiness with the prince (Step 1). One prediction statement might be "I predict she will be happy with the prince." This assertion can be supported (Step 2) by giving examples from the story that describe what a nice person Cinderella is and how happy she always is regardless of her situation. Next, I might ask them to consider their prediction based on other sources or information (Step 3). Students might support their prediction by saying that fairy tales always end happily ever after. In Step 4, students have the opportunity to reconsider predictions and modify the original prediction. For example, someone may have raised doubts about Cinderella's chances for long-term happiness because they think of Princess Diana and how she was not perceived as happy in her marriage. It may occur to students to consider what demands royalty would place on a peasant girl such as Cinderella. This might lead some students, who started out believing she would have long-term happiness, to change their prediction. In Step 5, one group of students may be 100 percent certain their prediction is correct. Another group that came to a different conclusion may be equally adamant. Of course, we will never know who is right. I do like this last step, however, because I want my students to think about the likelihood that their prediction is correct. Most of my fourth graders would not know percentages, so I would use a Likert-type scale that goes from "not sure" to "positive" that the prediction is correct. It really doesn't matter to me where the students make a slash mark, because I've added this step for our enjoyment. I do reflect on the lesson, however, to make sure it meets my objective: for students to review the story and their own knowledge to find supporting evidence to support their prediction.

5. The next step is turning the process into a graphic organizer. This is where teachers tend to get very nervous. They think they could never come up with a visual they could really use. But you can and here's how. First of all, think of the number of steps you used in your process. In my example, I used five, which means I need five places for my students to make a response. If I can't draw and have limited computer skills, I can always use boxes, circles, and arrows. High school teachers prefer these types of formats because their students often think pictorial formats are too cutesy and are only for elementary students. This is unfortunate because students often remember images. It's more likely they will remember the predicting process if it is embedded in labeled steps in a picture (Figure 6.9) as opposed to isolated boxes and lines (Figure 6.10).

When I created the Birthday Wishes graphic organizer, it started out as a staircase. After I made the steps, I thought it looked like a birthday cake, so I named it that. This is easy to draw on the computer but I could have drawn it by hand or asked the art teacher for help. When I use this organizer with students, the first thing they say is that it's an awesome birthday cake because it's so big.

I like to create two graphic organizer formats. One is usually pictorial and the other is a linear format. One style format may appeal to you more than another. But make sure you create different styles of organizers because if you always use boxes and arrows, you will be shortchanging learners who prefer to see pictorial formats. If you use a whole lot

Figure 6.9 Birthday Wishes Graphic Organizer (Predict)

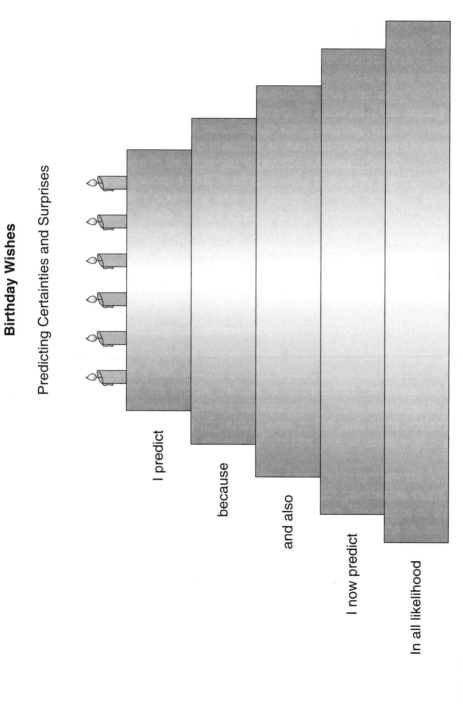

Birthday Wishes

Predicting Certainties and Surprises

I predict

because

and also

I now predict

In all likelihood

Figure 6.10   Linear Graphic Organizer (Predict)

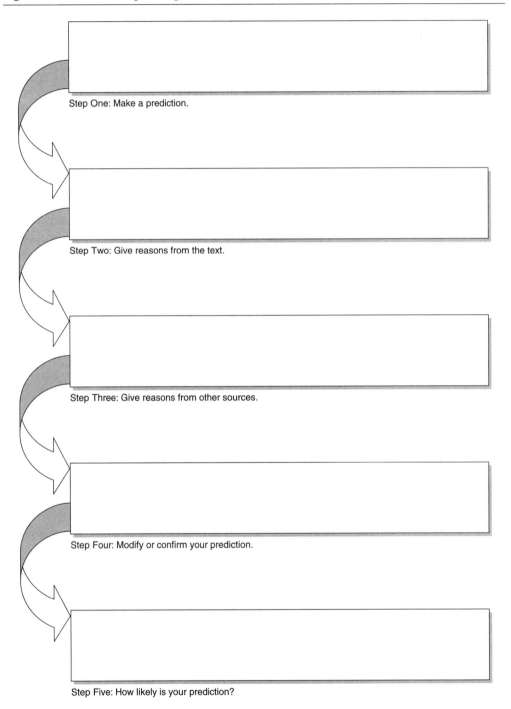

Step One: Make a prediction.

Step Two: Give reasons from the text.

Step Three: Give reasons from other sources.

Step Four: Modify or confirm your prediction.

Step Five: How likely is your prediction?

of pictures, you won't be helping learners who prefer information presented in simple, linear sections. Through variety, you reach all learners.

Once you know the steps for creating graphic organizers, you can help your students create their own. You may be surprised to discover that some students are really good at this. In fact, they may be better at it than you are. In *Great Teaching With Graphic Organizers* (Drapeau, 1998), there are examples of fourth-grade, student-generated creative thinking graphic organizers. Even though students can be successful doing this, they still need teacher support to understand how to analyze the verb, create procedural steps to process the verb, think about the information they are studying to make sure it works in the content area, and come up with a graphic design. Not all students will be up for this challenge. Perhaps students can generate their own thinking tools and share them with one another. Any tool that helps students be successful in the classroom is always welcome.

The pitfalls (see Figure 6.11) of allowing students to create or modify graphic organizers are numerous: Some of their creations will not make sense, and some students will simply be unable to create organizers. They may not be able to come up with logical steps, create a visual from the words, or the visual may be random and confusing to use. You will need to review the organizer (which of course is not part of the curriculum content), understand what the student is trying to say or do, and provide feedback. This takes time and can be a frustrating experience for both you and the student. Unless doing so is part of the curriculum, I do not recommend a whole class activity that asks students to create organizers. There should be opportunity to do this, but no requirement.

The benefits of students creating or modifying their own organizers, however, are numerous and can be well worth the time and effort. Students who can do it show evidence of developing awareness of their own thinking, the ability to articulate their thinking processes, and the ability to articulate this process visually. This is motivational for some students and fosters their self-esteem because they are usually proud of their original work. It is an opportunity for students to not feel restricted by someone else's design and for visual learners to see how the thinking process looks on paper. Students really learn about quality thinking when they come up with their own visual. Often, when they see the process, they understand it and remember it. Once it is embedded, they have access to the process whenever they want to use it again. This transference does not happen quickly—it takes practice across content and over time (Black & Black, 1990, cited in Burke, 1994).

Figure 6.11   Advantages and Disadvantages of Student-Created Graphic Organizers

Pros	Cons
1. Customize to fit responses.	1. Some of the original graphic organizers will not make sense.
2. Great for creative learners.	2. Takes time to correct original formats.
3. Great for visual learners.	3. Not all students will be able to or want to create their own graphic organizers.
4. Students and/or teachers create formats.	
5. Fosters self-esteem and motivation.	

DECIDING WHEN TO USE WHICH DIFFERENTIATION APPROACH

We've examined six different ways to differentiate using cognitive graphic organizers, but it should be noted that not all of the graphic organizers work well in every context in all content and with every student. Therefore it is important to consider some factors before you decide which differentiation approach to use in a lesson with a graphic organizer.

First, you need to consider nonnegotiable factors and situations, for example, the time allotted for a lesson. Consider how to use your time efficiently and effectively and to maximize the payoff. If you turn a graphic organizer lesson into a great activity that takes 45 minutes (because the discussion based on the responses on different organizers takes more time), as opposed to just having students fill out the same graphic organizer in 15 minutes and moving on, the 30 extra minutes was time well spent. When students create their own graphic organizers, it usually takes more time than any of the other options.

Next, consider at what point in the lesson students begin to really show a difference in what they know, remember, and can apply content. At what point in the lesson do some learners understand the information, whereas others need to review it? Use the directed prompt approach to address these different rates of learning.

If you choose to deepen the instruction by providing advanced extension resources, you need to have the resources or find them. When remediating the material, you might seek out supplemental materials. If you do not have the resources readily available or do not have time to search them out, then this is not a viable option. This creates a problem when your target differentiation approach is resources make the difference.

Factors to Consider When Selecting Graphic Organizers

- Time when lesson must end
- Point in lesson when students learn at different rates
- Point in lesson when supplemental or extension information is needed
- Point in unit that is not interesting and needs a lift
- Meeting needs of the students
- Meeting needs of the teachers

Brain research consistently supports the notion that learning must be novel, challenging, and meaningful (Jensen, 2006). In looking at a unit of study, take note of when activities, questions, or lessons fall flat. This might be a great place to give your unit a lift by substituting graphic organizer lessons for the ones that you previously used. If it's an introductory lesson, an open-ended prompt might spark discussion. If it's a lesson that occurs midway through a unit, different but the same might be an effective activity. Have students use different organizers with different prompts based on the same reading material. They can then come back as a group and share their ideas. In a follow-up lesson at the end of a unit, use the variety plus approach so that students can recap the information they have learned in their preferred style.

Meeting the needs of students can feel overwhelming. That is why it is important to collect data and form groups of students who have similar abilities, interests, and styles.

Student inventories are helpful in collecting data (Gregory & Kuzmich, 2004; Heacox, 2002). This information helps teachers to form groups of students and target their cognitive styles. Students who have a creative thinking preference can use the "brainstorm," "connect," "create," or "elaborate" graphic organizers, while the critical thinkers can use the critical thinking graphic organizers. In this situation, teachers can use the different but the same approach.

Teachers should consider their own needs as well. Research shows that if you're happy and enjoy teaching, you will be more effective in the classroom. Enthusiasm is contagious—the role of emotion in the classroom is well documented (Sousa, 2001; Sylwester, 2003; Wolfe, 2001). These graphic organizers can help you make changes in your teaching and differentiation practices.

CREATING A RATING SCALE OR RUBRIC

Once you've selected a graphic organizer, decide if you want to create a rating scale or rubric to go with it. The rating scale or rubric is based on a specific verb and provides guidance and direction for the student (see specific examples in Chapters 3–11). Let's take a look at how a rating scale might be created for our prediction example. Think about each step of making a prediction and ask questions about it based on the various criteria. For example, in Step 1, when the student is asked to make a prediction, the first question you might think about is: How *relevant* is the prediction? In Steps 2 and 3, you might want students to consider how *important* are the reasons found in- or outside of the text supporting this prediction? This might be a particularly important criterion for students who give reasons based on minutia or inconsequential facts. Another criterion you might want students to consider is how logical their final prediction is based on their reasons and sources. You can then ask students to score their responses on a 1 to 5 scale, with 5 being highest. The rating scale might look something like Figure 6.12.

There is no set number of criteria and probing questions that teachers need to use. Figure 6.13 presents a list of possible criteria and probing questions. This list is meant to help you get started in considering criteria that you can use with graphic organizers. You and/or your students can develop criteria and questions that are age-appropriate and specific to your content.

Have students use the rating scale to check their thinking, or, after they hand in their work, you can also use the rating scale to assess the graphic organizer and provide the student with feedback. When students rate themselves, the questions are personalized. They sound like this: How clear are my statements or how relevant are my predictions? A third way to use the rating scale is to have both the teacher and the student fill it out. If the two scores are discrepant, the teacher should meet with the student to discuss why.

Figure 6.12   Sample: Critical Thinking Rating Scale (Predict)

Criteria	Probing Questions	Rating
Relevancy	How relevant is the prediction?	5
Importance	How important are the reasons?	4
Logic	How logical is the prediction?	5

Figure 6.13   Generic Rating Scale Criteria and Prompts

Criteria	Probing Questions
Clarity	How clear are the statements?
Relevancy	How relevant are the statements?
Importance	How important are the reasons?
Logic	How logical is the reasoning?
Consistency	How consistent are the statements?
Reasonableness	Do the statements seem reasonable?
Connections	To what degree are connections made?
Accuracy	How accurate are the examples?
Creativity	To what degree are the ideas unusual?
Detail	To what degree are details included?

Figure 6.14   Sample: Critical Thinking Rubric (Predict)

1	2	3
The prediction is irrelevant.	The prediction is somewhat relevant.	The prediction is relevant.
Reasons reflect lack of evidence.	A few of the reasons are not that relevant.	All reasons are relevant.
The conclusions are not logical.	The conclusions are logical.	The logical conclusions reflect inferential reasoning and informed judgment.

Some teachers prefer to use a rubric rather than a rating scale. In Chapters 3–11, I include samples of both. The rubric provides more description and guidance than the rating scale. In Figure 6.14, the prediction rating scale is converted into a rubric that addresses each of the probing questions from the rating scale and describes a range of performances.

I design my assessment tools to be used as feedback. I rarely use them to grade the graphic organizers, although some teachers do. I generally use other summative performance tools for grading purposes. Most of the time, I use graphic organizers as a stepping-stone for the next activity. By that, I mean I use them as a pre-writing tool, a tool for a discussion format, a review for a test, a homework assignment, and so on. I often decide whether to grade or not based on the use of the graphic organizer. When I use the graphic organizer as a pre-writing tool, I grade the writing piece, not the graphic organizer. When I use the graphic organizer as a format for a shared discussion, I use the graphic organizer as a way for students to organize their thinking so that they can effectively participate in the discussion. I do not grade the discussion. When I ask students to use the graphic organizer as a tool to review for a test, it is the test I grade. When I ask them to use the graphic organizer as a homework assignment, I might grade the graphic organizer or I might just check off the homework as complete. I also do not use rating scales or rubrics every time I use a graphic organizer. That would be overkill! Just decide when the lesson or activity warrants using feedback tools such as these. In quick lessons, it is often not necessary to use the assessment tools, as opposed to in-depth lessons, where students are sorting through a lot of complex content.

KEY POINTS TO REMEMBER ABOUT DIFFERENTIATING WITH GRAPHIC ORGANIZERS

1. The six ways to use graphic organizers presented in this chapter are effective instructional techniques that help us apply the principles of differentiation.

2. Through the many applications of graphic organizers, teachers are able to modify the content, process, and product of a lesson; adjust pacing of instruction; and provide different levels of assistance.

3. Teachers can offer controlled choice by focusing graphic organizer options according to student needs, and foster active learning through group work.

4. Rating scales and rubrics provide specific tools that can be used for feedback.

5. The different ways to use the organizers allow for resource variety and assignment modifications.

6. The teacher provides the supportive classroom and creates a management system for this to work.

PAUSE FOR REFLECTION AND DISCUSSION

1. Summarize what you know about the six ways to use graphic organizers as differentiation tools.

2. How do you decide which graphic organizer to use and when?

3. In what situation or unit might you decide to create your own graphic organizer and who might you need to help you accomplish this task?

4. Do you think the use of rating scales will help your students to create better, clearer, more logical responses? Why or why not?

7

Differentiation and Adolescent Development

Glenda Beamon Crawford

Chapter 1 defined differentiation as the strategic approach to curriculum design and instruction that builds meaningfully and responsively on students' developmental needs and learning strengths. Box 7.1, "Adolescent-Centered Design Principles," identifies six Es that are key principles for adolescent-centered differentiation.

❖ BOX 7.1 Adolescent-Centered Design Principles

Principle 1: Evaluation. Seek to know students' developmental and individual learning needs, strengths, interests, and preferences through initial, multiple, and ongoing assessments.

Principle 2: Expectation. Use assessment knowledge strategically to design meaningful curriculum and appropriately challenging learning opportunities for a range of learners.

Principle 3: Engagement. Use varied, multiple, and engaging instructional strategies for students to learn and demonstrate understanding.

Principle 4: Exploration. Organize flexible opportunities for students to collaborate, explore, and practice under guidance and feedback.

Principle 5: Extension. Promote learning management by making cognitive strategies explicit and structuring time for reflection and metacognitive extension.

Principle 6: Environment. Create and maintain a learning environment that is supportive for adolescents' intellectual, social, physical, and emotional development.

Adolescent-centered differentiation additionally requires an understanding of the ever-changing developmental nature that defines adolescents as learners. Chapter 7 explores the relationship between adolescents' unique intellectual, personal, and social learning needs and the way their brains generally function during the learning process. It draws parallels between adolescent learning needs and the six differentiation design principles and illustrates these with implications for classroom practice. The chapter also reveals pivotal findings from the field of neuroscience associated with adolescents' intellectual and emotional maturity.

ADOLESCENT DEVELOPMENT

Adolescence is a developmental time of erratic physical growth, social exploration, and unfolding intellectual capacity. It is a time of awakening, realization, anticipation, confusion, awkwardness, transition, change, identity defining, and self discovery. As a unique population, adolescents share distinguishing developmental tendencies. Although there is great variation in intellectual capability and learning strengths, culture and language, and interests and experiences, several interrelated generalizations can be made that have implications for adolescent learning (Crawford, 2007).

Adolescence
The transitional time between late childhood and young adulthood characterized by rapid changes in physical, social, emotional, and intellectual development.

Adolescents' expanding cognitive capacity, for example, enables them to think abstractly and conceptually about more sophisticated content. Their capacity for intellectual reasoning and reflection is emerging faster than their ability to make rational decisions about personal health and lifestyle. They are eager to tackle relevant problems, discuss and share viewpoints about critical issues, and talk about ethical choices that impact their actions. They are also developing the capacity to reflect upon and regulate their own learning. Academically, adolescents are more self-motivated and push to direct their own learning, yet they may become easily discouraged if they fail to accomplish their goals.

Physically, adolescents' bodies are developing adult features and sexuality; personally they yearn for independence and autonomy. On a personal level, they crave normalcy and tend to obsess about appearance, physical differences, and perceived self-inadequacies. They frequently measure their personal worth and define self-identity by what they believe others think and feel about them. This self-identity is in a state of tentative and precarious negotiation as they move into who they are becoming.

Socially, adolescents crave acceptance and validation. They are entering a "brave new world" of peer negotiation and peer pressure, yet emotionally, they may lack the judgment to contain their feelings or to make healthy or appropriate decisions. Table 7.1, "Adolescent Developmental Tendencies, Implications for Learning," aligns adolescents' personal, intellectual, and social developmental inclinations with associated learning needs.

Table 7.1   Adolescent Developmental Tendencies, Implications for Learning

Adolescent Developmental Tendencies	Implications for Learning
Personal	*Learning Needs*
Anxious for developmental normality	Climate of acceptance, tolerance
Easily angered, slow to recover	Emotional safety, guidance
Push for independence, autonomy	Choice, responsibility, accountability
Easily discouraged if do not achieve	Appropriate challenge, relative success
Intellectual	*Learning Needs*
Have diverse knowledge, interests, abilities	Opportunities to develop range of skill and to pursue variety of content areas
Can see relationships among similar concepts, ideas, and experiences	Complex subject matter, relevant issues
Capable of inferential thinking, reasoning	Higher-level, analytical questioning
Capable of critical evaluation, extended focus	Time and opportunity for critical thinking
Reflective, metacognitive, self-motivated	Self-evaluation, choice
Social	*Learning Needs*
Can be indifferent to adult figures	Opportunity to interact with knowledgeable adults in collaborative projects
Concerned about self-presentation to peers	Emphasis on cooperation, inclusiveness, group contribution
Strive to conform for peer acceptance	Structured, positive student interaction

ADOLESCENTS AS LEARNERS

Adolescent learning is an intellectual process highly influenced by social interaction, situational context, personal beliefs, dispositions, and emotions (Bransford, Brown, & Cocking, 2000; Vygotsky, 1978). Teaching that capitalizes on adolescents' developmental tendencies is responsive to their associated developmental learning needs (Crawford, 2007). These developmental learning needs are identified and described below.

- **Personal connection**. Adolescents need to connect learning with prior knowledge, personal experience and interests, and mode of learning. They respond to relevance and authenticity in learning experiences that enable them to make meaningful personal connections and relate learning to the larger world of their experience.
- **Appropriate intellectual challenge**. Adolescents need to be cognitively engaged within the reach of their capabilities. Their developing cognitive capacities enable them to think about, question, and grapple with the pertinent issues and problems found in substantive content.
- **Emotional engagement**. Adolescents need to be motivated by relevant experiences that intrigue, activate their emotions, and actively involve

them—physically, intellectually, and socially. They are captivated by multi-sensory engagement, and they thrive on the opportunity for choice based on personal interests, strengths, and preferences.

- **Purposeful social interaction**. Adolescents need guided and meaningful collaboration with peers and others in the learning community. This interaction allows them to explore, experiment, and socially construct knowledge and learning.
- **Metacognitive development**. Adolescents are developing the capacity to think about, reflect on, and take ownership of their own learning. They need opportunities to acquire the cognitive and metacognitive skills and strategies to manage their learning and to extend it to other learning situations in and beyond the school.
- **Supportive learning environment**. Adolescents need a safe, structured, and supportive learning space where they can express and shape ideas, articulate developing thinking without fear of embarrassment, and feel included, accepted, and valued. In this space they can develop naturally, intellectually, socially, personally, and emotionally; be successful; and gain both competence and self-efficacy.

These six categories of adolescent developmental learning needs are supported by current research in learning, cognition, and brain development and functioning, as discussed in the following sections. This classification aligns with the six adolescent-centered differentiation principles identified in Chapter 1. Table 7.2, "Adolescent-Centered Differentiation," indicates this alignment.

Table 7.2   Adolescent-Centered Differentiation

Differentiation Principle	*Brain-Based/Developmental Learning Needs*
Knowledge of students through multiple and ongoing assessments	Personal connection, or the need to connect learning with prior knowledge, experience, interests, and learning preference
Design of consequential content and intellectually motivating instruction	Appropriate challenge, or the need to be cognitively engaged within the reach of personal capability
Varied, multiple, and engaging instructional strategies	Emotional engagement, or the need to be motivated by multisensory experiences that intrigue and actively involve
Flexible opportunities for guided collaboration, exploration, and practice with feedback	Purposeful social interaction, or the need for guided and meaningful collaboration with peers and others in the learning community
Strategy instruction for reflection and metacognitive extension	Learning ownership, or the need to acquire the metacognitive cognitive strategies for personal learning management and extension
Supportive learning environment that is emotionally and intellectually safe for adolescent thinking, learning, and development	Supportive learning environment, or the need to feel supported, valued, accepted, and protected in a community of learners.

PERSONAL CONNECTION

Learning is internally mediated, controlled primarily by the learner, and dependent on the knowledge, skills, and experiences that the learner brings to the learning experience (Bransford, Brown, & Cocking, 2000). Learning occurs when students actively construct personal meaning based on how they relate to or make sense of what they are trying to know or understand. Since adolescents bring a diverse range of knowledge and interests that are shaped by varying biological, cultural, and experiential factors, the challenge for teachers is to find a point of connection with what students know, believe, and feel (Crawford, 2007). When teachers pay attention to the knowledge and beliefs that learners bring to the learning task and use this knowledge as a starting point for new instruction, learning is enhanced (Bransford, Brown, & Cocking, 2000). Making personal connections with adolescents not only facilitates learning, but also validates who they are and what they can contribute as learners.

Supporting Brain-Based Research

Learning is a brain-based function that similarly relies on the need for personal connection. The brain is a pattern-seeking organ that chunks together, organizes, and integrates pieces of new information with what is familiar. It works like a sieve to filter out incoming sensory information that it cannot associate within its memory structure (Wolfe, 2001).The brain's key "sorter" is the internal perception of whether or not incoming information can connect with existing, related neural structures. The brain's filtering activity is thus directly linked to what it selects to pay attention (Sylwester, 2004).

The brain's active and dynamic nature enables adolescents to construct and reconstruct knowledge over time as they interact within learning environments. Even before adolescents are born, their brains rapidly develop complex, interrelated networks of neural structures that form the basis for memory and association (Caine, Caine, McClintic &, Klimek 2005; Diamond & Hopson, 1998; Sousa, 2001, 2003; Sylwester, 2003; Willis, 2006; Wolfe, 2001). These neural structures are influenced and shaped by the factors in the external environmental, including home life, culture, hobbies, interests, and level and amount of stimulation. All adolescents are capable of learning; yet the way their individual brains are structurally "wired" to learn differs. As a result of varying environmental and biological factors, what each brings to the learning situation varies.

Implications for Practice

The implication for teachers is to design instruction that enables adolescents' brains to make personally relevant connections. "Whenever new material is presented in such a way that students see relationships, they generate greater brain cell activity (forming new neural connections) and achieve more successful long-term memory storage and retrieval" (Willis & Horch, 2002, p. 15). As adolescents increase the quantity and quality of neural connections, they expand the ability to recognize, use, and communicate these connections.

In other words, they have a stronger capacity for executive functioning, or personal learning management.

Wolfe (2001) suggests that teachers "hook the unfamiliar with something familiar" by comparing a new concept with one known or by using analogies, similes, and metaphors (p. 104). The mathematical concept of parallel lines is illustrated by the tracks of a railroad or sides of a sheet of paper, for example. Prior knowledge of the circulatory system in the human body is useful when adolescents learn to dissect frogs. The ecosystem of a neighborhood creek is a stepping stone for them to understand the delicate balance of plant and fish life in saltwater marshes. Adolescents' interest in music can be connected to research about culture and traditions of ancient civilizations. The challenge for teachers is to activate what is stored in the long-term memory by making learning experiences relevant to prior knowledge. Accordingly, adolescents connect to and form new mental associations.

Teachers have access to a range of strategies that capture the brain's attention and help adolescents make relevant connections with new learning (Beamon, 2001; Caine & Caine, 1997; Caine, Caine, McClintic, & Klimik, 2005; Jensen, 2000; LaDoux, 1996; Sousa, 2001, 2003; Sprenger, 1999; Sylwester, 2003, 2004; Willis, 2006; Wolfe, 2001). These strategies are varied, hands-on, multisensory, active, and interactive. They also connect with students' visual, verbal, kinesthetic, and other intelligence strengths (Gardner, 2006). Helping adolescents make personal connections magnifies their cognitive response capability and enhances their memory. Ways to practice making these connections in the classroom include:

- Music, art, dance, and sensory enhancements that enable hands-on learning.
- Visuals and graphic organizers that help organize and "chunk" information.
- Physical movement for its interactive and kinesthetic value.
- Periodic processing time, in small discussion groups and individually, that gives opportunity for consolidation and internalization of new learning.
- Humor to heighten emotional response and promote relaxation.
- Other sensory-engaging experiences such as pantomime, simulations and role plays, real-life problems, field trips, mock trials or debates related to historical and current issues, experiments, model building, and mind mapping.

EMOTIONAL ENGAGEMENT

Emotional engagement is closely linked with adolescents' learning and thinking. Gardner (1999) explains the importance of emotions in the learning process: "[If] one wants something to be attended to, mastered, and subsequently used, one must be sure to wrap it in a context that engages the emotions" (p. 76). He further observes that students are "more likely to learn, remember, and make subsequent use of those experiences with respect to which they had strong—and one hopes—positive emotional reactions" (p. 77). Introducing a problem-based learning unit, for example, with the arrival of a mysterious telegram immediately stirs adolescents' curiosity. Students who engage in debate over current issues and events, such as immigration policy, digital privacy, censorship, or global warming, grapple with matters of high emotional investment. Reading and discussing adolescent literature related to the teen issues of friendship, death, peer pressure, and cultural identity rouse emotions related to who they are as young people.

Emotional engagement is also closely linked to the quality of classroom relationships. When adolescents feel marginalized because of differences in race, ethnicity, capabilities, or economic advantages, they may be angry or sad, and these emotions can directly interfere with learning (Jensen, 1998). Conversely, when students feel affirmed and purposeful, they are more likely to find emotional joy in learning.

Supporting Brain-Based Research

Current neuroscience technology confirms that emotions play a critical role in learning (Damasio, 1994; Feinstein, 2004). Unlike feelings, which are conscious expressions, emotions are beneath the level of conscious and are deeply rooted in memory. Wolfe (2001) notes that emotion is a primary catalyst in the learning process. She likens emotional response to a biological thermostat that alerts the brain and body to something in the environment that warrants attention. "The brain is programmed to attend first to information that has strong emotional content" (p. 88). Whether the determination is potentially dangerous or not, emotions capture attention and "get a privileged treatment in our brain's memory system" (p. 108).

Jensen (1998) writes that "emotions give us a more activated and chemically stimulated brain, which helps us recall things better" (p. 79). Emotional arousal stimulates the *amygdala*, the area in the middle brain that processes emotions, and starts a chain of physiological responses that determine the emotional relevance (i.e., is it harmful or something I'll like? Should I engage or should I withdraw?). A fraction of a second later, the incoming information goes from the thalamus, another sensory relay station, to the prefrontal cortex, the part of the brain that enables a more rational response and memory recall (i.e., have I confronted this before? How should I respond or act? How can I solve this problem?)

> **Amygdala**
>
> The area in the middle brain that is stimulated by emotional arousal and processes incoming information based on emotional relevance. Incoming information subsequently travels to the thalamus, another sensory relay station, and on to the prefrontal cortex where rational responses are made. In stressful situations, emotions dominate the ability for higher-level cognitive processing.

In stressful situations where the brain perceives threat, such as instances of humiliation or alienation, embarrassment or physical harm, such as bullying or boredom, emotions can dominant cognition and the rational/thinking part of the brain is less efficient (Beamon, 1997). When teaching engages adolescents' interests, stress is reduced and they are, as

Willis (2006) describes, "more successful and happier learners" (p. 59). Willis continues:

> The common theme to the brain research about stress and knowledge acquisition is that superior learning takes place when stress is lowered and learning experiences are relevant to students' lives, interests, and experiences. Lessons must be stimulating and challenging, without being intimidating. . . . Otherwise the stress, anxiety, boredom, and alienation that students experience block the neuronal transmission, synaptic connections, and dendrite growth that are the physical and now visible manifestations of learning. (p. 59)

Implications for Practice

Learning experiences that positively stimulate adolescents' curiosity and activate their senses are more likely to engage them emotionally (Crawford, 2007). Novelty, intrigue, and humor "hook" adolescents' interests. Teachers can introduce a problem scenario that is authentic and urgent; stage a mystery to solve by selectively bringing in clues; rearrange a room to simulate a coffee house for a poetry reading; bring in real props related to the lesson for background effect, dress in costume, or wear a hat for a role play (Kaufeldt, 2005).

Feinstein (2004) notes that emotional experiences affect what adolescents pay attention to, their motivation, reasoning strategies, and their ability to remember. She recommends music, played softly to welcome students to class or to accompany a content area, for example, Gustav Holst's *The Planets* during a science lesson. She writes of a physics teacher who skates into a classroom to demonstrate force and speed with two different masses. Another teacher turns cartwheels to simulate molecular rotation.

Willis (2006) determines several low-stress strategies that captivate students' attention and improve the brain's receiving, encoding, storing, and retrieval capacities. These are staging an element of surprise through unexpected classroom events; showing dynamic videos; creating a state of positive anticipation to stir students' curiosity; using humor and unique visuals, such as illusions; asking intriguing open-ended questions followed by quick writes or think-pair-share; and designing enriched and varied sensory learning experiences that are student centered and include choice. Engaging and holding students' attention enhances their readiness to use higher-order thinking. She suggests one strategy called "popcorn" reading, which is a read-aloud technique where students "jump in" and read at any time (p. 21). Crawford (2007) lists other emotionally engaging experiences, all presented in a physically safe and inviting classroom climate, as follows:

- drama, role play, and debate
- problem-based learning, problem solving
- games and simulations
- classroom celebrations
- seminars and class discussions

- cooperative learning and team events
- storytelling, personal expression, and journal writing
- mock trials, experiments, and projects
- field-based projects and service learning
- interactive technology

APPROPRIATE INTELLECTUAL CHALLENGE

In a period when rapid growth appears in the prefrontal cortex, or thinking part of the brain, cognitive capacity is unfolding and adolescents are intellectually primed for inquiry, critical thinking, and problem solving (Beamon, 1997). Adolescents thrive on challenge that is meaningful, appropriate, and relevant. "They love to play with words, to write limericks, to delve into science fiction, to debate political and environmental issues (the more controversial the better), to give opinions, to solve real life problems—the possibilities are endless" (p. 23). Intellectual challenge is not passively receiving information; it rather "gives adolescents the freedom to experiment with their imaginations, to release their passion for make-believe, to explore their fascination for fantasy, and to use developing psychomotor skills" (p. 24).

Adolescents are increasingly capable of abstract thinking and moral reasoning, which makes them responsive to ethical problems that impact them personally. They can consider hypothetical questions, analyze complex situations, and make reflective conclusions (Feinstein, 2004). Topics such as stem cell research, immigration regulations, deforestation of rain forests, genetic sequencing, human and civil rights, animal protection, and issues related to war justification and world peace generate engaging discussion and debate. Appropriate challenge brings novelty, interaction, movement, and emotional engagement to the learning experience.

Since all adolescents do not develop a capacity for abstraction simultaneously, teachers can reduce failure and frustration by providing hands-on, concrete learning strategies (Feinstein, 2004). Dissecting frogs helps adolescents understand the complex circulatory system, and manipulatives assist in the study of geometry. Vygotsky's (1978) concept of *zone of proximal development* contends that students are able to navigate challenge that is set one step above their readiness levels if they have adequate supports (Bransford, Brown, & Cocking, 2000). These supports, or *scaffolding*, can be human, such as the teacher, other students, and other adults, or symbolic, such as computers or graphing calculators, or graphic organizers and thinking maps that help students retrieve, manipulate, and organize new information in meaningful ways.

> **Zone of Proximal Development**
>
> Vygotsky's (1978) concept that students can navigate challenge that is one step above their readiness levels with adequate supports, or scaffolding.

Supporting Brain-Based Research

Challenge within a stimulating environment changes the brain's structure, density, and size (Kaufeldt, 2005). The brain is incredibly malleable, referred to as *brain plasticity*, and responsive to challenging experiences within the

---

Scaffolding

Supports in the learning environment that are human, such as the teacher, peers, or other adults, or symbolic, such as computers, graphing calculators, or graphic organizers.

---

learning environment (Diamond, 1967). On a cellular level, the adolescent brain's 30 billion intricate nerve cells connect with trillions of dendrites in an elaborate information-processing system (Beamon, 1997). Axons extend from cell bodies and transmit chemical signals across connective pathways to neighboring neurons. These synapses literally "fire" with conductive electrochemical transmissions as adolescents' brains process incoming stimuli and make connections with previously-learned knowledge in the long-term memory (Willis, 2006). With repeated practice and activation, the brain constructs more permanent and complex circuits of axons and dendrites, and neural associations become faster, richer, and more efficient.

As neural structures form, change, and alter, a fatty tissue of white glial cells called myelin forms around, stabilizes, and thus strengthen axons. This myelin sheath aids in the transmission of information between neurons and among brain regions and facilitates more integrated brain functioning. When the adolescent brain is actively engaged with new information—such as through questioning, discussion, problem solving, small group activities, and processing and application—cognitive connections are reinforced and new learning more potentially moves into long-term memory (Wolfe, 2001). Within an enriched environment, the brain can literally grow new and increasingly complex synaptic connections.

Brain Plasticity

The brain's responsiveness to a challenging learning environment by the development of dendrites and new, increasingly synaptic connectivity, which facilitates more integrated brain functioning.

Implications for Practice

When teachers present new material to be learned in multiple and multisensory ways, and allow time for practice, process, and review, neural connections become more numerous and more interrelated (Willis, 2006). In learning about the abstract concept of acceleration, for example, eighth graders learn a formula, visualize the process in small groups by conducting a series of lab trials with rulers, wind-up toys, and clock watchers, then discuss observations, analyze collected data, calculate speed and negative acceleration, figure in velocity, are reminded of the distinction between average velocity and final velocity through a graph the teacher draws on the board, write up the lab results in interactive notebook, share findings, and discuss evidences of acceleration in the real world (i.e., How can we determine the negative acceleration of the skateboard you are riding across the school parking lot?). With each activity, different parts of the brain are connecting and making associations with the new concept. The new information is thus stored in multiple brain regions, connected through memory circuits, and more easily accessed.

PURPOSEFUL SOCIAL INTERACTION

Adolescent learning is socially motivated through a natural inclination to interact with peers and a cognitive need to collaboratively construct knowledge and new learning.

Cognitive psychologists have contended for some time that learning is a social process that is supported by meaningful interaction with resources, human and symbolic, in the learning environment (Perkins, 1992; Resnick, 1987). Socially shared interaction, or *shared cognition*, makes internal conversations visible so that knowledge can be built upon, strengthened, or reshaped. Others (Pea, 1993; Gardner, 1999) assert that knowledge and intelligence are distributed among humans and supported by technology. When adolescents are able to interact with peers, whether solving a problem, conducting an investigation, creating a play, or planning for a debate, they benefit socially and cognitively from shared perspectives and shared resources.

> **Shared Cognition**
>
> The theory that learning and knowledge construction is supported by meaningful social interaction with resources in the learning environment, human and symbolic.

Similarly, the constructivist approach promotes the value of social interaction and shared knowledge within a local or global community of learners (Bransford, Brown, & Cocking, 2000; Perkins, 1999). Constructivism is a view of learning based on the belief that adolescents adjust prior knowledge to accommodate new experiences as their brains actively seek connections with what is already known and make meaning (Brooks & Brooks, 1993). This view supports the purposeful design of instruction that relates to adolescents' prior learning and experiences and that emphasizes hands-on problem solving. A key tenet of constructivism is that knowledge and understanding are socially constructed in dialogue with others.

As social as adolescents naturally are, however, they are not readily adept in social and personal skills to work together in a group toward a common academic goal. Social interaction is meaningful if it is well planned and if teachers instill in students the skills for purposeful collaboration. When structure and accountability are apparent through specific guidelines for learning tasks, when expectations for behavior and demonstration are clearly communicated, and when procedures for evaluation and reflection are organized, social interaction is more likely to work (Crawford, 2007).

Supporting Brain-Based Research

Brain research gives further credibility to the importance of social interaction. Renate Caine, one expert in brain-compatible learning, stresses the social dimension of the brain (Caine as cited in Franklin, 2005). "Remember, the mind is social . . . You're embedding this knowledge in their experiences and everyday worlds" (p. 3). Siegal (1999), author of *The Developing Mind*, suggests that the social interactions among people—within families, classrooms, cultures, or the larger world culture via the Internet—enhance the flow of energy and information into the brain where it is processed actively by the mind.

Sylwester (2006) explains the brain's maturation during late childhood and early adolescence ("the tween brain") as a progression from "childhood acceptance of dependence" to "an adolescent reach for independence' (p. 1). As the frontal lobes mature during the preteen years, thinking and actions shift from reactive to proactive thinking and behavior. As young children, adolescents depended on adults to make executive decisions; however, with maturation in the frontal cortex, adolescents begin to expect to make their own decisions and solve their own problems. With this cognitive shift, they crave exploration, peer interaction, and personal autonomy.

Implications for Practice

Instructional strategies abound that enable adolescents to work collaboratively to explore problems (Crawford, 2007). Problem- or project-based learning, service learning, simulations, cooperative learning structures, literature circles, and other grouping strategies provide opportunities for students to communicate ideas and learn collaboratively. Through interpersonal connections adolescents' "brain energy" is shared and the cognitive potential of thinking and learning is enhanced. Teachers accordingly can select among numerous available strategies to incorporate peer grouping into instruction. For adolescents, purposeful, shared interaction can promote positive self-concept, academic achievement, critical thinking, peer relationship, positive social behavior, and motivation to learn (Johnson, 1979; Johnson &, Johnson, 1988).

For social interaction to be successful, instruction, practice, and feedback must be purposeful, and the teacher's interactive role is essential. Ongoing assessment that supplies constructive feedback can help adolescents direct a learning activity productively and positively manage their actions toward one another. Interactive group work, implemented effectively, can benefit adolescents socially, personally, and intellectually.

METACOGNITIVE DEVELOPMENT

A critical goal of learning is to help adolescents to become responsible managers of their own cognition (Bransford, Brown, & Cocking, 2000). Important to this goal is that students develop the strategic competence for metacognition and self-regulation. "In order to develop strategic competence in learning, children need to understand what it means to learn, who they are as learners, and how to go about planning, monitoring, revising, and reflecting upon their learning and that of others" (p. 100). For self-management to be realized, however, guidance and structure from others more expert in learning is necessary. This relationship between teachers and adolescent learners is known as *cognitive apprenticeship* (Collins, Brown, & Newman, 1989). Under a teacher's guidance, adolescents become increasingly more competent and self-directed over time.

> **Cognitive Apprenticeship**
>
> Also referred to as metacognitive coaching, the process by which teachers model strategic thinking and guide as students practice and obtain the cognitive strategies for self-directed learning. Teacher assistance gradually decreases and student strategic competence increases.

Adolescents' emerging ability for metacognitive thinking enables them to think more strategically about personal learning. A powerful phenomenon, metacognition enables adolescents to set goals, plan, problem solve, and monitor and evaluate learning progress. Through ongoing feedback from teachers or more expert others in the learning context, adolescents can make adjustments and increasingly develop competence. In the final stage, the teacher gives less assistance, referred to as fading, and students assume more responsibility and a sense of ownership over their own learning. The goal of metacognitive coaching is to help adolescents think strategically about knowledge while they progressively strengthen cognitive skills.

Supporting Brain-Based Research

Similar to the teacher's role in the cognitive apprenticeship model is the brain-based strategy of elaborate rehearsal (Wolfe, 2001). *Elaborate rehearsal strategies* help adolescents interact with and process new information until it is learned. Repeated associations of pieces of information enable long-term memory circuits to form (Martin & Morris, 2002). Elaborate rehearsal strategies motivate adolescents through movement, emotion, multisensory engagement, social interaction, and intellectual challenge. They activate a new dendrite network and increase the probability that new information will be retained. Another benefit for the adolescent brain is more efficient neural processing. This increase in the speed of synaptic activity enables the brain to process information and make connections between previous and current learning more readily.

> **Elaborate Rehearsal Strategies**
>
> Strategies that activate the brain's natural capacity to build long-term memory circuits through repeated association. They motivate through movement, emotional stimulation, multisensory engagement, social interaction, and intellectual challenge.

Implications for Practice

The brain-based literature identifies many elaborate rehearsal strategies (Crawford, 2007; Caine & Caine, 1994; Jensen, 1998; Sousa, 2001, 2003; Sylwester, 1999; Wolfe, 2001). They include the following:

- Writing activities across the curriculum, including journaling, poetry, stories, speeches, letters, newspaper eulogies, dialogues, and Quickwrite/Quickdraw diagrams or interactive notebooks
- Mneumonic devices, including music, rap, jingles, acronyms, rhymes, phrases, key word imagery, location association, and narrative chaining
- Peer teaching and other cooperative learning structures that enable summarization, discussion, analysis, and evaluation
- Reciprocal teaching
- Active review, including student presentations and game format
- Reading punctuated with intervals of note taking, discussion, and reflection
- Thinking maps, including webs, graphic organizers, story-plots, diagrams, data organization charts, matrixes, and t-charts
- Physical movement, including role play, simulations, and reenactment

A SUPPORTIVE LEARNING ENVIRONMENT

Learning environments are multidimensional entities of physical space, structure, and time; social interaction and intellectual interplay; and emotional, affective interchange (Crawford, 2004). Teachers create learning environments when they make decisions about furniture arrangement and wall displays, routines and procedure, expectations for student behavior, materials and resources, student grouping, curriculum development and instruction, and teacher-student and student-student relationships. Learning environments comprise visible and invisible classroom structures and processes that are designed to benefit individual students and the whole class (Tomlinson & Eidson, 2003).

A learning environment that is conducive to adolescent thinking and learning is responsive to their personal, intellectual, and social needs (Crawford, 2007). Adolescents learn and think better in a flexible, yet structured community-oriented environment where they move, talk, and interact. They thrive in a learning environment where they are motivated personally, challenged intellectively, and supported intentionally; where they engage in relevant and meaningful learning activities; and where they can accomplish and experience academic success.

Supporting Brain-Based Research

In a physically, social-emotionally, and intellectually safe classroom environment, the brain operates at maximum capacity. In her book, *Differentiation Through Learning Styles and Memory,* Sprenger (2003) writes that physical characteristics such as natural lighting, cooler temperatures, natural colors, music, water, orderliness, and safety are linked to attention, learning, and retention. A learning environment that helps students understand and manage emotions, develop empathy toward the feelings of others, and build skills for interpersonal relationships is important for the brain's social-emotional development. A brain-compatible cognitive environment includes "predictability, feedback, novelty, choice, challenge, and reflection" (p. 18). Predictability reduces stress; continuous, interactive feedback enables the brain to learn; appropriate levels of novelty stimulate attention; and opportunities for choice appeal to the brain's emotional amygdala and motivate the capacity for decision making, planning, and critical thinking. Appropriate challenge and opportunity for reflection enable deeper processing and long-term memory.

Implications for Practice

Chapters 4 and 5 provide an extensive discussion of the developmentally appropriate learning environment and how the physical, affective, and cognitive dimensions can be differentiated to meet the varying needs of adolescents. They address interrelated research-based practices for structuring and managing an adolescent-centered environment for learning.

A PRIME TIME FOR LEARNING

Sophisticated neuroimaging and brain-mapping studies in neuroscience yield insight into adolescent brain development associated with learning and behavior (Giedd et al., 2004; Strauss, 2003; Willis, 2006). These findings are imminent in understanding the relationship among brain functioning, development, and instructional practice. Educators who write about *brain-compatible instruction* caution against a simplistic and causal interpretation (Caine, Caine, McClintic, & Klimik, 2005; Crawford, 2007; Jensen, 2000; Sylwester, 2005; Wolfe, 2001), yet they do agree that understanding how the brain learns is "an essential element in the foundation on which we should base educational decisions" (Wolfe, 2001, p. 191). Several new adolescent brain discoveries follow.

Scanned Exuberance

Important to teaching and learning is neural imaging documenting that the adolescent brain is still growing, maturing, and evolving. Strauss (2003), author of *The Primal Teen: What the New Discoveries about the Teenage Brain Tell Us About Our Kids*, explains the phenomena in this way:

> The teenage brain, it's now becoming clear, is still very much a work in progress, a giant construction project. Millions of connections are being hooked up; millions more are swept away. Neurochemicals wash over the teenage brain, giving it a new paint job, a new look, a new chance at life. The teenage brain is raw, vulnerable. It's a brain that's still becoming what it will be. (p. 8)

The adolescent brain's gray matter thickens as neurons grow more and more synaptic connections, or new pathways for nerve-cell communication. This overproduction, or *neural exuberance*, occurs just prior to puberty in the frontal lobes of the cerebral cortex (Strauss, 2003). Gray matter in this outer area of the cerebrum, associated with reasoning, metacognition, planning, problem solving, attention focusing, emotional self-regulation, and language specialization, actually thickens "as tiny branches [dendrites] of brain cells bloom madly . . ." (p. 15). This region of the adolescent brain is the last to mature and does not fully develop until early adulthood. As mentioned earlier, the brain's white matter, the fatty myelin sheaths that insulates the axons and carry information away from the neurons, additionally thickens. This myelin coating makes the nerve signals between cellular neurons transmit faster and more efficiently (Willis, 2006).

Brain growth in the prefrontal cortex is associated with adolescents' development of executive functioning, or the ability to plan and organize thinking, use reason, access working memory, engage in risk assessment, moderate emotions, and reflect on personal strengths and weaknesses (Caine, Caine, McClintic, & Klimek, 2005). While adolescents eventually become capable of executive functioning, it does not happen instantaneously. What remains "under construction," at times to the dismay of teachers and parents, is the adolescent brain's ability to resist impulses, to control emotions, to think out decisions, and to plan ahead (Strauss, 2003).

Brain-Compatible Instruction

Teaching that is responsive to the way the human brain receives and organizes new information through association with prior knowledge, processes information in long-term memory, and retrieves information previously learned. Conditions conducive for brain-compatible instruction include emotional stimulation and cognitive engagement within a supportive and safe learning environment.

Neural Exuberance

The overproduction of neurons and synaptic connections in the frontal lobes of the cerebral cortex just prior to the onset of puberty as the adolescent brain matures.

Neural Sculpting

Another relevant discovery is that between the ages of thirteen and fifteen, following the phase of neural overproduction, the adolescent brain goes through a "pruning back" phase known as *neural sculpting.* A small percentage of synaptic connections are actually lost. Neuroscientist Jay Giedd, in an interview for Frontline's *Inside the Teenage Brain* (Spinks, 2002) notes that "there is a fierce, competitive elimination, in which brain cells and connections fight it out for survival" (p. 2). Adolescent brains appear to go through a period of circuit refinement when synapses that are more frequently activated are strengthened at the expense of those less used (Wilson & Horch, 2002). Brain maturation thus involves a fine tuning of neural connections as the brain consolidates, focuses, and prepares for the adult years.

> **Neural Sculpting**
>
> The phase of circuit refinement following neural exuberance when neural connections that are used frequently strengthen and those less used are lost. Neural sculpting is susceptible to experiences as the adolescent brain matures.

Interestingly, the experiences in which adolescents are involved can play a role in determining which neural structures survive the pruning process (Spinks, 2002) As adolescents explore and shape their identities, what they do in their social, personal, and academic experiences factors into the brain's maturation. Those who engage actively in music, sports, or academics, for example, potentially strengthen and sustain synaptic connections in the associated brain areas. An associated and cruel irony, however, is that the maturing teen brain is highly susceptible to drug, alcohol, and nutrition abuse during a time when experimentation, need for social acceptance, and personal perceptions of infallibility are developmentally characteristic. These functional changes in the adolescent brain carry both potential and risk.

Crazy by Design

For years, the erratic, unpredictable behaviors of adolescents have been dismissed as the by-product of an oversupply of hormones. Recent brain research, however, may explain why teens make impulsive decisions or act out in reckless ways. The emotional turmoil associated with adolescence has less to do with raging hormones than the "complex interplay of body chemistry, brain development, and cognitive development" (Price, 2005, p. 22). The area of the brain associated with impulse control and self-regulation is still undergoing change. As Strauss (2003) humorously writes, "[t]he teenage brain may, in fact, be briefly insane. But, scientists say, it is crazy by design. The teenage brain is in flux, maddening and muddled. And that's how it's supposed to be" (p. 8).

An adolescent's underdeveloped prefrontal cortex is linked to an inability to regulate and refrain from certain behaviors. Feinstein (2004) notes that "[s]erotonin, the neurotransmitter that makes us feel calm and at peace, is at a natural low during adolescence" (p. 108). Not thinking of consequences for potentially harmful decisions and actions, adolescents are more prone to sensation-seeking or risky behavior that includes sexual engagement, cigarette smoking, and substance use (Caine, Caine, McClintic, & Klimek, 2005). Even a cognitive awareness of the associated dangers of thrill-seeking behavior does not appear to control adolescents' impulsive actions.

Although neuroscientists are wary to draw a direct relationship between brain functioning and teen behavior, they do speculate that brain development explains why adolescents at times have trouble regulating their emotional responses (Thompson, Giedd, & Woods, 2000). In emotion-inducing situations, adolescents tend to respond more on the "gut responses" of the amygdala, as mentioned earlier, than to the executive or regulating function of the prefrontal cortex. As teens grow older, however, the brain activity shifts to the frontal lobes, and emotional responses are more reasoned and justifiable. With support and structure, adolescents can develop the skills for responsible decision making and personal management.

A Physically Responsive Entity

Two other regions are of interest in the adolescent developing brain: the *cerebellum* and the mid-brain. A small area located above the brain stem, the cerebellum is responsible for balance, posture, muscle coordination, and physical movement (Jensen, 2000; Sylwester, 2006). Current brain research associates the cerebellum with cognitive functions, including the coordination of thinking processes (Wilson & Horsch, 2002). Neuroscientists speculate that growth in the cerebellum during adolescence is not genetically controlled and thus is susceptible to environmental influence. The traditional classroom where adolescents sit passively and memorize discrete, minimally relevant information is not an environment that primes cognitive development.

The association of the adolescent brain and physical activity is not new to brain research. Jensen (1998), who calls the brain a physically-responsive entity, writes of the connection of movement with learning. The cerebellum, according to Jensen, may be the brain's "sleeping giant because it is so neurologically connected to the frontal cortex" (p. 83). The cerebellum consists of approximately one-tenth of the brain's volume, yet contains over half of its neurons.

Multiple studies have linked physical movement and kinesthetic activity such as sculpture and design to enhanced visual thinking, problem solving, language development, and creativity (Greenfield, 1995; Silverman, 1992; Simmons, 1995). Physical exercise, including recess, sports, and in-class activities, fuel the brain with a high amount of food, called neurotropins, which enhance growth and connectivity among neurons. Movement associated with neural development includes physical activities such as a "living" graphic organizers, body sculpture, human bingo, summary ball toss, in-school field trips, and simple stretching exercises.

> **Cerebellum**
>
> The small area located above the brain stem responsible for balance, posture, muscle coordination, physical movement, and coordination of thinking processes. The cerebellum is responsive to conditions in the learning environment.

BRAIN-COMPATIBLE INSTRUCTION: A SUMMARY

Crawford (2007) highlights several brain-compatible instructional strategies that are appropriate for adolescent learning and development. These are recommended in the professional literature and have been implemented in middle and high school classrooms (Caine, Caine, McClintic, & Klimek, 2005; Jensen, 1998; Nelson, 2001; Sousa, 2001, 2003; Sylwester, 2003; Wolfe, 2001). These include:

- **Integrated thematic units of study** that encourage adolescents to make thematic connections across disciplines related to social issues and personal concerns

- **Problem/project-based units of study** that engage adolescents as stakeholders in investigation and critical analysis of authentic problems
- **Academic service-learning units of study** that promote collaborative inquiry, civic action, and community outreach
- **Real-life apprenticeships** that involve adolescents in internships with adults in jobs related to the curriculum or based on their personal interests
- **Simulations and games** that cast adolescents in roles where they consider alternate perspectives and pertinent ethical issues
- **Music and arts integration** that heightens emotion through sensorimotor stimulation and thus enhance memory
- **Peer collaboration and cooperative learning structures** that give adolescents the opportunity to share and construct knowledge, problem solve, and hone social and interpersonal skills
- **Thinking maps** that provide a visual and tangible mechanism for adolescents to organize and analyze their thinking
- **Reflective writing** that offers a vehicle for adolescents to process, consolidate, and think metacognitively about personal learning
- **Puzzles and word problems** that serve as "brain teasers" for adolescents to improve thinking skills and strengthen synaptic connectivity
- **Physical movement and exercise** that keeps the brain alert and attending
- **Physical group challenges** that promote collaboration and problem solving
- **Internet activities** that open the world to adolescents as they research relevant and timely issues; collaborate with mentors, experts, and peers; and actively manipulate data and skills

SUMMARY AND LOOKING AHEAD

Chapter 7 discusses the interrelationship of adolescents' developmental tendencies, learning, and brain functioning. It aligns the six differentiated design elements with associated developmental, brain-based elements that support adolescent learning. These are personal connection, appropriate intellectual challenge, emotional engagement, purposeful social interaction, metacognitive development, and supportive learning environment. The chapter also examines pivotal research on the developing adolescent brain related to adolescent learning and emotional management and suggests responsive classroom practices.

The next chapter expands the discussion of adolescent-centered differentiation through elaboration and application of four of the six design principles: evaluation, expectation, engagement, and exploration. Subsequent chapters discuss extension and the learning environment. The next chapter also introduces and illustrates multiple differentiation strategies in the content areas of science, social studies, math, and English.

8

Interface Between Gifted Education and General Education

Toward Communication, Cooperation, and Collaboration

Carol Ann Tomlinson, Mary Ruth Coleman, Susan Allan, Anne Udall, and Mary Slade

Gifted education has often seemed isolated from general education, in part because of differing perspectives on equity and excellence goals and tensions resulting from those divergent viewpoint. Recently however, there have been

Editor's Note: From Tomlinson, C. A., Coleman, M. R., Allan, S., Udall, A., & Landrum, M. (1996). In the public interest: Interface between gifted education and general education: Toward communication, cooperation and collaboration. *Gifted Child Quarterly, 40*(3), 165–171. © 1996 National Association for Gifted Children. Reprinted with permission.

calls from both educators of the gifted and general educators for an increased interface between the two fields. This article reports findings and suggestions from a study conducted by a task force commissioned by the National Association of Gifted Children to determine attitudes of educators of the gifted and general educators regarding linkage between the practices, and to provide guidance from practitioners in both fields on increasing communication, cooperation and collaboration between the fields.

BACKGROUND

During the current educational environment characterized by serious and sustained efforts at school reform (as often in past times as well), there have been evident tensions between general education and gifted education born largely from (1) the view of gifted education by general educators as elitist (Margolin, 1994; Oakes, 1985; Sapon-Shevin, 1995; Wheelock, 1992), and (2) the view of general education by educators of the gifted as insensitive to the needs of high ability learners (Council for Exceptional Children, 1994; Renzulli & Reis, 1991). Flashpoints representative of differences between the two groups of educators have included reform initiatives such as heterogeneous grouping, cooperative learning, site-based management, and the middle school concept (Council for Exceptional Children, 1994; Gallagher, 1991, 1992; Robinson, 1990; Rogers, 1991; Tomlinson, 1992, 1994).

Tensions notwithstanding, many educators of the gifted have noted that gifted learners also suffer from classrooms with a drill and skill, teacher-centered, text-based, test-driven profile (Tomlinson & Callahan, 1992), and that the school reform movement embodies many potential benefits for gifted learners as for all students (Council for Exceptional Children, 1994; Dettmer, 1993; Ford & Harris, 1993; Frank, 1992; Ross, 1993; Tomlinson & Callahan, 1992). The literature of gifted education has also recently included numerous calls for a closer linkage between gifted education and general education (Council for Exceptional Children, 1994; Hanninen, 1994; Treffinger, 1991; VanTassel-Baska, 1994). Nonetheless, there have been no systematic attempts to investigate ways in which practitioners in the two fields perceive the idea of linkage or to determine channels through which such a relationship might evolve.

During his tenure as President of the National Association for Gifted Children, James Gallagher established an NAGC Task Force commissioned to explore ways in which the field of gifted education might more effectively interface with the field of general education. The task force was charged with making recommendations to the NAGC Board for increased collaboration between the two fields. This article capsules the method and the content of the report of the NAGC Task Force on Interface Between Gifted Education and General Education with the expectation that both the general message of the report and many of its specific recommendations are useful not only at the national level, but at university, district, school and classroom levels as well.

METHOD: PROCESS EMPLOYED BY THE TASK FORCE

To encourage input from a larger number of participants than would likely be the case in a more typical committee structure, the task force chair devised a three-tiered data gathering process which would solicit ideas from a variety of professionals and parents across the country. The first tier of the process involved a collaboration between three members of a task force steering committee to develop an interview protocol and outline processes for data gathering and analysis. Each of the task force members had had lengthy professional experience with both general education and gifted education, each had served in both public school and university positions, and each had extensive training and practice in research. These participants also served as interviewers in the second tier of the process as well.

In the second tier of the process, steering committee members each contacted educators from various regions of the country, inviting them to participate in the work of the task force by interviewing two people in the field of gifted education whose role and contribution they respected, and two people from the field of general education whose role and contribution they respected. Those who accepted received an interview packet containing an explanation of the project and their role in it, a semi-structured interview protocol (Bogdan & Biklen, 1982), guidelines for interviewing (Bogdan & Biklen, 1982), and procedures for reporting data to the task force steering committee. (Supporting documents are available upon request.)

Interviewers tape recorded interviews, developed synthesis papers of each interview as well as reflection papers (Bogdan & Biklen, 1982) on their set of interviews, and submitted complete interview notes and syntheses to the steering committee who received and analyzed approximately 50 interviews. Interviews were conducted with professionals and parents in Arizona, California, Georgia, Illinois, Louisiana, Michigan, Missouri, New Mexico, North Carolina, South Dakota, Texas, Virginia, Washington, and Wisconsin. Categories of persons interviewed included: regular classroom teachers, school-level specialists in gifted education, district level administrators of programs for the gifted, state level administrators in gifted education, state level administrators in general education, university professors, school principals, assistant principals, superintendents of schools, assistant superintendents, a director of student learning and assessment, a program manager for federal funding, and parents. The goal of the task force was not to systematically sample from a universe, but rather to hear broadly ideas from a variety of individuals who have a stake in both gifted and general education. Members of the task force steering committee, joined by an additional member who had not been a part of the original design process, analyzed interview notes and syntheses, looking first for recurrent themes via content analysis (Lincoln & Guba, 1985), and then organizing those themes in a way which represented both the patterns and flow of ideas in the interviews as a group (Miles & Huberman, 1984). An audit trail for the project has been maintained (Lincoln & Guba, 1985).

The third tier of the task force process involved a review of the draft report by a committee convened by a public school educator with extensive professional experience in both gifted and general education. The intent of the review was to examine both the content and form of the report. The review committee was supportive of many of the recommendations in the draft version of the report. They were skeptical, however, of the draft focus on collaborative efforts between gifted education and general education, preferring instead to seek out and emphasize other avenues of interface which did not imply specific collaboration. Following review of the draft, the committee chair revised the draft to include the intent of the review committee report, presented it to steering committee members for approval, and subsequently to the President of NAGC who commissioned the work of the task force.

While those involved with the work of the task force do not doubt that other perspectives on the issue of a gifted education/general education collaboration exist, we do feel that the fifty interviews analyzed present noteworthy trends in thinking as well as an interesting and worthwhile range of suggestions.

AN OVERVIEW OF THE MESSAGE OF THE REPORT

The inescapable message which prevailed throughout the interviews, from educators of the gifted and general educators alike, was the urgency of need for communication, cooperation and/or collaboration between the fields. Virtually all interviewees talked about a rationale for joint efforts, included caveats in pursuing collaboration, noted obstacles to cooperation and collaboration, emphasized potential benefits to cooperation and collaboration, and made specific recommendations about how cooperation and collaboration might be nurtured. This report follows that format. In many instances, the words of interviewees are used to support or amplify generalizations developed through analysis of interview documents. It is important to note that interviewees as well as steering committee members and review committee members understand that cooperation and collaboration are not synonymous with assimilation. There was clarity among all participants that the field of gifted education has a unique mission in the larger field of education which must be preserved. Nonetheless, there was also a clear sense that communication, cooperation and collaboration between gifted education and general education are compelling goals which should be initiated and pursued by educators of the gifted. In this article, the term "collaboration" should be taken to mean those efforts which support mutual understanding and mutual action between the two fields, understanding that the missions of the two will not and should not be identical.

Rationale for Collaboration

Interviewees presented three distinct and recurrent rationales for fostering a collaboration between gifted education and general education.

1. *Collaboration between the two fields would facilitate balancing the roles of equity and excellence to the benefit of all students.* Often, general education emphasizes equity concerns in education while gifted education focuses on excellence concerns. When the two fields remain relatively distinct in dialogue, planning and execution of plans, the result is a sense of "haves" and "have nots" among identified gifted and non-identified students respectively. Collaboration would promote the idea of talent development for all students. It would "break the mold of treating all students the same" in general education, and yet be more inclusive in gifted education by intent "to provide a quality program for all students, not just a select few." Blending and balancing equity and excellence seems a compelling rationale for cooperation and/or collaboration to many interviewees. Equity becomes concerned with opportunity to maximize capacity for all learners, including the gifted. Excellence becomes concerned with talent development at all levels, including those not identified as gifted. American education (and democracy) benefits from recognition of the legitimate roles of both excellence and equity in schools (and society) and from balancing rather than devaluing either role.

2. *Collaboration between the two fields would reinforce the reality that we share many of the same goals.* Gifted students spend most of their time in the regular classroom setting. What benefits the health of the regular classroom contributes to the robustness of learning for all students, including the gifted. Therefore, rich content, regular expectations for critical and creative thinking, development of meaningful products, establishing expectations for high quality and hard work are goals shared by both sets of educators. (Reflecting opportunity rather than blame, one general educator said, "If you can't help make general education better, you're shortly not going to have the opportunity to make education of gifted students better, because there will be no public schools as we know them today.") Similarly, gifted students are part of the developmental continuum of learners, all of whom have specialized needs as well as shared needs. Therefore, "meeting the individualized needs of the child is a common philosophy of both groups (of educators)." Shared goals do not erase clear disagreements between general educators and educators of the gifted about how such goals should be enacted. They do, however, provide an important basis for discussion and cooperation between members of the two educational practices in developing implementation strategies beneficial to a broader group of students than might be the case without such dialogue and cooperation.

3. *Collaboration between the two fields would maximize the strengths of both generalists and specialists to the benefit of the total school community.* "General educators have an essential role to play in schools, but so do specialists, and they aren't

the same role, and they ought not to have to compete for status or recognition." Said a general educator, "As a teacher, I'd like to do a better job of providing for children. To do that, I need better training and support. I need a better repertoire of instructional strategies. I need to know about more resources and materials. And I need to have a better connection with what gifted education is all about." Said an educator of gifted learners, "The education a gifted student gets in my classroom could not be duplicated in the regular classroom, but I also know that gifted kids need to be a part of the larger environment." Gifted education has had and continues to have a role as a laboratory for testing, refining and disseminating ideas generated by and applicable to general education. Both generalists and specialists have particular contributions to make to the success of education, and a symbiotic relationship would enhance the possibilities of both groups of educators—and the children whom they serve.

The overall rationale for collaboration seemed to suggest the metaphor of an orchestra. Gifted education is one section of the larger group, with an important line of the score to contribute. The full expression of the music is only possible when all sections do their best to play their part—with regard for that part, and for the artistry of parts blended to become a more impressive end product. Gifted education is neither the whole orchestra—nor is the orchestra whole without it.

A Cautionary Note

A number of interviewees, while not veering from their commendation of collaboration, injected a caution. "We (gifted education) can be more collaborative with general education . . . Certainly we should share strategies and techniques that work broadly. It used to be that (these) strategies were used with just gifted students. Now we see the importance of using them with all students, and that's where we should collaborate. But we also have to have (a means) to meet the unique needs of gifted students." "Inclusion of students with unique needs into the regular classroom has a chance only if someone is out there insisting that we must address those needs in differing ways." "If we lose our identity, we lose our opportunity for advocacy."

One interviewee suggested that gifted education errs when it becomes exclusive, but not when it understands its separateness. Gifted education plays a role in advocating high-end excellence which no other group in education plays. "Don't reject your birthright," cautioned one general educator. "You must be what you are." An educator of the gifted said, "While our job must increasingly be to develop all talent, to take all kids as far as they can go, we must continue to be the models of high-end talent development in the context of general talent development." Another said, "Views of intelligence are broadening, but there are students still at the upper ends of each intelligence who are just putting in time in classrooms. We have to be there for them, even if it is not politically popular to do so."

Anthropologists are sometimes described as lumpers (those who look at commonalities of cultures) and splitters (those who look at cultural differences).

Currently, general education tends to take a "lumper" role. The similarities among students are real and important. Those similarities call upon gifted education to promote those instructional mechanisms which enrich all students. Nonetheless, educators of the gifted also have a role as "splitters." "Educators have to stop looking for a single way that will work for everybody. Kids need treatments according to their differing needs. Gifted education has to remind us that it is not acceptable to treat everybody the same—that one size never has fit all." "We cannot succumb to the bandwagon, to the mentality of the single quick fix." "Stop taking the temperature every 15 seconds. Stop saying the sky is falling. Let some things play out. Things are changing, and we need to see where they are going." "We tell our students that it is okay to be different. We'd better have the courage to be different when it's necessary too."

Clearly, gifted education exists to advocate for and serve a group of learners often overlooked in the planning and advocacy of other facets of educational practice. Articulating goals of and championing high-end excellence would likely be greatly diminished without the unique voice of gifted education. Collaborative efforts are not acceptable if they erode those roles. The caution seems to be that the field of gifted education adopt a sort of Janusian stance— looking both in the direction of our heritage and toward new opportunity.

Obstacles to Establishing Collaboration

Clearly there are obstacles which have impeded collaboration between general education and gifted education in the past. Some are implicit or explicit in previous sections of the article. Failure to understand the obstacles impairs our capacity to move forward toward collaboration. Three obstacles to collaboration pervaded the interviews of participants in the task force project: mutually negative attitudes between general educators and educators of the gifted, isolationism, and scarcity of resources.

Chief among the barriers to collaboration noted by interviewees falls under the heading of mutual suspicion and mistrust which permeates relationships between educators of the gifted and general educators. Educators of the gifted often seem to operate from an assumption that what happens in the regular classroom is not worthwhile, unimportant. "Gifted educators often exhibit an 'I know best' attitude. It's alienating." General educators seem to dismiss the value of gifted education. A regular classroom teacher said, "I'm a pessimist when it comes to this subject. I don't know if it's the times or the locality where I work, but among 45 faculty working in my school, I'd say there are about 44 who don't believe that gifted education exists or that gifted children do. It's very overt. People are filled with animosity . . ."

Related to mutually offensive attitudes about colleagues are defeating attitudes about students as well. "I get the feeling that educators of the gifted think the only important talent is in their classes. It's not true, of course. But sometimes, I don't think gifted educators want to see that." "There's misunderstanding, even fear of, gifted students on the part of many classroom teachers. This kind of negative reaction is born of a great . . . lack of information and knowledge about gifted students." A state-level general educator spoke from no-man's-land, "Many of us have a feeling of defensiveness, caused by so many little camps with their own focus and interests. None of them have what I believe ought to be the primary focus, and that is to educate the child. Children suffer because of it."

Related to the barrier of mistrust is one which stems from programs which appear remote and isolated from the general curriculum. Pullout programs per se were not cited as obstacles, but rather pullout programs which seem disintegrated from the regular education program were problematic. "I want to emphasize," said one regular classroom teacher, "that programs which separate do not support collaborative efforts." Another noted, "I have no ownership (in the pullout program) even though I am a gatekeeper for it." Another educator concluded, "This kind of program puts us into a 'my kids/your kids' mentality instead of an 'our kids' frame of mind."

A third impediment to collaboration recurrent in the interviews was the issue of resources. Paucity of time and money were evident concerns of both general educators and educators of the gifted. An educator of the gifted reflected, "I would like to collaborate with classroom teachers more. I think what it comes down to is time. I think they would like to work more with us too. It's hard to develop a working relationship when you are only in the building a few hours a week . . . (and when) the other person has no time to plan anyhow." A professor explained, "There are too few resources available to help teachers meet the needs of high ability learners. Teachers become overwhelmed and end up teaching to the middle."

Benefits from Establishing Collaboration

Obstacles to collaboration notwithstanding, virtually all interviewees elected to concentrate on benefits to education, educators and to learners which could result from collaborative relationships between general educators and educators of the gifted. In fact, it appeared evident that many respondents felt collaboration held the best promise to eroding the barriers, even as it held promise to enrich education.

Three categories of benefits of collaboration were common among interviews.

1. *Collaboration enhances understanding and trust between gifted education and general education.*

Collaboration:

- facilitates communication.
- promotes ownership of gifted learners by educators of the gifted.
- promotes ownership of non-identified students by educators of the gifted.

- encourages linking general and specialized learning opportunities for gifted students.
- helps each group of educators develop more accurate information about a broader group of learners.
- helps educators "act their way into new beliefs rather than believing their way into new actions."

2. *Collaboration supports professional development of all educators.*

Collaboration:

- encourages networking among educators.
- decreases the problem of the isolation of teaching.
- promotes sharing of competencies which could accelerate positive school change.
- promotes shared expertise, allowing educators of the gifted to share process skills and general educators to share content knowledge.
- promotes peer coaching and observation for professional growth.
- encourages mutually beneficial research on and evaluation of challenging instructional practices.

3. *Collaboration enhances student learning.*

Collaboration:

- promotes individualization and differentiation for all students.
- facilitates higher level thinking and higher expectations for content and production for more students.
- promotes talent development for all students.
- promotes continuity across school programs and services.
- promotes more fluid and flexible grouping of students.
- promotes speaking with a single voice for community support for education.

Several interviewees pointed to specific benefits to gifted education of collaboration. Said one, "It strengthens the voice of gifted education. Alone, gifted education has little impact on the field of education as a whole." Another explained that teachers of the gifted are often perceived as being "superhuman" and inaccessible simply because of their association with the term "gifted." "If educators of the gifted work in regular classrooms and take instructional and management risks right along with the classroom teacher, and make mistakes right along with the classroom teacher, we will ultimately become "real" teachers and our voices will be human voices again." By making themselves more accessible and inviting to general educators through collaboration, gifted educators who establish effective collaborations benefit general educators and gifted learners. One classroom teacher explained, "I need help . . . I'm frustrated . . . I have so many exceptionalities to deal with and I have only five front row seats." Another said, "Generalists don't feel they can do it all, even if reformers think so."

Recommendations in Behalf of Collaboration

Virtually all respondents emphasized the need for gifted education to take the lead in establishing collaborative efforts at national, state, district, school and classroom levels. Interviewees provided a diverse range of suggestions for moving toward gifted education/general education collaboration. Some of the recommendations would be best implemented by practitioners at the local level, some by organizations such as NAGC and at a national level. "We (gifted education) have to take the lead. We are not big, we are not valued (by the general education community), we are not important. We have to knock (on the wall that separates us) to see if someone is on the other side." Suggestions for enhancing collaboration are grouped here in six categories.

1. *Suggestions for Improved Perceptions about Gifted Education*

- Take clear, consistent, proactive public stands that make gifted education part of the movement to improve education for all students.
- Greet examples of acceptance and nurturing of gifted children by general educators with expressions of interest and excitement.
- Using broadened conceptions of intelligence, focus on gifted education as a resource for talent development in a broad range of students.
- Develop videotapes of effective examples of gifted education and share them broadly.
- Provide opportunities for general educators to see educators of the gifted at work in a variety of settings "to help more educators understand what gifted learners can do and what differentiation looks like."
- Provide in-depth training for educators of the gifted on topics which help them become active players in the larger perspectives of education (e.g. standards, rubrics, portfolios).
- "Plant the seed for the need." Create materials and conversations which help general educators understand the specific needs of gifted learners which could be effectively addressed by generalist/specialist collaborations.
- Provide assistance from public relations and communications professionals (through conferences such as those sponsored by state associations for the gifted and NAGC) to educators of the gifted in how to respond in positive ways to detractors and how to network with colleagues.
- In interactions with general education, be patient. Accept "a little progress each time. Don't push too hard."
- Support educators of the gifted in remaining active in professional organizations of general education.

2. *Suggestions Regarding Instructional Practice and Programming*

- Focus on how to assess student needs and interests, and how to design responsive instruction rather than focusing on identification and grouping.
- Provide leadership in using performance-based assessment.
- Focus on the regular classroom more than on special programs/classes.
- Share differentiated units broadly, demonstrating ways in which instructional strategies can be modified for most effective use with high ability learners.
- Focus on flexible use of time with gifted learners in the classroom.
- Emphasize a continuum of services necessary for and available to gifted learners in the school.
- Take the lead in establishing differential rubrics and performance outcomes for use with gifted learners in the regular classroom.
- Emphasize collaborative identification through the regular classroom.
- Emphasize both co-planning and co-teaching.
- Provide opportunities for general educators and educators of the gifted to swap roles.
- Proactively develop administrator understanding of the benefits of collaboration and support toward building collaboration.
- Promote collaboration between specialists in gifted education and special education as a means of addressing and supporting individualization and differentiation for more students in more settings.
- Create and share specific models of differentiated instruction and flexible grouping in the regular classroom.
- Find and share examples of general education teachers who are effective with gifted learners in the regular classroom.
- In special classes/learning opportunities for the gifted, be sure g/t specialists differentiate instruction rather than assuming all eligible students should fit a single mold.

3. *Suggestions Regarding Preservice, Inservice, and Graduate Preparation*

- Encourage university level educators of the gifted to volunteer to teach preservice courses, participate in preservice seminars, and serve as university supervisors for student teachers. "We need preservice teachers coming out of college ready to deal with student differences."
- Encourage university level educators of the gifted to collaborate with special educators to develop and teach models of differentiated instruction for academically diverse classrooms.
- Emphasize collaborative/consultative models and models of instructional differentiation in Master's level programs preparing educators of the gifted.

- Prepare educators of the gifted to model a variety of instructional strategies in the regular classroom.
- Take the lead in action research projects on topics related to high ability learners with general educators and educators of the gifted.
- Actively recruit and support minority teachers of the gifted at both preservice and graduate levels.
- Find out what kinds of collaboration and assistance general educators want and help educators of the gifted be ready to provide it. "Stay close to the classroom."

4. *Suggestions Regarding Policy and Political Action*

- Plan conferences such as state association conferences and NAGC conferences at times and in places where other professional groups are meeting, then encourage sharing of sessions, speakers, demonstrations.
- Give reduced cost or no cost admission to a general educator accompanying and state association or NAGC members to a state or NAGC conference, and plan sessions on collaboration designed to facilitate the working partnership between members of both groups.
- Become involved in the national standards movement.
- Seek involvement with the Holmes Group.
- Nurture support which now exists for gifted education in the National Education Association, American Federation of Teachers as well as state and local education associations.
- Link governors' schools and residential schools for the gifted to new mandates for alternative schools.
- Hold state association and NAGC conference sessions and strands on how to form liaisons with general education at the state department of education, school district, and school levels.
- Hold state association and NACG conference sessions and/or special workshops on political action and policy development. Provide financial support for a network of educators of the gifted with potential to make an impact in these areas to receive the training.
- Support educators of the gifted and other advocates for gifted child education in becoming administrators, school board members, site-based committee members, PTAs, and other policy-making groups and positions.
- Support educators of the gifted in attending and presenting at general education professional conferences at state and national levels (e.g., NCTM, ASCD, NMSA, NAASP, NCTE).
- Promote use of technology by educators of the gifted to form liaisons with general educators and general education groups.
- Encourage university level educators of the gifted to order general teacher education books, survey contents, and communicate with publishers regarding concepts which need to be included in future editions.

- Establish working relationships with businesses and industries which have an interest in high-end excellence.
- Assist in parent education with the goal of tapping into the political influence of parents of gifted learners in positive ways.

5. *Suggestions Regarding School Reform Issues*

- Advocate and work for educational environments in which all students have an opportunity to explore meaningful content, think critically and creatively, and become engaged in worthwhile production.
- Form alliances with other groups that have an interest in flexible classrooms designed to appropriately address student diversity.
- Stress teaching educators of the gifted how to understand and respond effectively to student diversity (including academic diversity, ethnic diversity, learning style diversity) and how to assist colleagues in doing likewise.
- Work closely with minority communities, learning from them ways in which the community would identify and develop talent.
- Encourage state association and NAGC conference proposals to integrate minority issues into topics presented rather than separating minority issues from other issues.
- Encourage development of curricula which are multicultural in emphasis and approach.
- Join other educators in working for reduced class size, longer blocks of instructional time, improved teacher salaries and other initiatives likely to improve the quality of instruction broadly in schools.
- Advocate adapting school schedules to accommodate collaborative teacher planning and shared instruction.
- Develop broad guidelines for working with gifted learners in site-based settings.

6. *Suggestions Regarding Research and Dissemination Efforts*

- Work to strengthen the research base for practices advocated for gifted learners.
- Provide leadership in reflective practitioner and action research to address issues of interest to teachers regarding gifted learners, diversity, and practices likely to impact instruction of gifted learners.
- Conduct longitudinal efforts to study and modify teacher attitudes about giftedness.
- Stress effective qualitative research as an evaluation tool for gifted education and as a way to help educators understand gifted learners.
- Invite more collaborative participation in gifted education journals.
- Develop publications for general educators discussing instructional issues and sharing instructional practices of interest to teachers. "Share your trade secrets broadly."

SUMMARY

A general educator said, "Generalists don't feel like they can do everything, even if reformers think they can," said one respondent. The broad consensus of the interviewees is that there is merit and urgency in collaboration, both from the vantage point of general educators as well as educators of the gifted. We both work at a moment in history when polar influences encourage us on the one hand to mask diversity and on the other to celebrate it. Gifted learners would benefit from the latter stance, as would many other learners in our schools. Gifted education has an opportunity and a history which could make a positive contribution toward moving in the direction of embracing diversity, There was a caution that gifted education must not jettison its reason for being in order to hop aboard educational bandwagons. Nonetheless, the voices of interviewees spoke as a chorus affirming that, with temperance and caution, the benefits of collaboration far outweigh the very real obstacles in the path of collaboration.

Gayle H. Gregory and Carolyn Chapman

IN OUR QUEST TO FIND THE BEST FIT FOR OUR STUDENTS, WE NEED to recognize that change is a process, not an event (Fullan, 1991), and that we are on a journey of continuous improvement.

Day-to-day planning takes time, especially when our planning involves the process of rethinking what we have done in the past in the one-size-fits-all classroom. We still "begin with the end in mind," focusing on the standards and expectations in the curriculum, but now we also adjust and redesign the learning activities, tailoring them to the needs and preferences of the unique learners in each classroom. We also need to consider how the brain operates, and we should always strive to use research-based best practices when planning instruction, to ensure that we are being effective in our efforts to maximize student learning.

Throughout this book, we have suggested many ideas and strategies to fill your tool kits. Coming full circle in this chapter, we will revisit the lesson-planning template from Chapter 1 and the adjustable-assignments grid from Chapter 5. We will apply the template (see Figure 9.1) and the grid (Figure 9.2) to a variety of differentiated lessons at various levels—early, elementary, middle, and high school—and we will also use them to differentiate by content, interest, readiness, and multiple intelligences for the diverse learners in our classrooms: those just beginning, those approaching content mastery, and those already at a high degree of content mastery (see Figures 9.2–9.8). Differentiation does *not* mean always tiering every lesson for three levels of complexity or challenge. It does mean finding interesting, engaging, and appropriate ways of honoring diversity and helping students learn new concepts and skills.

We think it is important to start small but to think big, too. If you aim for just 1 new "gourmet" lesson each week, you'll have 40 at the end of the year.

Teachers and schools should have a moral purpose, they say. But "they" usually present too few ideas about what that moral purpose should be. Not just any purpose will do. Schools should reach for higher educational purposes that truly are moral in transforming children's lives and building a better world for the generations of the future. Among the many purposes of schooling, four stand out to us as having special moral value: to love and care, to serve, to empower, and, of course, to learn (Hargreaves & Fullan, 1998). Educators need to celebrate how dedicated they are to meeting the needs of their students and how strategic teaching and learning have become.

The chart in Figure 9.9 offers questions for reflection by teachers as they move toward differentiated learning for their students.

Figure 9.1   The Six-Step Planning Model for Differentiated Learning: Template

Planning for Differentiated Learning	
1. STANDARDS: What should students know and be able to do?	Assessment tools for data collection: (logs, checklists, journals, agendas, observations, portfolios, rubrics, contracts)
Essential Questions:	
2. CONTENT: (concepts, vocabulary, facts) — **SKILLS:**	
3. ACTIVATE: Focus Activity: Pre-assessment strategy Pre-assessment Prior knowledge & engaging the learners	• Quiz, test • Surveys • K-W-L • Journals • Arm gauge • Give me • Brainstorm • Concept formation • Thumb it
4. ACQUIRE: Total group or small groups	• Lecturette • Presentation • Demonstration • Jigsaw • Video • Field trip • Guest speaker • Text
5. Grouping Decisions: (TAPS, random, heterogeneous, homogeneous, interest, task, constructed) **APPLY** **ADJUST**	• Learning centers • Projects • Contracts • Compact/Enrichment • Problem based • Inquiry • Research • Independent study
6. ASSESS Diversity Honored (learning styles, multiple intelligences, personal interest, etc.)	• Quiz, test • Performance • Products • Presentation • Demonstration • Log, journal • Checklist • Portfolio • Rubric • Metacognition

Figure 9.2   Adjustable-Assignments Grid to Record Data
About Student Readiness Levels: Template

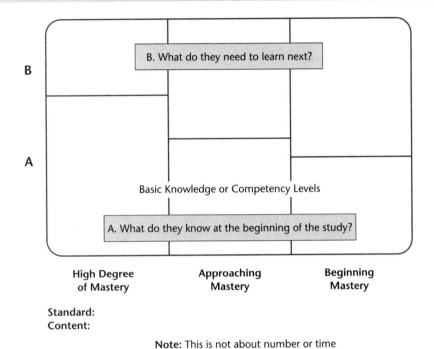

Figure 9.3   Planning for Differentiated Learning for Early Elementary Math: Reading the Analog Clock/Telling Time

Planning for Differentiated Learning	
1. STANDARDS: What should students know and be able to do? Read the clock to the minute. Count time using minutes. Count time using minutes and seconds. Learn how to read the clock for all times. Essential Questions: What time is it?	Assessment tools for data collection: (logs, checklists, journals, agendas, observations, portfolios, rubrics, contracts)
2. CONTENT: (concepts, vocabulary, facts) digital clock, hours, minutes, seconds, AM, PM	**SKILLS:** Reading the clock accurately in the same hour on most occasions. Reading the time on the digital clock when given a specific time and show it on the digital clock. Understanding a clock and how it works.
3. ACTIVATE: Focus Activity: Pre-assessment strategy Pre-assessment Prior knowledge & engaging the learners Label the minute and hour hands, seconds. Describe ½, ¼, and on the hour time. Name and discuss five important times in your daily schedule.	• Quiz, test • Surveys • K-W-L • Journals • Arm gauge • Give me • Brainstorm • Concept formation • Thumb it
4. ACQUIRE: Total group or small groups Use individual manipulative clocks to show various times. Partners explain how the hour and minute hands work. In a small group, have students brainstorm about when they would need a digital clock so they are aware of the value of learning the skill. Small groups race to find the assigned accurate time on their manipulative clocks.	• Lecturette • Presentation • Demonstration • Jigsaw • Video • Field trip • Guest speaker • Text

5. Grouping Decisions: (TAPS, random, heterogeneous, homogeneous, interest, task, constructed)
APPLY
ADJUST
Beginning Mastery
Count by 5s with minute hand.
Learn location of each hand:
    on the hour
    quarter past, 15 minutes
    half hour, 30 minutes
    quarter 'til, 45 minutes
Approaching Mastery
Read the clock to the minute.
Count time using minutes.
Count time using minutes and seconds.
Learn how to read the clock for all times.
High Degree of Mastery
Needs opportunities to read the clock for all times automatically.
	• Learning centers
	• Projects
	• Contracts
	• Compact/Enrichment
	• Problem based
	• Inquiry
	• Research
	• Independent study

6. ASSESS Students will show the right time on the clock faces when given a specific time. Test on the parts of the clock. Diversity Honored (learning styles, multiple intelligences, personal interest, etc.)	• Quiz, test • Performance • Products • Presentation • Demonstration • Log, journal • Checklist • Portfolio • Rubric • Metacognition

Figure 9.4   Adjustable-Assignments Grid for Early Elementary Math:
Understanding the Clock and Elapsed Time

Standard, Concept, or Skill: Elapsed Time
Level: Upper Elementary
Key

A.   What the learners know at the beginning of the study.
B.   What the learners need to learn next.

B	Needs to read the clock for all times automatically.	Read the clock to the minute. Count time using minutes. Count time using minutes and seconds. Learn how to read the clock for all times.	Count by 5s with minute hand. The hour hand moves more slowly than the minute hand. Learn location: ___ O'clock: On the hour and location of each hand: quarter past, 5 minutes, half hour, 30 minutes, quarter 'til, 45 minutes.
A	Uses the clock daily. Explains how the hour and minute hands work. Reads the clock accurately in the same hour on most occasions.	Tells time accurately on hour and half hour. Recognizes time on clock of routines such as lunch time or dismissal time. Understands and reads accurately elapsed time on the hour.	Reads a digital clock. Can name parts of the clock: minute hand, hour hand Knows 60 minutes is an hour. Knows 12 numbers represent hours.

High Degree of Mastery   **Approaching Mastery**   **Beginning Mastery**

Figure 9.5 Planning for Differentiated Learning for Upper Elementary Science: Interpreting the Periodic Table

Planning for Differentiated Learning

1. STANDARDS: What should students know and be able to do? Read and interpret the periodic table. Interpret charted data. Learn each element and its location on the periodic table.	Assessment tools for data collection: (logs, checklists, journals, agendas, observations, portfolios, rubrics, contracts)
Essential Questions: What does each element represent on the periodic table? What are the elements, and what do they mean?	

2. CONTENT: (concepts, vocabulary, facts) Element names and attributes of periodic table	**SKILLS:** Interpreting data and terminology. Learning how to read the periodic table. Learning how the periodic table is designed and its purpose. Needs a thorough explanation of the process of working with the periodic table.

3. ACTIVATE: Focus Activity: Pre-assessment strategy Pre-assessment Prior knowledge & engaging the learners Can use a given key on the table. Locates and changes substance particles. Recognizes the periodic table. Learn the terminology. Use the key on the table. Learn the common elements and characteristics.	• Quiz, test • Surveys • K-W-L • Journals • Arm gauge • Give me • Brainstorm • Concept formation • Thumb it

4. ACQUIRE: Total group or small groups Interpret the data on the entries on the table. Determine number and mass by using the table accurately. Name reasons behind columns and rows. Name basic formulas using the table.	• Lecturette • Presentation • Demonstration • Jigsaw • Video • Field trip • Guest speaker • Text

5. Grouping Decisions: (TAPS, random, heterogeneous, homogeneous, interest, task, constructed) **APPLY** **ADJUST** **Beginning Mastery** Recognize the periodic table. Learn the terminology. Use the key on the table. Learn the common elements and characteristics. **Approaching Mastery** Learn how the periodic table is developed. Needs a thorough explanation of the process of working the periodic table. **High Degree of Mastery** Apply combinations of elements. Use the table with real-world problems and situations.	• Learning centers • Projects • Contracts • Compact/Enrichment • Problem based • Inquiry • Research • Independent study

6. ASSESS The definition and process of using the periodic table. Interpreting the table key. What does each entry stand for and mean? How does the table work? Who uses the periodic table, and when? Diversity Honored (learning styles, multiple intelligences, personal interest, etc.)	• Quiz, test • Performance • Products • Presentation • Demonstration • Log, journal • Checklist • Portfolio • Rubric • Metacognition

Figure 9.6   Adjustable-Assignments Grid for Upper Elementary Science:
Interpreting the Periodic Table

Standard, Concept, or Skill: Interpreting the Periodic Table
Key
A. List specific knowledge base that the students know at the beginning of the study. This
    has been determined by a well-planned pre-assessment.
B. To determine B, the teacher lists what each group of learners need to learn next. This
    challenges those who have a strong background at the high degree of mastery level,
    determines what those learners who are ready for the information need, and determines
    the gaps of those who do not have the basic knowledge needed to learn the informa-
    tion being taught.

	High Degree of Mastery	Approaching Mastery	Beginning Mastery
B	Apply combinations of elements. Use the table with real-world problems and situations.	Learn how the periodic table is developed. Needs a thorough explanation of the process of working with the periodic table.	Recognize the periodic table. Learn the terminology. Use the key on the table. Learn the common elements and characteristics.
A	Determines number and mass by using the table accurately. Understands reasons behind columns and rows. Is able to write basic formulas using the table.	Understands the terminology. Can use a given key on the table. Locates and changes substance particles.	Knows a few common elements. Has heard the term *periodic table*.

Figure 9.7   Planning for Differentiated Learning for Middle School Science: Exploring the Functions of the Body's Skeletal and Muscular Systems

Planning for Differentiated Learning

1. STANDARDS: What should students know and be able to do? Skeletal and muscular systems work together to carry out the life function of locomotion.	Assessment tools for data collection: (logs, checklists, journals, agendas, observations, portfolios, rubrics, contracts)

Essential Questions:
What functions do skeletal and muscular systems provide? How do we better care for these systems?

2. CONTENT: (concepts, vocabulary, facts) Muscles, skeleton, functions, ligaments, bones	**SKILLS:** Visual representations Cause and effect	

3. ACTIVATE: Focus Activity: Pre-assessment strategy Pre-assessment 3 Functions of skeletal/muscular system Prior knowledge & 2 Questions you would like to ask engaging the 1 Reason why this is good to know learners Label the parts of the skeletal & muscular systems	• Quiz, test • Surveys • K-W-L • Journals • Arm gauge • Give me • Brainstorm • Concept formation • Thumb it
4. ACQUIRE: Total group or small groups View video in groups of 3 with an advanced organizer. Small group discussion and fill in advance organizer as a summarizing and note-taking piece. Compare information from video with textbook reading working with a random partner.	• Lecturette • Presentation • Demonstration • Jigsaw • Video • Field trip • Guest speaker • Text

5. Grouping Decisions: (TAPS, random, heterogeneous, homogeneous, interest, task, constructed)			• Learning centers • Projects • Contracts • Compact/Enrichment • Problem based • Inquiry • Research • Independent study
APPLY ADJUST	Students will group according to the choices they make from the choice board	Students will work alone, in pairs or trios to complete two projects on the choice board.	Students will present their projects from the choice board. Teacher and peers provide feedback with rubric.

6. ASSESS Students will individually write a paper on the necessity and functions of the skeletal and muscular systems and their efforts to take care of these systems for healthy living. Test on parts and functions of the two systems. Diversity Honored (learning styles, multiple intelligences, personal interest, etc.)	• Quiz, test • Performance • Products • Presentation • Demonstration • Log, journal • Checklist • Portfolio • Rubric • Metacognition

In this lesson, the strategies for learning are being differentiated. The teacher does a quick informative pre-assessment to find out what the students know. Their interest is stimulated with a variety of audio, visual, and print materials and ongoing discussion in cooperative small groups. Choice is provided with a Tic-Tac-Toe or Choice Board so that students can rehearse content and present their understandings in a variety of ways.

Differentiation is not always three levels of complexity or challenge, but interesting, engaging, and appropriate ways of learning new concepts and skills.

| **Figure 9.8** | Planning for Differentiated Learning for High School Social Studies: Examining the Impact of European Immigration on American Culture |

Planning for Differentiated Learning

1. STANDARDS: What should students know and be able to do? Examine the influx of European immigrants and their contributions to American society.	Assessment tools for data collection: (logs, checklists, journals, agendas, observations, portfolios, rubrics, contracts)

Essential Questions:
How has the ethnicity of immigrants in the early 21st century influenced and affected our lives in the United States?

2. CONTENT: (concepts, vocabulary, facts) Immigration, culture, emigration, relocation, ethnicity, employment, religion	**SKILLS:** Compare and contrast. Research and data collection. Visual representation.

3. ACTIVATE: Focus Activity: Pre-assessment strategy Pre-assessment Prior knowledge & engaging the learners Students create a four-corner organizer to fill in what they know about immigration at the beginning of the 21st century. Each student will generate a personal question. Guest speaker: immigrant grandparent.	• Quiz, test • Surveys • K-W-L • Journals • Arm gauge • Give me • Brainstorm • Concept formation • Thumb it
4. ACQUIRE: Total group or small groups From an interest survey, students identify which groups of immigrants they would like to investigate more thoroughly. Students will use the Internet, text, resource center, and community resources to gather information on a W5 chart.	• Lecturette • Presentation • Demonstration • Jigsaw • Video • Field trip • Guest speaker • Text
5. Grouping Decisions: (TAPS, random, heterogeneous, homogeneous, interest, task, constructed) **APPLY** **ADJUST** Students in small groups will present their findings to the total class. Each student will partner with another student who investigated a different ethnicity of immigrants using a cross-classification matrix. Students will regroup until the entire chart is filled in and all students have discussed all immigrant groups.	• Learning centers • Projects • Contracts • Compact/Enrichment • Problem based • Inquiry • Research • Independent study
6. ASSESS Students will create a "mindmap" in small groups to symbolize the contributions of immigrants to the American culture. Test on immigration in the early 21st century and the impact of the different ethnic groups. Diversity Honored (learning styles, multiple intelligences, personal interest, etc.)	• Quiz, test • Performance • Products • Presentation • Demonstration • Log, journal • Checklist • Portfolio • Rubric • Metacognition

This lesson focuses on best practices of note taking and summarizing using the four-corner organizer, so students can record the information about immigrant groups as a pre-assessment activity. Generating personal questions commits students to further investigation of the topic. Using an interest survey also helps students connect to the content in a personal way.

There are a variety of resources to facilitate investigation of immigrant groups. TAPS is used throughout the learning experience. The total group completes an interest survey. Learners identify personal interests independently. Students work in pairs and small groups at various different times. Students have multiple rehearsals using a variety of instructional strategies. Learning styles are respected: auditory, visual, tactile/kinesthetic.

Figure 9.9	Checklist of Questions for Teachers Planning Differentiated Learning for Their Students

B uilding Safe Environments

- Do students feel safe to risk and experiment with ideas?
- Do students feel included in the class and supported by others?
- Are tasks challenging enough without undo or "dis" stress?
- Is there an emotional "hook" for the learners?
- Are there novel, unique, and engaging activities to capture and sustain attention?
- Are "unique brains" honored and provided for? (learning styles & multiple intelligences)

R ecognizing and Honoring Diversity

- Does the learning experience appeal to the learners' varied and multiple intelligences and learning styles?
- May the students work collaboratively and independently?
- May they "show what they know" in a variety of ways?
- Does the cultural background of the learners influence instruction?

A ssessment

- Are pre-assessments given to determine readiness?
- Is there enough time to explore, understand, and transfer the learning to long-term memory (grow dendrites)? Is there time to accomplish mastery?
- Do they have opportunities for ongoing, "just in time" feedback?
- Do they have time to revisit ideas and concepts to connect or extend them?
- Is metacognitive time built into the learning process?
- Do students use logs and journals for reflection and goal setting?

I nstructional Strategies

- Are the expectations clearly stated and understood by the learner?
- Will the learning be relevant and useful to the learner?
- Does the learning build on past experience or create a new experience?
- Does the learning relate to their real world?
- Are strategies developmentally appropriate and hands on?
- Are the strategies varied to engage and sustain attention?
- Are there opportunities for projects, creativity, problems, and challenges?

N umerous Curriculum Approaches

- Do students work alone, in pairs, and in small groups?
- Do students work in learning centers based on interest, need, or choice?
- Are some activities adjusted to provide appropriate levels of challenge?
- Is pretesting used to allow for compacting/enrichment?
- Are problems, inquires, and contracts considered?

References

Chapter 1

Burke, K. (1993). *The mindful school: How to assess authentic learning.* Thousand Oaks, CA: Corwin.

Caine, R. N., & Caine, G. (1997). *Education on the edge of possibility.* Alexandria, VA: Association for Supervision and Curriculum Development.

Campbell, D. (1998). *The Mozart effect.* New York: Avon.

Cardoso, S. H. (2000). *Our ancient laughing brain. Cerebrum: The Dana Forum on Brain Science, 2*(4), 15–30.

Csikszentmihalyi, M. (1990). *Flow: The psychology of optimal experience.* New York: HarperCollins.

DePorter, B., Reardon, M., & Singer-Nourie, S. (1998). *Quantum teaching.* Boston: Allyn & Bacon.

Diamond, M., & Hopson, J. (1998). *Magic trees of the mind.* New York: Penguin.

Driscoll, M. E. (1994, April). *School community and teacher's work in urban settings: Identifying challenges to community in the school organization.* Paper presented at the annual meeting of the American Educational Research Association, New Orleans, LA. (Available from New York University)

Gibbs, J. (1995). *Tribes: A new way of learning and being together.* Santa Rosa, CA: Center Source.

Glasser, W. (1990). *The quality school.* New York: Harper & Row.

Glasser, W. (1998). *Choice theory in the classroom.* New York: HarperCollins.

Goleman, D. (1995). *Emotional intelligence.* New York: Bantam.

Goleman, D. (1998). *Working with emotional intelligence.* New York: Bantam.

Green, E. J., Greenough, W. T., & Schlumpf, B. E. (1983). Effects of complex or isolated environments on cortical dendrites of middle-aged rats. *Brain Research, 264,* 233–240.

Gregory, G. H., & Parry, T. S. (2006). *Designing brain-compatible learning* (3rd ed.). Thousand Oaks, CA: Corwin.

Harmin, M. (1994). *Inspiring active learning.* Alexandria, VA: Association for Supervision and Curriculum Development.

Healy, J. (1992). *Endangered minds: Why our children don't think.* New York: Simon & Schuster.

Jensen, E. (1998a). *Introduction to brain-compatible learning.* Thousand Oaks, CA: Corwin.

Jensen, E. (1998b). *Teaching with the brain in mind.* Alexandria, VA: Association for Supervision and Curriculum Development.

Marzano, R. J. (1992). *A different kind of classroom teaching with dimensions of learning.* Alexandria, VA: Association for Supervision and Curriculum Development.

Maslow, A. (1968). *Toward a psychology of being.* New York: Van Nostrand Reinhold.

McTighe, J. (1990). *Better thinking and learning* [Workshop handout]. Baltimore: Maryland State Department of Education.

O'Keefe, J., & Nadel, L. (1978). *The hippocampus as a cognitive map.* Oxford, UK: Clarendon.

Ornstein, R., & Thompson, R. (1984). *The amazing brain.* Boston: Houghton Mifflin.

Pert, C. B. (1998). *Molecules of emotion.* New York: Scribner.

Rozman, D. (1998, March). *Speech at Symposium on the Brain.* University of California, Berkeley.

Sapolsky, R. M. (1998). *Why zebras don't get ulcers.* New York: Freeman.

Chapter 2

Dunn, K., & Dunn, R. (1987). Dispelling outmoded beliefs about student learning. *Educational Leadership, 44*(6), 55–61.

Grinder, M. (1991). *Righting the educational conveyor belt.* Portland, OR: Metamorphous Press.

Guild, P., & Garger, S. (1998). *Marching to different drummers* (2nd ed.). Alexandria, VA: Association for Supervision and Curriculum Development.

Kittredge, M. (1990). *The senses.* New York: Chelsea House.

Kline, P. (1997). *The everyday genius: Restoring children's natural joy of learning, and yours too.* Arlington, VA: Great Ocean.

LeDoux, J. (2002). *Synaptic self.* New York: Penguin.

Markova, D. (1992). *How your child is smart.* Emeryville, CA: Conari.

Markova, D., & Powell, A. (1998) *Learning unlimited.* Berkeley, CA: Conari.

Meltzoff, A. (2000). Nurturing the young brain: *How the young brain learns* [Audio cassette]. Alexandria, VA: Association for Supervision and Curriculum Development.

Rose, C., & Nicholl, M. (1997). *Accelerated learning for the 21st century.* New York: Dell.

Chapter 3

Diamond, M. C., Scheibel, A. B., Murphy, G. M., Jr., & Harvey, T. (1985). On the brain of a scientist: Albert Einstein. *Experimental Neurology, (88),* 198–204.

Doidge, N. (2007). *The brain that changes itself: Stories of personal triumph from the frontiers of brain science.* New York: Penguin.

Jackson, R. R. (2009). *Never work harder than your students & other principles of great teaching.* Alexandria, VA: Association for Supervision and Curriculum Development.

Jensen, E. (1997). *Completing the puzzle: The brain-compatible approach to learning.* DelMar, CA: TurningPoint.

Jensen, E. (1998). *Introduction to brain-compatible learning.* Del Mar, CA: Turning Point.

Jensen, E. (2006). *Enriching the brain: How to maximize every learner's potential.* SanFrancisco: John Wiley and Sons.

Marzano, R. J. (2001a). *Designing a new taxonomy of educational objectives.* Thousand Oaks, CA: Corwin.

Marzano, R. J. (2001b). *What works in schools.* Alexandria, VA: Association for Supervision and Curriculum Development.

Prensky, M. (2006). *Don't bother me Mom—I'm learning.* St. Paul, MN: Paragon House.

Sousa, D. (2006). *How the brain learns* (3rd ed.). Thousand Oaks, CA: Corwin.

Sprenger, M. (2002). *Becoming a "wiz" at brainbased teaching.* Thousand Oaks, CA: Corwin.

Tileston, D. W. (2004a). *What every teacher should know about effective teachingstrategies.* Thousand Oaks, CA: Corwin.

Tileston, D. W., (2004b). *What every teacher should know about learning, memory, and the brain.* Thousand Oaks, CA: Corwin.

Tileston, D. W. (2004c). *What every teacher should know about media and technology.* Thousand Oaks, CA: Corwin.

Tileston, D. W. (2004d). *What every teacher should know about student assessment.* Thousand Oaks, CA: Corwin.

Chapter 4

Ainsworth, Larry. (2003a). *Power standards: Identifying the standards that matter the most.* Denver, CO: Advanced Learning Press and Center for Performance Assessment.

Ainsworth, Larry. (2003b). *Unwrapping the standards: A simple process to make standards manageable.* Denver, CO: Advanced Learning Press and Center for Performance Assessment.

Caine, Renate, & Caine, Geoffrey. (1991). *Making connections: Teaching and human brain.* New York: Addison-Wesley.

Caine, Renate, & Caine, Geoffrey. (1997). *Education on the edge of possibility.* Alexandria, VA: Association for Supervision and Curriculum Development (ASCD).

Elder, Linda, & Paul, Richard. (2002). *The art of asking essential questions.* San Francisco: Foundation for Critical Thinking.

Fogarty, Robin, & Bellanca, Jim. (1993). *Patterns for thinking, patterns for transfer: A cooperative team approach for critical and creative thinking in the classroom.* Arlington Heights, IL: IRI/Skylight.

Hart, Leslie. (1993). *Human brain and human learning.* Arizona: Books for Education.

Healy, Jane. (1990). *Endangered minds: Why our children don't think.* New York: Simon & Schuster.

Jacobs, Heidi Hayes. (1997). *Mapping the big picture: Integrating curriculum and assessment K–12.* Alexandria, VA: ASCD.

Kuzmich, Lin. (1998). *Data driven instruction: A handbook.* Longmont, CO: Centennial Board of Cooperative Services.

Kuzmich, Lin. (2002). *Scenario-based learning.* Paper presented to New Orleans Archdiocese administrators.

Parry, Terence, & Gregory, Gayle. (2003). *Designing brain compatible learning.* Arlington Heights, IL: Skylight.

Reeves, Douglas B. (2000). *Accountability in action: A blueprint for learning organizations.* Denver, CO: Advanced Learning Press and Center for Performance Assessment.

Reeves, Douglas B. (2003). *The daily disciplines of leadership.* Denver, CO: Advanced Learning Press and Center for Performance Assessment.

Silver, Harvey, Strong, Richard, & Perini, Matthew. (2000). *So each may learn: Integrating learning styles and multiple intelligences.* Alexandria, VA: ASCD.

Stiggins, Richard J. (1997). *Student-centered classroom assessment* (2nd ed.). Columbus, OH: Merrill, an imprint of Prentice Hall.

Vail, Priscilla. (1989). *Smart kids with school problems.* New York: New American Library.

Chapter 5

Aronson, E. (1978). *The jigsaw classroom*. Beverly Hills, CA: Sage.

California Department of Education. (1994). *Differentiating the core curriculum and instruction to provide advanced learning opportunities*. Sacramento, CA: Author.

Campbell, B., & Campbell, L. (1999). *Multiple intelligences and student achievement: Success stories from six schools* (p. 69). Thousand Oaks, CA: Corwin.

Clarke, J. (1994). Pieces of the puzzle: The jigsaw method. In S. Sharan (Ed.), *Handbook of cooperative learning methods* (pp. 34–50). Westport, CT: Greenwood Press.

Clarke, J., Widerman, R., & Eadie, S. (1990). *Together we learn*. Scarborough, ON: Prentice Hall.

Cohen, E. (1994). *Designing groupwork: Strategies for the heterogeneous classroom* (2nd ed.). New York: Teachers College Press.

Covey, S. (1989). *Seven habits of highly effective people*. New York: Free Press.

Daniels, H. (1994). *Literature circles: Voice and choice in the student-centered classroom*. Portland, ME: Stenhouse Publishers.

Dunn, R., & Dunn, K. (1987). Dispelling outmoded beliefs about student learning. *Educational Leadership, 44*(6), 55–61.

Fisher, D., & Frey, N. (2007). *Checking for understanding: Formative assessment techniques for your classroom*. Alexandria, VA: Association for Supervision and Curriculum Development.

Gardner, H. (1993). *Multiple intelligences: The theory in practice*. New York: Basic Books.

Gregory, G. H., & Chapman, C. (2007). *Differentiated instructional strategies: One size doesn't fit all* (2nd ed.). Thousand Oaks, CA: Corwin.

Joyce, M., & Tallman, J. (1997). *Making the writing and research connection with the I-search process*. New York: Neal-Schuman Publishers.

Kelly, R. (2000). Working with WebQuests: Making the Web accessible to students with disabilities. *Teaching Exceptional Children, 32*(6), 4–13.

Lyman, F. T. (1981). The responsive classroom discussion: The inclusion of all students. In A. Anderson (Ed.), *Mainstreaming digest* (pp. 109–113). College Park: University of Maryland Press.

Lyman, F. (1992). Think-pair-share, thinktrix, and weird facts. In N. Davidson & T. Worsham (Eds.), *Enhancing thinking through cooperative learning*. New York: Teachers College Press.

Macrorie, K. (1988). *The I-search paper*. Portsmouth, NH: Boynton/Cook Publishers.

McTighe, J., & O'Connor, K. (2005, November). Seven practices for effective learning. *Educational Leadership, 63*(3).

Palincsar, A. S. (1986). Reciprocal teaching. In *Teaching reading as thinking*. Oak Brook, IL: North Central Regional Educational Laboratory.

Palincsar, A. S., & Brown, A. L. (1985). Reciprocal teaching: Activities to promote read(ing) with your mind. In T. L. Harris & E. J. Cooper (Eds.), *Reading, thinking and concept development: Strategies for the classroom*. New York: The College Board.

Reis, S. M., Burns, D. E., & Renzulli, J. S. (1992). *Curriculum compacting: The complete guide to modifying the regular classroom for high-ability students*. Mansfield Center, CT: Creative Learning Press.

Santa, C. M. (1988). *Content reading including study systems*. Dubuque, IA: Kendall/Hunt.

Sharon, Y., & Sharon, S. (1992). *Expanding cooperative learning through group investigation.* New York: Teachers College Press.

Slavin, R. E. (1994). *Cooperative learning: Theory, research, and practice.* Boston: Allyn & Bacon.

Sternberg, R. (1996). *Successful intelligence: How practical and creative intelligence determines success in life.* New York: Simon & Schuster.

Tomlinson, C. (1999). *The differentiated classroom: Responding to the needs of all learners.* Alexandria, VA: Association for Supervision and Curriculum Development.

Tomlinson, C. (2001). *How to differentiate instruction in mixed-ability classrooms* (2nd ed.). Alexandria, VA: Association for Supervision and Curriculum Development.

Winebrenner, S. (2001). *Teaching gifted kids in the regular classroom: Strategies and techniques every teacher can use to meet the academic needs of the gifted and talented.* Minneapolis, MN: Free Spirit Publishing.

Chapter 6

Anderson, L. W., & Krathwohl, D. R. (Eds.). (2001). *A taxonomy for learning, teaching, and assessing: A revision of Bloom's Taxonomy of educational objectives.* New York: Longman.

Beers, S. Z. (2003). *Reading strategies for the content areas: Vol. 1. An ASCD action tool.* Alexandria, VA: Association for Supervision and Curriculum Development.

Burke, K. (1994). *How to assess authentic learning.* Palatine, IL: IRI/Skylight.

Drapeau, P. (1998). *Great teaching with graphic organizers.* New York: Scholastic.

Drapeau, P. (2004). *Differentiated instruction: Making it work.* New York: Scholastic.

Fogarty, R. (1994). *Teach for metacognitive cognition.* Palatine, IL: IRI/Skylight.

Forsten, C., Grant, J., & Hollas, B. (2003). *Differentiating textbooks strategies to improve student comprehension and motivation.* Peterborough, NH: Crystal Springs Books.

Gangwer, T. (2005). *Visual impact, visual teaching: Using images to strengthen learning.* San Diego, CA: The Brain Store.

Gardner, H. (1999). *Intelligence reframed.* New York: Basic Books.

Glasser, W. (1999). *Choice theory.* New York: Perennial.

Gregory, G., & Chapman, C. (2002). *Differentiated instructional strategies: One size doesn't fit all.* Thousand Oaks, CA: Corwin.

Gregory, G., & Kuzmich, L. (2004). *Data driven differentiation in the standards-based classroom.* Thousand Oaks, CA: Corwin.

Heacox, D. (2002). *Differentiating instruction in the regular classroom.* Minneapolis, MN: Free Spirit Publishing.

Howard, D. L., & Fogarty, R. (2003). *The middle years: The essential teaching repertoire.* Chicago, IL: Fogarty and Associates.

Intrator, S. (2004). The engaged classroom. *Educational Leadership, 62*(1), 23.

Jacobs, H. H. (2006). *Active literacy across the curriculum.* Larchmont, NY: Eye on Education.

Jensen, E. (2006). *Enriching the brain.* San Francisco, CA: Jossey-Bass.

Kaplan, S. N. (2005). Layering differentiated curriculum for the gifted and talented. In F. A. Karnes & S. M. Bean (Eds.), *Methods and materials for teaching the gifted* (pp. 107–132). Waco, TX: Prufrock Press.

Kenney, J. M., Hancewicz, E., Heuer, L., Metsisto, D., & Tuttle, C. L. (2005). *Literacy strategies for improving mathematics instruction.* Alexandria, VA: Association for Supervision and Curriculum Development.

Marzano, R. J., Pickering, D. J., & McTighe, J. (1993). *Assessing student outcomes: Performance assessment using the dimensions of learning model.* Alexandria, VA: Association for Supervision and Curriculum Development.

Nunley, K. F. (2006). *Differentiating in the high school classroom.* Thousand Oaks, CA: Corwin.

Paul, R. (1999). *Critical thinking: Basic theory and instructional structures.* Sonoma, CA: Foundation for Critical Thinking.

Polette, N. (1987). *The ABCs of books and thinking skills: A literature-based thinking skills program K–8.* O'Fallon, MO: Book Lures.

Reid, L. (1990). *Thinking skills resource book.* Mansfield, CT: Creative Learning Press.

Sousa, D. A. (2001). *How the brain learns.* Thousand Oaks, CA: Corwin.

Sprenger, M. (2005). *How to teach so students remember.* Alexandria, VA: Association for Supervision and Curriculum Development.

Sternberg, R. J. (1996). *Successful intelligence: How practical and creative intelligence determine success in life.* New York: Simon & Schuster.

Sylwester, R. (2003). *A biological brain in a cultural classroom* (2nd ed.). Thousand Oaks, CA: Corwin.

Tomlinson, C. A. (1999). *The differentiated classroom: Responding to the needs of all learners.* Alexandria, VA: Association for Supervision and Curriculum Development.

Tomlinson, C. A., & Edison, C. (2003). *Differentiation in practice: A resource guide for differentiating curriculum grades K–5.* Alexandria, VA: Association for Supervision and Curriculum Development.

Tomlinson, C. A., & McTighe, J. (2006). *Integrating differentiated instruction and understanding by design.* Alexandria, VA: Association for Supervision and Curriculum Development.

Wolfe, P. (2001). Brain matters: *Translating research into classroom practice.* Alexandria, VA: Association for Supervision and Curriculum Development.

Wormelli, R. (2006). *Fair isn't always equal: Assessing and grading in the differentiated classroom.* Portland, ME: Stenhouse.

Chapter 7

Beamon, G. W. (1997). *Sparking the thinking of students, ages 10–14: Strategies for teachers.* Thousand Oaks, CA: Corwin.

Beamon, G. W. (2001). *Teaching with adolescent learning in mind.* Thousand Oaks, CA: Corwin.

Bransford, J. D., Brown, A. L., & Cocking, R. R. (2000). *How people learn: Brain, mind, experience, and school: Expanded edition.* Washington, DC: National Academy Press. Retrieved June 29, 2006, from http://www.nap.edu/openbook/0309070368/html/

Brooks, J. G., & Brooks, M. G. (1993). *In search of understanding: The case for constructivist classrooms.* Alexandria, VA: Association for Supervision and Curriculum Development.

Caine, R. N., & Caine, G. (1994). *Making connections: Teaching and the human brain* (Rev. ed.). Menlo Park, CA: Addison-Wesley.

Caine, R. N., & Caine, G. (1997). *Understanding the power of perceptual change: The potential of brain-based teaching.* Alexandria, VA: Association for Supervision and Curriculum Development.

Caine, R. N., Caine, G., McClintic, C., & Klimek, K. (2005). *12 brain/mind learning principles in action: The fieldbook for making connections, teaching, and the human brain.* Thousand Oaks, CA: Corwin.

Collins, A., Brown, J. S., & Newman, S. E. (1989). Cognitive apprenticeship: Teaching the crafts of reading, writing, and mathematics. In L. B. Resnick (Ed.), *Knowing, learning, and instruction: Essays in honor of Robert Glaser* (pp. 453–494). Hillsdale, NJ: Lawrence Erlbaum.

Crawford, G. B. (2004). *Managing the adolescent classroom: Lessons from outstanding teachers.* Thousand Oaks, CA: Corwin.

Crawford, G. B. (2007). *Brain-based teaching with adolescent learning in mind* (2nd ed.). Thousand Oaks, CA: Corwin.

Damasio, A. (1994). *Descartes' error: Emotion, reason, and the human brain.* New York: Putman.

Diamond, M. C. (1967). Extensive cortical depth measurements and neuron size increases in the cortex of environmentally enriched rats. *Journal of Comparative Neurology, 131,* 357–364.

Diamond, M., & Hopson, J. (1998). *Magic trees of the mind: How to nurture your child's intelligence, creativity, and healthy emotions from birth through adolescence.* New York: Dutton.

Feinstein, S. (2004). *Secrets of the teenage brain: Research-based strategies for reading and teaching today's adolescents.* Thousand Oaks, CA: Corwin.

Franklin, J. (June 2005). *Mental mileage: Education update.* Alexandria, VA: Association for Supervision and Curriculum Development.

Gardner, H. (1999). *The disciplined mind: What all students should understand.* New York: Basic Books.

Gardner, H. (2006). *Multiple intelligences: New horizons.* New York: Basic Books.

Giedd, J. N., Gogtay, N., Lusk, L., Hayashi, K. M., Greenstein, D., Vaituzis, A. C., et al. (2004). *Dynamic mapping of human cortical development during childhood through early adulthood.* Proceedings of the National Academy of Sciences. *627,* 231–247.

Greenfield, S. (1995). *Journey to the center of the mind.* New York: W. H. Freeman Company.

Jensen, E. (1998). *Teaching with the brain in mind.* Alexandria, VA: Association for Supervision and Curriculum Development.

Jensen, E. (2000). *Different brain, different learners.* Thousand Oaks, CA: Corwin.

Johnson, D. W. (1979). *Educational psychology.* Englewood Cliffs, NJ: Prentice Hall.

Johnson, D. W., & Johnson, R. (1988). Critical thinking through structured controversy. *Educational Leadership, 45*(8), 58–64.

Kaufeldt, M. (2005). *Teachers, change your bait!: Brain-based differentiated instruction.* Norwalk, CT: Crown House Publishing Company.

LaDoux, J. (1996). *The emotional brain.* New York: Simon & Schuster.

Martin, S. J., & Morris, R. G. M. (2002). New life in an old idea: The synaptic plasticity and memory hypothesis revisited. *Hippocampus, 12,* 609–636.

Nelson, K. (2001). *Teaching in the cyberage: Linking the Internet and brain theory.* Thousand Oaks, CA: Corwin.

Pea, R. D. (1993). Practices of distributed intelligence and designs in education. In G. Saloman (Ed.), *Distributed cognitions: Psychological and educational considerations* (pp. 47–87). Cambridge, England: Cambridge University Press.

Perkins, R. (1992). *Smart minds: From training memories to educating minds.* New York: The Free Press.

Perkins, R. (1999). The many faces of constructivism. *Educational Leadership, 57*(3), 6–11.

Price, L. F. (April 2005). The biology of risk taking. *Educational Leadership, 62*(7), 22–26.

Resnick, L. B. (1987). *Education and learning to think.* Washington, DC: National Academy Press.

Siegal, D. J. (1999). *The developing mind: Toward a neurobiology of interpersonal experience.* New York: Guilford.

Silverman, S. (1993). Student characteristics, practice, and achievement in physical education. *Journal of Educational Research, 87,* 1.

Simmons, S. (December 1995). Drawing as thinking. *Think Magazine*, 23–29.

Sousa, D. A. (2001). *How the brain learns: A classroom teacher's guide*. Thousand Oaks, CA: Corwin.

Sousa, D. A. (2003). *How the gifted brain learns*. Thousand Oaks, CA: Corwin.

Spinks, S. (2002). *Adolescent brains are works in progress: Here's why*. Retrieved June 25, 2006, from http://www.pbs.org/wgbh/pages/frontline/shows/teenbrain/work/adolescent .html

Sprenger, M. (1999). *Learning and memory: The brain in action*. Alexandria, VA: Association for Supervision and Curriculum Development.

Sprenger, M. (2003). *Differentiation through learning styles and memory*. Thousand Oaks, CA: Corwin.

Strauss, B. (2003). *The primal teen: What the new discoveries about the teenage brain tell us about our kids*. New York: Anchor Books.

Sylwester, R. (1999). *A celebration of neurons: An educator's guide to the human brain*. Alexandria, VA: Association for Supervision and Curriculum Development.

Sylwester, R. (2003). *A biological brain in a cultural classroom: Enhancing cognitive and social development through collaborative classroom management*. (2nd ed.). Thousand Oaks, CA: Corwin.

Sylwester, R. (2004). *How to explain a brain: An educator's handbook of brain terms and cognitive processes*. Thousand Oaks, CA: Corwin.

Sylwester, R. (2006). Connecting brain processes to school policies and practices. Retrieved June 28, 2006, from http://www.brainconnection.com/library/?main=talkhome/columnists

Thompson, P. M., Giedd, J. N., Woods, R. P. et al. (2000). Growth patterns in the developing brain detected by using continuum mechanical tensor maps. *Nature, 404*(6774), 190–193.

Tomlinson, C. A., & Eidson, C. C. (2003). *Differentiation in practice: A resource guide for differentiating the curriculum*. Alexandria, VA: Association for Supervision and Curriculum Development.

Vygotsky, L. S. (1978). *Mind in society: The development of higher psychological processes*. Cambridge, MA: Harvard University Press.

Willis, J. (2006). *Research-based strategies to ignite student learning: Insights from a neurologist and classroom teacher*. Alexandria, VA: Association for Supervision and Curriculum Development.

Wilson, L. M., & Horch, H. D. (September 2002). Implications of brain research for teaching young adolescents. *Middle School Journal, 34*(1), 57–61.

Wolfe, P. (2001). *Brain matters: Translating research into classroom practice*. Alexandria, VA: Association for Supervision and Curriculum Development.

Chapter 8

Bogdan, R., & Biklen, S. (1982). *Qualitative research for education: An introduction to theory and methods*. Boston: Allyn & Bacon.

Council for Exceptional Children (1994). Toward *a common agenda: Linking gifted education and school reform*. Reston, VA: Council for Exceptional Children.

Dettmer, P. (1993). Gifted education: Window of opportunity. *Gifted Child Quarterly, 37,* 92–94.

Ford, D., & Harris, J. III. (1993). Educational reform and the focus on gifted African-American students. *Roeper Review, 15,* 200–204.

Frank, R. (1992, March). School restructuring: Impact on attitudes, advocacy, and educational opportunities for gifted and talented students. In *Challenges in gifted education. Developing potential and investing in knowledge for the 21st century.* Columbus, OH: Ohio State Department of Education.

Gallagher, J. (1991). Educational reform, values, and gifted students. *Gifted Child Quarterly, 35,* 12–19.

Gallagher, J. (1992, March). Gifted students and educational reform. In *Challenges in gifted education: Developing potential and investing in knowledge for the 21st century.* Columbus, OH: Ohio State Department of Education.

Hanninen, G. (1994). Blending gifted education and school reform. ERIC Digest #E525.

Lincoln, Y., & Guba, E. (1985). *Naturalistic inquiry.* Beverly Hills, CA: Sage.

Margolin, L. (1994). *Goodness personified: The emergence of gifted children.* New York: Aldine De Gruyter.

Miles, M., & Huberman, A. (1984). *Qualitative data analysis: A sourcebook of new methods.* Newbury Park, CA: Sage.

Oakes, J. (1985). *Keeping track: How schools structure inequality.* New Haven, CT: Yale University Press.

Renzulli, J., & Reis, S. (1991). The reform movement and the quiet crisis in gifted education. *Gifted Child Quarterly, 35,* 26–35.

Robinson, A. (1990). Cooperation or exploitation? The argument against cooperative learning for talented students. *Journal for the Education of the Gifted, 14,* 9–27.

Rogers, K. (1991). *The relationship of grouping practices to the education of the gifted and talented learner* Storrs, CT: National Research Center on the Gifted and Talented.

Ross, R. (1993). *National excellence: A case for developing America's talent.* Washington, DC: Office of Educational Research and Improvement.

Sapon-Shevin, M. (1995). Why gifted students belong in inclusive schools. *Educational Leadership, 52*(4), 64–70.

Tomlinson, C. (1991). Gifted education and the middle school movement: Two voices on teaching the academically talented. *Journal for the Education of the Gifted, 15,* 206–238.

Tomlinson, C. (1992). Gifted learners: The boomerang kids of middle school? *Roeper Review, 16,* 177–182.

Tomlinson, C. & Callahan, C. (1992). Contributions of gifted education to general education in a time of change. *Gifted Child Quarterly, 36,* 183–189.

Treffinger, D. (1991). School reform and gifted education: Opportunities and issues. *Gifted Child Quarterly, 35,* 6–11.

Van Tassel-Baska, J. (1991). Gifted education in the balance: Building relationships with general education. *Gifted Child Quarterly, 35,* 20–25.

Wheelock, A. (1992). *Crossing the tracks: How "untracking" can save America's schools.* New York: The New Press.

Chapter 9

Fullan, M. (with Steigelbauer, S.). (1991). *The new meaning of educational change.* New York: Teachers College Press. teachers. Thousand Oaks, CA: Corwin.

Hargreaves, S., & Fullan, M. (1998). *What's worth fighting for out there?* New York: Teachers College Press.

CORWIN

A SAGE Company

The Corwin logo—a raven striding across an open book—represents the union of courage and learning. Corwin is committed to improving education for all learners by publishing books and other professional development resources for those serving the field of PreK–12 education. By providing practical, hands-on materials, Corwin continues to carry out the promise of its motto: **"Helping Educators Do Their Work Better."**